DATE DUE

SE 10 '99			

PRACTICES OF REASON

PRACTICES OF REASON

Aristotle's Nicomachean Ethics

C. D. C. REEVE

CLARENDON PRESS · OXFORD
1992

Oxford University Press, Walton Street, Oxford OX2 6DP
Oxford New York Toronto
Delhi Bombay Calcutta Madras Karachi
Petaling Jaya Singapore Hong Kong Tokyo
Nairobi Dar es Salaam Cape Town
Melbourne Auckland
and associated companies in
Berlin Ibadan

Oxford is a trade mark of Oxford University Press

Published in the United States
by Oxford University Press, New York

British Library Cataloguing in Publication Data
Data available

Library of Congress Cataloging in Publication Data
Reeve, C. D. C., 1948–
Practices of reason: Aristotle's Nicomachean ethics/C.D.C. Reeve.
p. cm.
Includes bibliographical references and indexes.
1. Aristotle. Nicomachean ethics. 2. Ethics. 3. Knowledge,
Theory of. I. Title.
B430.R46 1992 92–3648
171'.3—dc20
ISBN 0–19–823984–X

Typeset by Pentacor PLC
High Wycombe, Bucks.
Printed and bound in
Great Britain by Biddles Ltd.,
Guildford & King's Lynn

For
Peter and Linda

CONTENTS

Contents

ABBREVIATIONS

APo.	*Posterior Analytics* (Ross, 1949)
APr.	*Prior Analytics* (Ross, 1949)
Cael.	*De Caelo* (Allen, 1961)
Cat.	*Categories* (Minio–Paluello, 1949)
DA	*De Anima* (Ross, 1956)
EE	*Eudemian Ethics* (Susemihl, 1884)
GA	*De Generatione Animalium* (Lulofs, 1965)
GC	*De Generatione et Corruptione* (Forster, 1955)
HA	*Historia Animalium* (Peck, 1965)
MA	*De Motu Animalium* (Nussbaum, 1978)
MM	*Magna Moralia* (Armstrong, 1935)
Metaph.	*Metaphysics* (Ross, 1924)
Mete.	*Meteorologica* (Lee, 1952)
Mu.	*De Mundo* (Furley, 1955)
NE	*Nicomachean Ethics* (Bywater, 1894)
Po.	*Poetics* (Kassel, 1966)
PA	*De Partibus Animalium* (Peck, 1968)
Ph.	*Physics* (Ross, 1936)
PN	*Parva Naturalia* (Hett, 1936)
Pol.	*Politics* (Ross, 1957)
Prt.	*Protrepticus* (Düring, 1961)
Rh.	*Rhetoric* (Ross, 1959)
SE	*Sophistici Elenchi* (Ross, 1984)
Top.	*Topics* (Ross, 1984)

INTRODUCTION

It is not necessary that an active life be in relation to others, as some people think, nor is that thought alone practical which is for the sake of the consequences of the action, but much more so are the studies and thoughts that are their own ends and for their own sakes.

(*Pol.* 1325^{b}16–21)

THIS book is my attempt to elucidate the epistemological, metaphysical, and psychological foundations of Aristotle's *Nicomachean Ethics* by showing (or, in some cases, sketching) its place in the context of Aristotle's broader philosophical enterprise. A brief account of its genesis will serve to introduce its major findings.

I began by trying to grasp the difference between *phronēsis* or practical wisdom, which is the central notion of Aristotle's ethical epistemology, with *epistēmē haplōs* or unconditional scientific-knowledge, which is arguably the central notion of his general epistemology. Hence I was led to the *Posterior Analytics*, which is Aristotle's most detailed discussion of science. What struck me most forcibly in this discussion is the clear implication that most scientific-knowledge—and this includes pretty well everything that we would comfortably class under the rubric—is not unconditional at all, but holds only *hōs epi to polu* or for the most part. For Aristotle tells us explicitly that much *ethical* knowledge has this same somewhat mysterious status (*NE* 1094^{b}14–22).

Hōs epi to polu thus recommended itself as a promising topic for further investigation: why was some scientific-knowledge unconditional, while some—like ethical knowledge and presumably for the same reason—held only for the most part? Aristotle's answer seemed to be that some sciences—mathematics and theology—study essences or universals that are essentially matterless, and so give rise to unconditionally necessary truths, while others—physics, biology, part of psychology, and others—study essences or universals that are essentially enmattered, and so give rise to necessary truths that hold only for the most part. To figure out what this meant, and why Aristotle thought it was true, I had to explore form and matter, hypothetical necessity, 'the less and the more', and other topics from his biological writings, *Physics*, and *Metaphysics*. These explorations occupy §§1–2, and are intended to be no more detailed or well-armoured than my purposes require, though the Appendix provides more support for one especially controversial proposal than it seemed appropriate to provide in the text itself.

The next piece in the emerging story fell into place when I put together the following three ideas, two from the *Ethics* and one from the *De Anima*: *eudaimonia* is a first principle of ethics; *eudaimonia* is study or the theoretical activity of *nous*; *nous* and study are essentially matterless. For this led me to raise the question of whether unconditional scientific-knowledge is possible in ethics. The answer I uncovered is developed in §4. It is a controversial answer, but it seems to me to be largely compelling, especially in light of the remainder of the story.

First principles in a science are accessed by *nous*, but dialectic 'has a road towards the first principles of all types of inquiry' (*Top.* 101^{b}3–4). How, then, is dialectic related to *nous* in science, and does this relation carry over to ethics? §§4–10 are concerned with these questions, and hence with Aristotle's discussions of dialectic in the *Topics*, *Sophistici Elenchi*, and elsewhere, and with his discussion of *nous* in the *Posterior Analytics* and *Nicomachean Ethics*. First principles, I argue, are justified empirically and made true by the world, while the function of dialectic, whether in science or ethics, is to 'clarify' first principles by solving the *aporiai* to which they give rise. It is this clarification that results in full-blown *nous*.

By this point, I have tried to establish, first, that we have *nous* of the essentially matterless first principles of ethics as a result, in part, of producing dialectical solutions to the *aporiai* to which they (or our beliefs about them) give rise, and, second, that we have unconditional scientific-knowledge of the principles we demonstrate from those first principles. But ethics is manifestly not just knowledge of universal principles, it is also knowledge of how to apply them correctly in particular circumstances in order to achieve *eudaimonia*. And this, of course, is where *phronēsis* comes explicitly into the picture. In §§11–18 I develop an account of its nature by exploring its relations to practical perception, scientific-knowledge, craft-knowledge, the virtues of character, deliberation, decision, and, of course, *nous*. Two conclusions are particularly worth mentioning. First, deliberation, though it can be about ends, cannot be about the unconditional end, *eudaimonia*. Hence, the first principle of ethics is not, as is often argued, a topic for deliberation. Second, *nous* is involved with *phronēsis* not just in one way, but in two. *Nous* provides *phronēsis* with the knowledge of ethical universals that it needs to achieve its practical purposes. But *nous*—or rather its activation, study—is also the final cause of practical activity itself. For study, being primary *eudaimonia*, is the unconditional end of *phronēsis*. It is for this reason, as I explain most fully in §§26–7, that the first principles of *nous* and desire are the same (*Metaph.* 1072ᵃ25–7).

Eudaimonia is the next topic, and in a way it occupies the remainder of the book, illuminating *nous*, since in a way it—or, more accurately, one variety of it—just is the activity of *nous*, illuminating *phronēsis*, since it is what *phronēsis* aims to promote or achieve.

In §19, I try to explain what an *energeia* or activity is and why Aristotle thinks *eudaimonia* must be one. This involves another descent into the *Metaphysics*, which results in a new understanding of the various kinds of ends Aristotle recognizes and sets the scene for novel analyses of the major arguments of *NE* i. 1–6: the argument from politics (§20); the argument from completeness, self-sufficiency, and choiceworthiness (§21); and, the function argument (§22–5).

By the end of §25, I have argued in a number of different ways, first, that there are two kinds of *eudaimonia*, primary *eudaimonia*, which is identical to study, and secondary *eudaimonia*, which is identical to practical activity, and, second, that the human function or essence is study.

In §25–6, I argue by appeal to the *Posterior Analytics*, the *Metaphysics*, and the *De Anima* that study—'the most exact form of scientific-knowledge' (*NE* 1141ᵃ16–17)—is theology and that theology is first philosophy. Aristotle's account of substance in the *Metaphysics* ends, therefore, in the same place as his account of *eudaimonia* in the *Ethics*. For god is primary substance and he is also primary *eudaimonia*. These are wild doctrines, no doubt, but they are, I am persuaded, Aristotle's own. The conclusion I draw—though I recognize that others may be inclined to draw a rather different one—is that Aristotle is wilder and less commonsensical than we have often been urged to believe.

In §28, I argue that secondary *eudaimonia* must be for the sake of primary *eudaimonia* in order to be any kind of *eudaimonia* at all. In §§29–33, I discuss external goods, friends, and the virtues of character, and explain how they and primary *eudaimonia* are combined by and with *phronēsis* in the *eudaimōn* life. A distinctive feature of this discussion is that it makes far more use of the fact that *phronēsis* is the same state as politics (*NE* 1141^{b}23–4) than most others with which I am acquainted. This enables us to see *phronēsis* in a new light and to solve some otherwise intractable problems in a clear and, I think, convincing way.

If I am right about all of this, then, understanding the *Nicomachean Ethics* is very largely a matter of understanding the involvement of *phronēsis* with *nous* and the involvement of *nous* with *eudaimonia*. Since the latter involvement reveals, and *Pol.* 1325^{b}16–21 attests, that the exercise of *nous* expressing wisdom is even more practical than the exercise of *phronēsis*, both of these are included in the practices of reason to which my title refers.

In speaking of aetiology I have perforce said quite a lot about structure. Let me now add a few more words explicitly on that topic. The book has four main chapters. Chapter 1 is about our knowledge of ethical universals, and so deals with scientific-knowledge, dialectic, and *nous*. Chapter 2 is about how *phronēsis* uses the knowledge of ethical universals provided by *nous* to best achieve *eudaimonia* in a particular situation, and about what Aristotle thinks it has to be like in order to accomplish that task. Chapter 3 is about the three major arguments in *NE* i. 1–6, each of which throws important light on *phronēsis* and *eudaimonia* and so, since the activation of *nous* is primary *eudaimonia*, on *nous*. Chapter 4 deals with study, and with the arguments that Aristotle uses to establish that study is primary *eudaimonia* and that the activity expressing *phronēsis* is secondary *eudaimonia*. But its major topic is the way in which *phronēsis* combines these two activities with external goods in order to ensure a *eudaimōn* life. The four chapters thus represent four related perspectives on *phronēsis* and *nous* and their interrelations, which together lay bear the foundations—epistemological, metaphysical, and psychological —on which the *Nicomachean Ethics* is built. In the conclusion, I discuss some of the philosophical strengths and weaknesses of the *Ethics* and assess its significance for contemporary philosophy.

The audience I have had in mind consists of people who have read the *Ethics* a number of times, have looked at some of the secondary literature on it, and have been left with many uncertainties about its central arguments, concepts, and presuppositions. Some of this audience will naturally be specialists in Greek philosophy, some will be ethicists, political scientists, or classicists, some will be graduate students or advanced undergraduates, and some will simply be serious lay students of Aristotle. I have tried to write with the needs of all such readers in mind, but without any illusions about the challenge that some parts of my story—like some parts of the *Ethics* itself—will pose to them. For Aristotle, like Kant, is an unusually demanding author, and only those at home in philosophical argument and willing to read difficult texts with care and attention are likely to appreciate his brilliance and subtlety.

Though I have not presupposed any knowledge of Greek, I have retained a few transliterated Greek terms, mostly familiar, for which no entirely satisfactory or undisputed English synonyms exist. The discussion makes clear how these terms are best understood. I list them here, none the less, together with some of the rough equivalences translators have found for them:

aporiai	(problems, puzzles);
endoxa	(common beliefs, reputable opinions);
eudaimonia	(happiness, flourishing, well-being);
eudaimōn	(happy, flourishing);
nous	(intuitive intellect, understanding);
phainomena	(appearances, observed facts);
phronēsis	(practical wisdom, intelligence);
phronimos	(one who possesses *phroñesis*)

But for the awkwardness that results when corresponding verbs are needed, I would have added to the list:

epistēmē	(scientific-knowledge),
praxis	(action),
proairesis	(decision),
theōria	(study)

In translating and interpreting the *Nicomachean Ethics*, I have invariably found Irwin (1985*b*) of great assistance, even though I have seldom followed it in every particular. I have also made free use of the other translations of Aristotle's works listed in the references, emending them to suit my purposes.

I am indebted to Richard Kraut (whose provocative and to me largely congenial book on the *Ethics* appeared as my own neared completion) for providing characteristically useful and tactful comments on an early draft and for being helpful in many other ways, and to George Bealer for helping with some problems in §1. My debts to other writers on Aristotle—and there have been an astonishing number of good ones—will be clear from the notes, but Jonathan Barnes, David Charles, John Cooper, T. H. Irwin, and Jonathan Lear merit additional mention here.

Reed College generously gave me a sabbatical leave and a summer research award; Carrie Swanson retrieved library books, xeroxed papers, and discussed emerging arguments. I thank them both warmly.

1

DEMONSTRATION AND DIALECTIC

> The educated person seeks exactness (*takribēs*) in each area to the extent that the nature of the subject allows.
>
> (*NE* 1094^{b}23–5)
>
> The rational exactness (*akribologian*) of mathematics is not to be demanded in all cases, but only in the case of things that have no matter.
>
> (*Metaph.* 995^{a}14–16)

ARISTOTLE'S ethical epistemology—his account of ethical knowledge—has two major components. The first explains the nature of our knowledge of ethical universals such as justice, moderation, and *eudaimonia*. The second explains how, for example, we are able to use such knowledge in order to determine what justice requires of us in a given particular situation and how to accomplish it. In this chapter, we shall focus on the first of these components, leaving the second for discussion in Chapter 2. Our initial task will be to examine Aristotle's conception of unconditional scientific-knowledge or *epistēmē haplōs*.[1] This will allow us to explain why some knowledge of ethical universals holds only *hōs epi to polu* or for the most part (*NE* 1094^{b}14–22), and to explore the differences and the no less illuminating similarities that hold between ethical knowledge and scientific-knowledge.

I UNCONDITIONAL SCIENTIFIC-KNOWLEDGE

To understand what Aristotle means by unconditional scientific-knowledge, we need to begin at some distance from that notion and work towards it. The discussion, like Aristotle's own, is somewhat

---

[1] Burnyeat (1981) argues that *epistēmē* is understanding rather than knowledge. He is answered in Irwin (1988*b*, 530 n.24).

abstract and technical but it will be all the more succinct and clear for that.

An Aristotelian science is a structure of demonstrations from first principles. Hence it must be necessarily true, complete, and restricted to a single genus of beings. For, on Aristotle's view, demonstration is possible only from necessarily true premises in a complete science dealing with a single genus.[2]

Suppose that S is an Aristotelian science. P_i and P_j are the *archai* or first principles of S if and only if there are demonstrations of all the other propositions of S from P_i and P_j but no demonstrations of P_i or P_j from them.[3]

Now Aristotle thinks of first principles in a variety of ways, which we may distinguish as follows. There are ontological first principles, basic entities or fundamental explanatory causal factors out there in the world, and there are epistemic first principles, principles of our knowledge of the world. Thus both *eudaimonia* and beliefs about it are ethical first principles.[4] The former is an ontological first principle; the latter are epistemic first principles. But if our theories about the world are true, their structure will, on Aristotle's view, reflect or mirror the structure of the world, so that the truth of epistemic first principles depends on ontological ones.[5] Aristotle's is therefore a realist conception of truth.

An epistemic first principle could be either a concept or it could be a proposition. The ontological version of this distinction is between universals, conceived of as the non-particular aspects of the world that concepts pick out, and facts (or ways the world is), conceived of as what makes propositions either true or false. Aristotle sometimes seems to mark this distinction, but just as often he ignores it, so that it is sometimes difficult to determine whether he has a concept (universal) in mind or a proposition (fact).[6] This is not simple carelessness on his part, however. For, on his view, a first principle is paradigmatically a definition (*horismos*)—a type of

---

[2] See *APo.* 73ª21–74ª3 and below; *APr.* 46ª17–27 with §5; *APo.* 75ª28–b20, 87ª38–b4, 88ª30–b3.

[3] I have translated *archē* as 'first principle' throughout: 'For a principle (*archē*) is a first thing (*prōton*) and a first thing is a principle' (*Top.* 121b9–10).

[4] See *NE* 1095b6–7, 1102ª3, 1139b1–4; §3 The definition of first principles at *GA* 788a14–16 presents them as ontological, that at *APo.* 76ª31–2 as epistemic.

[5] See *Cat.* 14b11–23; *PA* 639ª1–646ª8; *Metaph.* 1011b26–8, 1034b20–2.

[6] The *locus classicus* is *APo.* ii. 19, discussed in §9. See Barnes (1975, 259–60), Kahn (1981), and Modrak (1987, 157–79).

proposition or fact—that articulates an essence—a concept or universal.[7] Hence, again, we can think of either *eudaimonia* or the definition of *eudaimonia* as being a first principle of ethics. If the definition in question is of a concept or universal proper to the genus studied by S, it is peculiar to S. But Aristotle also counts among S's first principles what he calls *axiōmata* or axioms (*APo.* 72^a15–20). These include the laws of logic, such as the Principle of Non-Contradiction, which hold at least analogically of all beings (76^a38–$^b2$), as well as such less general laws as the axioms of equality, which, though not universally applicable, are none the less not peculiar to a single science or single genus.

The notion of a demonstration (*apodeixis*), to which we now turn, is also a technical one. To get a grip on it, we must first understand four other technical notions. The first is *kath' hauto* predication. F is G *kath' hauto*—it is G *by itself*—if and only if G is part of the definition of F or F is part of the definition of G (73^a34–$^b24$).[8]

The second notion we need is the relevant sense of necessity. P_i is necessary, in this sense, if and only if it is of the form 'F is G' and F is G by itself. Thus, on Aristotle's view, both of the following are necessary:

1. A triangle is an arrangement of lines.
2. A number is either odd or even.

In (1) the predicate (an arrangement of lines) is part of the definition of the subject (triangle). For being an arrangement of lines is part of the definition of what it is to be a triangle (a triangle is a plane figure bounded by three straight lines). In (2) the subject (number) is part of the definition of the predicate (odd or even). For being a number is part of the definition of what it is to be odd or even (something is odd, for example, if and only if it is a number that is not divisible by two without remainder).

The third notion we need is this. P_i is prior to and more knowable by nature than P_n if and only if its demonstration from first principles is shorter than that of P_n. Or, in the formulation Aristotle

---

[7] See *APo.* 90^b24–7, *Top.* 158^b1–4, *DA* 402^b25–403^a2, *Metaph.* 1031^a12, §3. First principles seem also to include existence claims corresponding to those concepts or definitions (*APo.* 76^b3–6), although real definitions seem to have existential import on their own. See Gomez-Lobo (1981), Kahn (1981, 391–2), and below.

[8] For further discussion see §19.

prefers, P_i must be further away from sense experience than P_n in S.[9]

The final notion we need is the relevant sense of universality. P_i holds universally, in this sense, if and only if it is of the form 'F is G', every F is G, and F is G by itself (73^b25–74^a3).

If P_i and P_j have these features, if they are necessary, universal, and prior to and more knowable by nature than P_n, then a valid syllogistic deduction (*syllogismos*) of P_n from P_i and P_j is a demonstration of P_n.

We are now in a position to define unconditional scientific-knowledge. X has unconditional scientific-knowledge that P_n is true if and only if X knows P_i and P_j, knows that they are the first principles of S, and knows the demonstration of P_n from P_i and P_j. Thus: 'We think we have unconditional scientific-knowledge of something when we think we know (*ginōskein*) its causal explanation (*aitian*), know it to be its causal explanation, and when it is not possible for the thing itself to be otherwise' (71^b9–12). For causal explanations, in Aristotle's view, are demonstrations from first principles.

It follows from this account that we cannot have unconditional scientific-knowledge of first principles. For we cannot demonstrate them (*NE* 1140^b33–1141^a1). Aristotle is explicit, none the less, that the knowledge we have of first principles must be scientific-knowledge of some sort, if we are to have unconditional scientific-knowledge of the propositions we demonstrate from them:

> But we say that not all scientific-knowledge is demonstrative, but in the case of the immediates [first principles] it is nondemonstrable. That this must be so is evident. For if we must know the things that are prior and on which the demonstration depends and demonstration must come to a stop somewhere, then it is necessary for these immediates to be nondemonstrable. (*APo.* 72^b18–23)

For the only alternatives are an infinite regress of demonstrations, circular demonstrations, or demonstrations that begin in something less than scientific-knowledge, and none of these, Aristotle argues, is acceptable (72^b18–73^a20). The scientific-knowledge we have of first principles is *nous* (see §9).

The first principles special to a science must be necessary definitions, then. But are they nominal definitions or real defin-

---

[9] See 71^b16–72^a5, 74^b5–26; §§5, 26.

itions? Do they define nominal essences or real essences? Are they
necessary *de dicto* or necessary *de re?*
De dicto necessities are analytic; they are made true by words or
their meanings. *De re* necessities are made true by the world. Thus,
for example,

1. Bachelors are unmarried men.

is necessary only *de dicto*. Given the meanings of the words in it,
it must be true. But it is not necessary *de re*. It is not the case, for
example, that if John is a bachelor, he cannot ever marry. No
necessity is present in him just because it is present in (1). If John
marries tomorrow, he will cease to be a bachelor, but he will
neither have done the impossible nor falsified (1). Now consider

2. Gold has atomic number 79.

(2) does not seem to be analytic. It does not seem to be true
simply in virtue of the meanings of the words it contains. But
arguably, at least, (2) is necessary—*de re* necessary. For it seems
that the part of the world that is gold must have an atomic number
of 79, that if it ceased to have that atomic number it would
necessarily cease to be gold.[10]

Nominal definitions, as their very name suggests, are definitions
that are necessary *de dicto*. They state nominal essences. Real
definitions are definitions that are necessary *de re*. They state real
essences. Thus (1) is a nominal definition of the term 'bachelor' and
states the nominal essence of bachelors. (2) is a (partial) real
definition of gold and states (part of) the real essence of gold.

Returning to our question of what sorts of necessary definitions
P_i and P_j are, the most reasonable answer is that they are definitions
that are necessary *de re*, that they are real definitions that specify
real essences. For, first, Aristotle himself distinguishes between
nominal and real definitions of essences, and claims that the
definitions involved in demonstrative syllogisms must be of the
latter variety ($93^b29–94^a19$). Second, he states that it is difficult or
impossible to find definitions of what does not exist: 'To seek what
something is without grasping that it is, is to seek nothing' ($93^a26–$
7; see $93^b23–4$). The implication is that we discover essences by
investigating things in the world, not by *a priori* reflection on

---

[10] See Kripke (1980) and Putnam (1975, 215–71). Witt (1989, 180–97) usefully
contrasts Kripke's views on essences with those of Aristotle.

concepts or the meanings of words. Finally, many of Aristotle's own sample definitions of essences are clearly not analytic: 'thunder is noise in the clouds caused by the extinguishing of fire' (93^h7-9); deciduousness is 'the solidifying of the sap at the joint between leaf and stem' (99^a28-9).[11]

One final question about P_i and P_j. Are they definitions of universals or of particulars? Aristotle's answer is clear. Only universals have definitions: 'definition is of the universal and of the form' (*Metaph.* 1036^a27-8; see $1037^b8-1038^a35$). Only universals can be known unconditionally (*APo.* 75^b24-6). What we are explaining in biology, or any other science, are lawlike connections in nature, connections that Aristotle—in company with some contemporary philosophers—conceives of as necessary relations between universals.[12] Such explanations can be applied to particular cases, in Aristotle's view, but when they are, they do not yield unconditional scientific-knowledge (75^b21-36).

We now know—albeit in very abstract terms—how Aristotle thinks of demonstration or causal explanation in a science. An example may help to bring his views down to earth. Let us suppose that we want to explain why oak trees are deciduous. What we are looking for is some feature of oak trees that causally explains why they lose their leaves in autumn. Such a feature might be, Aristotle thinks, the fact that the sap at the joint between leaf and stem solidifies in colder autumn temperatures. If he is right, the appropriate explanatory syllogism would look something like this (see 98^b36-8):

1. All plants in which sap solidifies at the joint between leaf and stem in autumn are deciduous.
2. All oak trees have sap that solidifies at the joint between leaf and stem in autumn.
3. Therefore, all oak trees are deciduous.

---

[11] For further defence of the view that Aristotle's principles are necessary *de re* see Ackrill (1981*b*), Gomez-Lobo (1981), Irwin (1982), and Sorabji (1981).

[12] See Burnyeat (1981, 108–110). Armstrong (1983, 77–173) is a recent defence of the view that natural laws are best understood in terms of necessary relations between universals. Forms and essences are also definable objects of scientific-knowledge for Aristotle. This suggests that they are universals. But there is controversy about their classification as such. See Frede (1987, 72–80), Lear (1988, 273–93), Owen (1978), and Witt (1989, 144–79). For present purposes, there is no need to take sides in the controversy, and we can simply allow the knowability and definability of forms and essences to attract them into the class of universals. In §26, we shall see that greater refinement is needed.

But there are important conditions that (1) and (2) must satisfy if this syllogism is indeed to explain causally: for example, the demonstrations of them from biological first principles must be shorter than the demonstration of (3)—they must be further from experience in the structure of demonstrations that is complete biology than (3)—and they must be necessary *de re*. Why does Aristotle impose these austere conditions? It is sometimes thought that he does it because he mistakenly assimilates all the sciences to mathematics. There may be some truth in this, but the real reason surely has to do with the ideals of knowledge and explanation.

If (1) and (2) are not theoretically deeper than (3), they cannot be an adequate explanation of it. For in the true and complete biological theory (3) will be used to explain (1) and (2). Thus in using them to explain (3) we would be implicitly engaging in circular explanation, and circular explanation is not explanation at all (72^{b}25–73^{a}20). If (1) and (2) are not necessary, they will not adequately explain (3) either. For we would still have to explain why, given that plants with sap of the kind in question do not have to lose their leaves or that oak trees do not have to have sap of that kind, oak trees none the less do lose their leaves.[13]

2 Plain Scientific-Knowledge and *hōs epi to polu*

Unconditional scientific-knowledge is restricted to necessary relations between universals that guarantee the necessary truth of the corresponding universally quantified proposition. But *plain* scientific-knowledge, as we may call it, seems to enjoy wider scope: 'Scientific-knowledge (*epistēmē*) is of what holds always or of what holds for the most part (*hōs epi to polu*)' (*Metaph.* 1027^{a}20–1; see *Ph.* 197^{a}19–20). In other texts, however, the scope of even plain scientific-knowledge seems to be the same as that of its unconditional partner:

We all suppose that what we have scientific-knowledge of does not even admit of being otherwise . . . Hence what we have scientific-knowledge of is by necessity. Hence it is eternal. For the things that are by unconditional (*haplōs*) necessity are all eternal and eternal things are ingenerable and indestructible. . . . Scientific-knowledge is the grasp of universals and of things that are by necessity. (*NE* 1139^{b}20–1140^{b}32)[14]

[13] I have benefited here from Kosman (1973).
[14] See *APo.* 75^{b}21–36, 81^{a}40–^{b}1, 84^{a}11–17; *DA* 417^{b}23–4, 429^{b}10–22; *Metaph.* 1015^{b}6–7; §26.

To get at the doctrine behind these texts and to see whether or not they conflict we must investigate the nature of what holds for the most part.

What holds for the most part seems to hold among particulars not among universals: to say that for the most part Fs are Gs seems to be just to say that *most* Fs are Gs. But there is good reason to think that this is not at all what Aristotle intends. For he claims that the following deduction is valid even when the premises and conclusion hold only for the most part (*APo.* 96ᵃ8–17):

F is G (or All Fs are Gs)
G is H (or All Gs are Hs)
F is H (or All Fs are Hs)

The corresponding syllogism with 'most' is clearly not always valid, however: most centenarians are women; most women are under seventy; but most centenarians are not under seventy.[15] Moreover, in the discussion of law in the *Ethics* Aristotle speaks of the universal law that 'holds for the most part (*hōs epi to pleon*)' (1137ᵇ14–16), and in the *Historia Animalium* he writes that 'for the most part all (*hōs d'epi to polu pantes*) crabs have the right claw bigger and stronger than the left' (527ᵇ6–7).[16] Both texts suggest that what holds for the most part is, as we would say, universally quantified.

In the *Topics*, a deduction is said to be a demonstration 'when the premises from which the deduction starts are true first principles' (100ᵃ27–8). In the *Posterior Analytics*, it is allowed that 'there will be immediate first principles also in the case of what holds for the most part' (96ᵃ17–19). Together these texts suggest that holding for the most part is no obstacle to being demonstrable. In two other texts, the suggestion is explicit:

There is no scientific-knowledge through demonstration of what holds by luck. For what holds by luck is neither necessary nor does it hold for the most part but comes about separately from these; and demonstration is of one or other (*thaterou*) of the former. (*APo.* 87ᵇ19–22; see 75ᵇ33–6)

We next point out that what admits of being otherwise (*to endechesthai*) is said in two ways, in one it signifies what holds for the most part but falls short of the [unconditionally] necessary, for example a man's turning grey or growing or decaying, or everything that holds by nature . . . In another it

---

[15] See Barnes (1975, 184).
[16] This text was brought to my attention by Mignucci (1981).

signifies the indefinite . . . or everything that happens by luck . . . Scientific-knowledge and demonstration are not concerned with things that are indefinite, because the middle term is uncertain; but they are concerned with what holds by nature and as a rule arguments (*logoi*) and inquiries are made about things that are possible in this sense. (*APr.* 32^{b}4–21; see *EE* 1247^{a}31–2)

Aristotle is also explicit, however, that demonstration is restricted to the realm of necessary relations among universals. It follows that what holds for the most part must also be restricted to that realm. (We may infer from these texts that the more austere conditions that Aristotle sometimes imposes on demonstration, which require the premises of demonstrations to be true in every case, are intended as sufficient conditions only.)

But if what holds for the most part holds by some sort of necessity among universals, how are we to understand it and the sort of necessity it involves? Aristotle contrasts what holds for the most part with what holds in every case without fail and with what simply comes about by luck (*APo.* 87^{b}19–22, *Metaph.* 1026^{b}24–1027^{a}28).[17] It is luck when people find treasure while digging for potatoes or cultivating a field. But it is not just luck—even though it is not always and invariably the case—that 'honey water is useful to a person in a fever' (*Metaph.* 1027^{a}22–4) or that adult human males have hair on their chins (*APo.* 96^{a}9–11). Rather these things hold because there is a necessary, law-like connection between the relevant universals—between honey water and fever, between being an adult human male and having hair on the chin—that explains why, for the most part, they do hold. Relying on Aristotle's remark that 'the probable (*eikos*) is what holds not always but for the most part' (*Rh.* 1402^{b}20–1), let us say that the relation in question is one of *probabilizing*, so that if F probabilizes G, then it will hold for the most part that Fs are Gs.

The following text nicely draws the pertinent contrast between what is unconditionally necessitated and what is merely probabilized:

For a monster (*teras*) is something contrary to nature; not to every nature, but to that which holds for the most part. For nothing can happen contrary to nature considered as eternal and necessary, but only where things for the

---

[17] Aristotle's views on luck are further discussed in §29 and in Sorabji (1980, 3–25).

most part happen in a certain way, but may also happen in another way. (*GA* 770^{b}9–13)[18]

The unconditionally necessary holds always; the probabilized can fail to hold although it rarely does: 'The contrary of what holds for the most part is always comparatively rare' (*Top.* 112^{b}10–11; see *Metaph.* 1025^{a}14–21). That is why Aristotle sometimes refers to things that hold for the most part as *endechomena*, as things that admit of being otherwise. What he means to exclude by so doing is not necessity in every sense of the term, however, but only unconditional necessity.[19]

Unconditional necessity is a necessary, law-like relation between universals that guarantees the truth of the corresponding universally quantified proposition: if F and G are thus related, 'All Fs are Gs' is necessarily true. Probabilizing is a necessary, law-like relation between universals that guarantees that the corresponding universally quantified propositions will be for the most part true: if F and G are thus related, 'All Fs are Gs' will necessarily hold for the most part.

We are now in a position to understand why Aristotle's syllogism involving propositions that hold for the most part is valid. If F and G are related by a necessary, law-like relation guaranteeing that 'All Fs are Gs' is for the most part true, and G and H are related by a necessary, law-like relation guaranteeing that 'All Gs are Hs' is for the most part true, it follows that F and H must be related by a necessary, law-like relation guaranteeing that 'All Fs are Hs' is for the most part true. More succinctly: if F probabilizes G, and G probabilizes H, then F probabilizes H.

What, then, are we to make of *NE* 1139^{b}21–1140^{b}32, which seems to assure us that plain scientific-knowledge, too, is only to be had of unconditional necessities? The most reasonable answer— but certainly not the only possible one—is that in this passage Aristotle means to be referring to unconditional scientific-knowledge without bothering to say so explicitly. And, in fact, the purpose of the discussion in which the passages occur, which is surely to summarize the conclusions reached in the *Posterior Analytics*, makes this a very reasonable assumption (*APo.* 89^{b}7–9, *NE* 1139^{b}36–7). It follows that the *Ethics* and the *Metaphysics* are

---

[18] See *Ph.* 199^{b}34–5, *Metaph.* 1015^{a}33–^{b}9, *NE* 1139^{b}22–4.
[19] See *APr.* 25^{b}14–15, 32^{b}4–13. *Endechomena* are more fully discussed in §§12–13.

consistent. For the former is talking about unconditional scientific-knowledge, while the latter is talking about what we have called plain scientific-knowledge. Putting all this together we arrive at the following account. We have scientific-knowledge only of necessary relations holding between universals. If the relations in question are relations of unconditional necessity and we can demonstrate them from first principles, we have unconditional scientific-knowledge of them. If they are probabilizing relations and we can demonstrate them from first principles, we can have plain but not unconditional scientific-knowledge of them. Since what holds for the most part holds because universals are related by probabilization, we can have plain, but not unconditional, scientific-knowledge of what holds for the most part.

The question we must now pursue is this: why are some universals related by probabilization while others are related by unconditional necessity? A sketch and an Aristotelian illustration will provide the first part of the answer.

Some necessities are 'located', as we may put it, in the four elementary types of matter—earth, water, fire, air—out of which all enmattered things are made. Thus, for example, it is necessary that fire rises. Other necessities are located in enmattered things themselves and are not reducible to the necessities located in matter. Thus, for example, it is necessary in a way that is not reducible to facts about heart material that human beings have hearts. Necessities located in matter are none the less importantly related to those located in enmattered things. And one of the most important of these relations is the relation of hypothetical necessity (*anagkē ex hupoteseōs*), which Aristotle discusses in *Physics* ii. 9 and *De Partibus Animalium*.[20]

Given the nature of the various kinds of matter available, only one of them or a few of them, are possible means to the end that it is part of the essence of a type of enmattered thing to achieve (see §22). In such a case, the matter in question is hypothetically necessary to achieving that end. Hypothetical necessity is in general related to teleology in this sort of way.

To enable an enmattered thing to achieve a certain end, the hypothetically necessary matter typically needs to be shaped or

---

[20] 639^b21–640^a10, 642^a1–13, $^a31$–$^b4$. My discussion of hypothetical necessity is indebted to Cooper (1987a).

formed. The agent that does the shaping is form (*eidos*), which Aristotle identifies with essence (*to ti ēn einai*).[21] Hence we can represent the emergence of enformed things somewhat fancifully as a struggle between matter and form, or between the necessities definitive of each of them, matter resisting form to some degree depending on the extent to which it is or is not ideal for the purpose for which form is shaping it.[22]

Now for the Aristotelian illustration. In human reproduction, as Aristotle describes it (*GA* 763[b]25–769[a]6), the female provides the matter for the offspring, this being *katamēnia* or menstrual fluid, while the male provides the form, which is present in his semen. If the *katamēnia* were wholly receptive of form, if it had no nature, no necessities of its own, the offspring would resemble the male parent, who would pass on his own form to it unaltered. But the *katamēnia* has necessities of its own that resist to different degrees those present in the semen. If the *katamēnia* resists the imposition of some parts of the form being impressed upon it, the result may be a female offspring. If it resists a sufficient number of parts, the result will be a *teras*, a monster. For the most part, the *katamēnia* is sufficiently pliant that male or female offspring of the appropriate species come about. But sometimes, it is not sufficiently pliant. That is why the appropriate offspring do not always and invariably come about.[23]

The effect of this resistance of matter to form is that the same form, realized in different matter, may result in particular things with different qualities and capacities: a man's children typically resemble each other no more than they resemble him. Hence, while most Fs may be Gs, an occasional F, realized in a particularly recalcitrant piece of matter, may fail to be a G. If we could study F and G in separation from matter, however, this fact need have no epistemic consequences at the level of universals themselves. We can know unconditionally necessary truths about circles, even

---

[21] See *Phys.* 193[a]30–1, 193[b]1–2; *Metaph.* 1032[b]1–2, 1035[b]14–16, 1041[b]4–9; Witt (1989, 63–179).

[22] In common with Charlton (1970, 129–45), Furth (1988, 221–7), and Gill (1989, 243–52) I doubt that Aristotle believed in 'prime matter', which is a completely indeterminate and impassive substratum. But if he did, then this struggle between matter and form will occur only when the matter in question is not prime, but already, like the *katamēnia* described below, somewhat formed.

[23] For a more detailed defence of this account of Aristotle's embryology, see the Appendix.

though those truths fail to hold exactly of actual circles, because we can abstract the universal circle from matter. But if F and G are essentially enmattered, if matter is part of their very essences and definitions, the resistance of matter to form 'codes up', so to speak, to the universals F and G themselves, insuring that F and G are related at best by probabilization not by unconditional necessity.

To understand more precisely how this resistance 'codes up' to universals to ensure such an outcome, we need to introduce one other element in Aristotle's account of essentially enmattered universals, namely, 'the more and the less (*to mallon kai hētton*)'.[24] In *De Partibus Animalium*, Aristotle writes that 'all kinds that differ by degree and by the more and the less have been linked under one kind . . . I mean that bird differs from bird by the more or by degree; for one is long-feathered, another is short-feathered' (644ª16–21). The idea seems to be this. A kind (*genos*) is defined by a set of general characteristics or differentiae that are essential to every member of the kind. And different species of a single kind are distinguished by the ways in which these general differentiae are further specified by features that differ only in degree: 'they don't differ structurally, but only with respect to bodily affections such as larger or smaller, softer or harder, smoother or rougher, and so on, or, to put it generally, they differ by the more and the less' (*PA* 644ᵇ14–15; see *HA* 486ª23–ᵇ16). Thus the various species of the kind *bird* differ from one another because of possibly minute differences of degree in the size, texture, and so on of their differentiae. Since form or essence determines species, this means that there is a kind of vagueness or open-texture in the forms of the various species of living things that belong to the same kinds, which ensures that we can only define what they are more or less.

So far we have been dealing with differences of degree between forms and species within a single kind. But it seems clear that similar differences also exist between the forms of individuals belonging to a single species. Thus Socrates' form differs from that of Coriscus in ways that explain why their children have different characteristics (see *GA* 767ª36–768ᵇ30). Perhaps not all the differences in question are differences of degree, but Aristotle is clear that some of them are and that matter is responsible for them:

---

[24] My attention was drawn to the more and the less and to some of the passages I cite in this paragraph and the next by Lennox (1987). The idea originates in Plato's *Philebus* 25a–d.

'As number does not admit of the more and the less, neither does the substance in respect of the form, but if indeed any substance does, it's the one that involves matter' (*Metaph.* 1044ª10–11). Thus we have a route back from essentially enmattered forms or universals to the more and the less and from it to vagueness or open-texture in the forms or universals themselves. This provides the explanation of 'coding up' and its epistemic consequences that we were seeking. For vague or open-textured universals, as opposed to definite or precise ones, are just the sort that we would expect to be related by probabilization rather than by unconditional necessity, just the sort to be described by sciences whose principles hold only for the most part.[25]

In the following passage, Aristotle explicitly recognizes this, remarking on the crucial importance of determining whether we are studying essentially matterless or essentially enmattered universals:

Physics must be a theoretical science, but it studies being that admits of being moved and substance whose definition, not being separate from matter, holds only for the most part (*kai peri ousian ton logon hōs epi to polu hōs ou chōristēn*). Now, we must not fail to notice the mode of being of the essence and of its definition. For, without this, inquiry achieves nothing. Of things defined, that is the what something is, some are like snub, some like concave. These differ because snub is bound up with matter (for the snub is a concave *nose*), while concavity is without perceptible matter. If then all natural things are like snub (for example nose, eye, face, flesh, bone and, in general, animal or leaf, root, bark and, in general, plant; for none of these can be defined without reference to movement; they always have matter), it is clear how we must seek and define what a natural thing is. It is also clear that it belongs to the physicist to study even psyche in a way, that is, so much of it as is not without matter. (*Metaph.* 1025ᵇ26–1026ª6)[26]

[25] It is notorious that Aristotle does not mention matter or hylomorphic analysis in the supposedly early works that compose the *Organon*. But *hōs epi to polu*, which presupposes both these things, is used throughout those works. This is strong evidence, in my view, that matter and form are not later additions to Aristotle's arsenal of philosophical notions. If I am right about this, it has significant consequences for our understanding of Aristotle's thought and its development. See Graham (1987).

[26] See *Metaph.* 1033ᵇ24–6, 1035ᵇ28–32, 1036ᵇ21–32, 1037ª5–10, 1037ª21–ᵇ7, 1039ᵇ27–31. Gill (1989, 111–44) argues that Aristotle limits the notion of essence to the matterless form of a hylomorphic compound. This makes the contrast drawn at the beginning of the passage very difficult to understand; for it would mean that all essences were epistemically on a par. How, then, could we explain the fact that principles in physics, unlike in mathematics or theology, hold only for the most part? For further discussion and references see Balme (1984, 306–12).

The universals studied by physics are all essentially enmattered, but other universals, such as those studied by mathematics and theology, do not involve matter (see *Metaph.* 1026ª6–32, §§26–27). Hence, for reasons we now understand, physical principles hold only for the most part, while mathematical and theological ones hold universally and unconditionally.

It is not surprising, then, that, on Aristotle's view, exactness (*akribeia*) in a science is a function of its level of abstraction from matter (see §26). We can have exact, unconditional scientific-knowledge of an essentially matterless universal or its definition, but when we turn to essentially enmattered universals exactness is lost (*Metaph.* 995ª14–17, 1027ª13–15). And the reason it is lost is the indeterminateness of matter:

The aim of nature, then, is to measure the generation and decay of animals by the regular motions of these bodies [the sun and the moon], but nature cannot bring this about exactly because of the indeterminateness of matter and because there are many causes that hinder generation and decay from being according to nature and often cause things to occur contrary to nature. (*GA* 778ª4–9)[27]

Since the universe consists largely of enmattered things, we can understand why Aristotle identifies nature (in one sense of the term) with what holds for the most part.[28]

Matter, which prevents essentially enmattered universals from being objects of unconditional scientific-knowledge, is even more of a problem when it comes to moving and changing particulars. So much so, in fact, that we cannot have any kind of scientific-knowledge of particulars at all. Of them, Aristotle is explicit, we can have only perception.[29] But neither this fact, nor the fact that scientific-knowledge is rigidly theoretical, should make us think that unconditional scientific-knowledge, even of the most exact kind, has no bearing either on practice or on the particulars with which, as we shall see in §§11–12, it is essentially involved. For Aristotle is clear that the theoretical sciences, though essentially

[27] Balme (1987, 283–5) is useful on how not to understand this passage. The nature that things are caused by matter (and other things) to act contrary to must, of course, be what holds for the most part. See *GA* 770ᵇ9–13 and above.
[28] See *PA* 663ᵇ28–9; *GA* 727ᵇ29–30; *Metaph.* 1027ª8–28; *Rh.* 1357ª34–ᵇ6, 1369ª33–ᵇ2.
[29] See *APo.* 81ª40–ᵇ1; *NE* 1109ᵇ20–3, 1126ᵇ2–4, 1142ª14–18; *Metaph.* 1039ᵇ27–1040ª7; §11.

concerned only with truth, are 'incidentally useful to us for many of the things we need' (*EE* 1216^{b}15–16). Indeed, he believes, just as Plato did, that the first principles of *nous* and of desire are the same (*Metaph.* 1072^{a}27).[30]

3 ETHICS

Ethics as Aristotle conceives of it is a practical investigation or *methodos* (NE 1094^{b}10–11) that aims not merely at theoretical knowledge but at personal change: 'The purpose of our examination is not simply to know what virtue is, but to become good, since otherwise the inquiry would be of no benefit to us' (1103^{b}27–9).[31] And because ethics is a practical investigation, its first principle is an end: 'In action the end we act for is the first principle (*to hou heneka archē*), as the hypotheses are the first principles in mathematics' (1151^{a}16–17). And one of the first principles or ends in question is *eudaimonia*: '*eudaimonia* is a first principle. For the first principle is what we all aim at in all our other actions' (1102^{a}2–3; see 1176^{a}30–1).[32]

Ethics has at least one first principle, then. We shall see that it also has others. But are they first principles in the same way that a first principle in science is a first principle? Are all other ethical principles demonstrable from them? Is ethics like a science or is it something completely different?

Science studies universals and discovers some necessary truths about them that hold universally and some that hold for the most part. Of the former we can have unconditional scientific-knowledge; of the latter plain scientific-knowledge. In which of these respects, if either, does ethics differ from science?

Some passages in the *Ethics* suggest that there is no equivalent in ethics of unconditional scientific-knowledge:

Moreover, what is fine and just, the topics of inquiry in politics [and so in ethics], differ and vary so much that they seem to rest on convention only, not on nature. Goods, however, also vary in the same sort of way, since

[30] See §§20, 26. On Plato see R. 505a2–4, 511b3–c2; Reeve (1988, 43–117).

[31] See 1095^{a}5–6, 1099^{b}29–32, 1179^{a}34–^{b}31.

[32] This does not mean that all voluntary actions have *eudaimonia* as their end. An Aristotelian action must not only be voluntary it must be be caused by wish and by decision (see §15) and be its own *allo* end (see §19). And what it then aims at will actually be *eudaimonia* or the good only if the agent has acquired *nous* and *phronēsis* (Rh. 1363^{b}12–15, §14).

they cause harm to many people. For it has happened that some people
have been destroyed because of their wealth, others because of their
courage. Since these, then, are the sorts of things we argue from and about,
it will be satisfactory if we can indicate the truth roughly and in outline
(*tupō(i)*); since we argue from and about what holds for the most part, we
must be content (*agapēton*) if we can draw conclusions of the same sort.
(1094ᵇ14–22)

If we begin in ethics with things that hold only for the most part
and end with them, we never reach things that hold always and in
every case. And if we never reach such things, we never achieve
unconditional scientific-knowledge in ethics. The same message
might also be extracted from the following text:

But let us take it as agreed in advance that every account of the actions we
must do has to be stated in outline (*tupō(i)*), not exactly, and as we also
said at the beginning, the type of accounts we demand should reflect the
subject-matter; and questions about actions and expediency, like questions
about health, have no fixed answers. And when our universal account is
like that, the account of particular cases is all the more inexact. For these
fall under no craft or profession and the agents themselves must consider in
each case what the opportune action is, as doctors and navigators do.
(1103ᵇ34–1104ᵃ10)

Exactness is required for unconditional scientific-knowledge. But in
ethics exactness is not available. Hence unconditional scientific-
knowledge is not available in ethics.³³
   On one reading of these texts, then, they seem to exclude the
possibility of unconditional scientific-knowledge in ethics. But is
that reading the only one? Is it even the right one? Aristotle refers to
his discussion of the good as a sketch or *tupos*. He insists, however,
that it could easily be filled out in detail, if digressions were not a
problem:

This, then, is an outline of the good. For, presumably, we must first sketch
it (*hupotupōsai*) and then later fill in the details. If the outline is good,
anyone, it seems, can advance and articulate it, and in such cases time is a
good discoverer, a good co-worker. This is also how the crafts have
improved, since anyone can add what is lacking in the outline. However,
we must also remember our previous remarks and not look for the same

---

³³ See Irwin (1985*b*, 398–9), (1988*b*, 600n. 3); MacDowell (1979); and
Nussbaum (1986*a*, 235–421). 1140ᵃ31–ᵇ4, which might seem relevant here, is
discussed in §13.

degree of exactness in all areas, but the degree that suits the subject-matter
... so that digressions do not overwhelm our main task. (1098ᵃ20–33)

1094ᵇ14–22 says that we must be content with a sketch. But what we must be content with need not be something that we cannot improve upon. 'We must be content (*agapēton*) to acquire and preserve the good even for an individual', but it is possible, indeed 'it is finer and more divine' to acquire and preserve it for a people or a city (1094ᵇ9–10). Hence neither text gives us a compelling reason to believe that Aristotle's sketch *of the good* is intrinsically sketchy, that it could not be filled out in detail and made exact. And this in fact is how his account of the good actually sounds as we read it. For Aristotle never suggests for a moment that *it* is intrinsically inexact or that it holds only for the most part. Indeed, it is hard even to make sense of the idea that he might think that *eudaimonia* is for the most part the activity expressing the most complete virtue.

Ethics is a practical investigation. Hence much of it has to do with what things are fine, just, or good, with what actions are obligatory or expedient. And both 1094ᵇ14–22 and 1103ᵇ34–1104ᵃ10 seem explicit that ethical principles bearing directly on such topics will be inexact and will hold only for the most part. Since ethics as a whole incorporates such principles, ethics as a whole will be no better epistemically speaking than its weakest components. But this does not mean that ethics does not have stronger components. It does not mean that *no* ethical principles are objects of unconditional scientific-knowledge.

It would be cavalier, given these facts, to rush to judgement either way. The texts may suggest that unconditional scientific-knowledge is impossible in ethics. But it is far from clear that they rule it out altogether. And, as we are about to see, there is compelling additional reason to rule it in.

In the *Topics*, Aristotle defines unconditional knowing as follows: 'Knowing unconditionally (*to haplōs gnōrimon*) is not knowing in general but knowing when in a good intellectual condition, just as the unconditionally healthy is what is healthy for someone in a good bodily condition' (142ᵃ9–11).³⁴ Hence if Aristotle recognizes the existence of a characteristically ethical good intellectual condition, he should also recognize the existence

---

³⁴ APo. 71ᵇ9–12 specifies in more detail what the good intellectual condition in question actually is.

of unconditional knowledge in ethics. But he does recognize such a condition, and in terms that show the clear relevance of the *Topics* definition to it:

If, then, these views do not satisfy us, should we say that, unconditionally (*haplōs*) and in truth, what is wished for is the good, but to each person what is wished for is the apparent good? To the excellent person (*tō(i) spoudaiō(i)*), then, what is wished for will be what is truly wished for, while to the base person what is wished for is whatever it happens to be that he wishes for. Similarly in the case of bodies, truly healthy things are healthy to people in good condition, while other things are healthy to sickly people, and the same is true of what is bitter, sweet, hot, heavy, and so on. For the excellent person judges each thing correctly and in each the truth appears to him. For each state of character has its own individual view of what is fine and pleasant and the excellent person differs most from the others because he sees the truth in each, being a sort of standard and measure of what is fine and pleasant. (1113ᵃ22–33; see 1176ᵃ15–19)

It is hard to escape the conclusion that, for all the variations that there are among fine and pleasant things, there are yet unconditionally fine and pleasant ones of which the excellent person has unconditional knowledge. Hence, if unconditional knowledge is the same as unconditional scientific-knowledge, these texts provide compelling evidence that the latter is possible in ethics. In any case, they clearly suggest that the variation mentioned at 1094ᵇ14–22; and 1104ᵃ2–10 may be a consequence not of there being no unconditionally true view of these things, but of there being different character types in the world each with its own distinctive view of them.

A second argument for this conclusion is more controversial, but if it is right, as we shall see reason to believe it is, then it has considerable probative force. We could not have unconditional scientific knowledge of an ethical principle in either of two circumstances: (1) we cannot demonstrate it from ethical first principles of which we have *nous*; (2) ethical first principles, being definitions of enmattered universals, hold only for the most part. But (1) is false because we do have *nous* of ethical first principles and can demonstrate other ethical principles from them (§9 and below). And (2) is also false. For primary human *eudaimonia* is study or the activity of *nous* expressing wisdom (§28). And neither study nor *nous* is enmattered (§§24, 26–7). Hence a major obstacle to our having unconditional scientific-knowledge in ethics is removed. For matter, and matter alone, poses an obstacle to such knowledge.

The third and final argument on this head is also the least conjectural. It is this. Wisdom (*sophia*) is a part of virtue as a whole (1144ª5–6). Activity expressing *phronēsis* is for the sake of activity expressing widom (§17). Hence the fully virtuous person, the *phronimos*, must possess wisdom. But wisdom is 'the most exact form of scientific-knowledge' (1141ª16–17). And this most exact form is, as we might expect, entirely unconditional (§26). Hence the *phronimos* must possess not just unconditional scientific-knowledge, but the most exact form of it. Now this most exact form of scientific-knowledge is in fact knowledge of primary *eudaimonia* (§26). It follows that one of the most important kinds of ethical knowledge, knowledge of the first principle of ethics, is the most exact form of unconditional scientific-knowledge.

Turning, now, to plain scientific-knowledge our way forward is somewhat less controversial. Aristotle is explicit that in ethics we are often if not always dealing with things that hold for the most part. But he is also explicit that we can have plain scientific-knowledge of what holds for the most part. It follows that we can have plain scientific-knowledge in ethics.[35] Since plain scientific-knowledge is demonstrative, it is not surprising, therefore, that Aristotle actually speaks of ethical demonstrations: 'We must attend, then, to the undemonstrated remarks and beliefs of experienced and older people or of people with *phronēsis*, no less than to their demonstrations (*tōn apodeixeōn*)' (1143ᵇ11–13).[36] What is perhaps surprising, at least on some views of the *Ethics*, is the importance he attributes to them. For if we must attend to the voice of experience and *phronēsis* no less than to ethical demonstrations, we must surely give the demonstrations a lot of attention.

It seems certain, then, that we can have at least plain scientific-

---

[35] Cf. Barnes (1969, 73–7). Joachim (1951, 15) sees that ethics and science ought to be analogous in this way for Aristotle, but thinks—mistakenly—that Aristotle rejected the analogy.

[36] It is possible that Aristotle means that we must attend to undemonstrated *ethical* remarks and beliefs of experienced and older people and people with *phronēsis*, no less than to their non-ethical scientific demonstrations. But this results in a very unnatural reading, which no one, so far as I know, has tried to defend. For why should we assume that older people or people with *phronēsis* will know any non-ethical science? Irwin (1988*b*, 600 n. 3) overlooks this passage when he writes that 'Aristotle never contemplates demonstration of ethical conclusions'.

knowledge of ethical universals. And it follows that our knowledge of such universals can be as exact and scientific as our knowledge of physics, biology, or any other science whose first principles are essentially enmattered. But, since some of the first principles of ethics are essentially matterless, it is at least possible that some of our knowledge of ethical universals is, like our knowledge of theology and mathematics, unconditional scientific-knowledge. In what follows I shall often have this stronger conclusion in view, but the weaker one, which follows simply from the fact that ethical principles hold for the most part, is sufficient to establish that Aristotelian ethics is much more like a science than it is usually represented as being.

Eudaimonia is a first principle of ethics and it is essentially matterless, but if demonstration is to be possible in ethics, there must be at least one other first principle as well. For, since a syllogism must have two premises (*APo.* 73ᵃ7–11, 94ᵃ24–6), the smallest number of principles from which we can demonstrate is two. And if any of these ethical demonstrations is to result in unconditional scientific-knowledge, at least one other ethical first principle must also involve only universals that are essentially matterless. For unconditional scientific-knowledge is possible only of demonstrable principles that are unconditionally necessary, and such principles are unconditionally necessary if and only if *all* of the first principles from which they are ultimately derived are themselves unconditionally necesssary, and so essentially matterless.

Now a plausible additional ethical first principle has already passed before us. It is this: we all aim at *eudaimonia* (or what we take to be *eudaimonia*) in all our other actions (see §§15, 19). For without some such principle there would be no explicit connection between *eudaimonia* and our will and desires. This principle, however, almost certainly involves matter, since we are hylomorphic compounds of matter and form (see §24). But it has what we might call an essentially matterless analogue, namely, 'every *nous* chooses what is best for itself' (1169ᵃ17).[37] Since *nous* is essentially matterless, and we are most of all our *nous* (see §24), this principle gives us all we need for demonstration of unconditionally necessary ethical propositions, all we need for unconditional scientific-knowledge in ethics. Thus the following, for example,

---

[37] This text is discussed in §24.

might well be a demonstration of the proposition that every human being aims most of all at study:

Primary *eudaimonia* is study.
Every *nous* aims at primary *eudaimonia*.
Every *nous* aims at study.

Every *nous* aims at study.
Every human being is most of all its *nous*.
Every human being aims most of all at study.[38]

This demonstration suggests, no doubt, that the extent of unconditional scientific-knowledge in ethics may be rather limited, but it also makes clear that what such knowledge lacks in extent it may well make up for in controversiality.

Are there other ethical first principles besides the two we have been considering? Undoubtedly, there are. For example, various other psychological principles, such as those bearing on the division of the psyche into parts and faculties or those dealing with *akrasia* or weakness of will, may well count as first principles, if not of ethics proper, then of ethical psychology (1102^a12–23). But are there other first principles that are, so to speak, quintessentially ethical, that do belong to ethics proper? There seem to be just three viable candidates: the fine (*to kalon*), the just (*to dikaion*), and the right (*to deon*).

Aristotle speaks of the fine and just as 'what we argue from and about' in ethics (1094^b14–22), suggesting that they might be first principles. He is explicit that virtue is chosen because of itself or for its own sake (1097^b2–4) and that virtuous actions are done 'for the sake of what is fine' (1115^b13), suggesting that virtue and the fine may be ends ethically on a par with *eudaimonia*. For 'of all goods those are ends that are worth having for their own sakes' (*EE* 1248^b18–19). In characterizing virtue, he resorts to the concept of the right:

We can be afraid, or be confident, or have appetites, or get angry, or feel pity, or, in general, be pleased or pained, either too much or too little and in both ways not well; but having these feelings at the right times, about the right things, towards the right people, for the right end, and in the right way, is the mean and best condition and this is proper to virtue. (1106^b18–23)[39]

[38] The enthymematic second syllogism relies for its validity on the account of its minor premise developed in §24.
[39] See 1119^a16–18, 1120^a9–13, 1121^a1–2.

This suggests that the right may also be a first principle of ethics. The fine and the just are ends. They are choiceworthy because of themselves. The right may also be choiceworthy because of itself. But this does not mean that ethical agents—of whom the *phronimos* is the paradigm—will always choose them. We can see this most readily by considering the example of pleasant amusements. Pleasant amusements are choiceworthy because of themselves, but they sometimes fail to promote *eudaimonia* (1176^b9–11, §28). Hence, a *phronimos* would sometimes reject them (1176^b32–1177^a1); for he reliably does what best promotes *eudaimonia* (see §§11–18). By parity of reasoning, we reach a similar conclusion about the fine, the just, and the right: their intrinsic choiceworthiness does not entail that an ethical agent will always choose them or that he will not sometimes reject them.

In fact, however, an ethical agent would always choose these ends, but this is so because the fine, the just, and the right are actually determined by their essential relationships to *eudaimonia*. It is by reference to *eudaimonia* that the mean states are determined to which the virtues are identical (1138^b21–3, §30). Actions are in every way right if they express the reason that the actions of the *phronimos* express (1107^a1–2). And that reason is itself determined by what best promotes *eudaimonia* (see §30). Finally, the fine, being 'what is both choiceworthy because of itself and praiseworthy' (*Rh.* 1366^a33–4), is determined by virtue. For, since *eudaimonia* is beyond praise (1101^b21–7), only virtue and virtuous action have the features definitive of the fine: 'fine things are the virtues and the actions resulting from virtue' (*EE* 1248^b36–7).[40]

It follows that the fine, the just, and the right are not first principles of ethics, but derived principles. For their place as ethical ends is determined by *eudaimonia*, which is the best good (1094^a14–16, 1176^b30–1), the unconditional end (1097^b1, 1139^b1–4).[41]

Eudaimonia is not just a first principle of ethics, then, it is the quintessentially ethical first principle of ethics. The other first principles of ethics are principles of ethical psychology or the like rather than of ethics proper. These distinctions are rough and ready, certainly, and are not intended to bear too much weight, but

---

[40] See *NE* 1097^b1–5, 1101^b31–2, 1103^a8–10, 1105^b31–1106^a2, 1109^a29–30, 1144^a26, 1155^a28–30; *EE* 1248^b17–36.
[41] For opposing argument see Irwin (1986).

they convey the right idea about the *Ethics* in just the way that it conveys the right idea about Mill's utilitarianism to say that its ethical first principle is maximal universal utility. (When I speak of *eudaimonia* as *the* first principle of ethics in what follows, I mean that it is the quintessentially ethical first principle of ethics, not that it is the only one.)

Now to have scientific-knowledge of something other than a first principle, one must know its causal explanation, its demonstration from first principles. Is this also true in ethics? Aristotle is clear that it is. In ethics we begin with the *hoti* and search for the *dioti* (1095^b4–8); we begin with the belief that something is true and try to discover why it is true (see §5). But is it true if *eudaimonia* is the first principle of ethics? Is discovering what *eudaimonia* is, discovering the causal explanation of our other ethical principles? There is every reason to think so. *Eudaimonia* is 'what we all aim at in all our other actions' (1102^a2–3). Hence it is the cause—the final or teleological cause—of our actions and of those principles that guide us towards itself.[42]

Eudaimonia is the first principle of ethics, then. By demonstrating other principles from it—together with the relevant principles of ethical psychology—we acquire plain or unconditional scientific-knowledge of them. But how do we acquire knowledge of *eudaimonia* itself? A natural thought is that we should ask people who have lived and experienced different sorts of lives. But when we ask them, we make a disquieting discovery. Everyone agrees that 'the best good' (1094^a22)—'the human good' (1094^b7), 'the highest of all the goods pursued in action' (1095^a16–17)—is called *eudaimonia* (1095^a17–22). But about what *eudaimonia* actually is they completely disagree. The vulgar think that it is pleasure or wealth; the more cultivated think that it is honour; the wise think that it is the good itself (see §28).

Eudaimonia could be pleasure, then, or honour or the good itself —it could be something else altogether. But which is it? Experience tells us incompatible things. Demonstration is impotent because *eudaimonia* is a first principle. What we want is some way to argue to a first principle. And that—although it may seem impossible—is to some degree, at least, what we are about to get.

---

[42] See *APo.* 94^a20–4; §§17, 19–27.

4 ARGUING TO A FIRST PRINCIPLE

Scientific-knowledge of a principle P_n is not easy to achieve, it is clear. To know P_n scientifically, we must be able to demonstrate it from other principles P_i and P_j, which are themselves known. If P_i and P_j are demonstrable, this requirement poses no immediate problem, but, eventually, if we are to have scientific-knowledge of anything, we must come to first principles that are known. The question is, how do we acquire knowledge of first principles and what justifies us in claiming to have it?

In the *Ethics*, Aristotle warns us that 'we must notice, however, the difference between arguments from first principles and arguments to first principles' (1095^a30–2). It is judicious advice for a reader of the *Posterior Analytics* to bear in mind. For, with the possible exception of the discussion of *nous* in ii. 19, it is absolutely clear that the account of science Aristotle gives in that work applies almost exclusively to arguments from first principles not to them (see §§9–10). If we want to know how to argue to first principles, the *Posterior Analytics* is of little help.

But what would help? How could we possibly argue to a first principle? Aristotle's answer is explicit and in due course it will become intelligible. Arguments to first principles, he claims, must be dialectical arguments:

> Dialectic is also useful in relation to the first principles of each science. For we cannot say anything about them from the first principles proper to the science in question, since they are prior to everything else. Hence it is necessary to discuss them by considering the *endoxa*[43] on each subject. And this is peculiar to, or most of all proper to, dialectic. For since it examines (*exetastikē*)[44] it has a road towards the first principles of all types of inquiry. (*Top.* 101^a37–$^b4$)

Arguments from first principles, by contrast, are scientific arguments. Thus when dialectic actually uncovers first principles, and we begin to argue from them rather than to them, our discussion ceases to be dialectical and becomes scientific: 'The happier someone is in his selection of premises, the more he will unconsciously produce a science quite different from dialectic . . .

---

[43] *Endoxa* are explained in §5.

[44] *Exetastikē* here surely refers to the process of examining arguments and *endoxa* in order to solve *aporiai*. See *NE* 1095^a28–30, *EE* 1215^a6–7, *Rh.* 1354^a4–6.

For if he once chances upon first principles, he won't be doing dialectic any more but that very science whose first principles he has discovered' (*Rh.* 1358ª23–6; see *APr.* 46ª29–30). It seems reasonable to conclude that Aristotle's normative account of our knowledge of first principles, his account of how we argue to them, is to be found in his discussions of dialectic and in his own use of dialectical methods.

Once we have acquired knowledge of the first principles of biology (say), by arguing to them dialectically, and we then begin to argue from those principles, our arguments belong to the science of biology, a science that is a structure of demonstrations at once true and complete. What we are doing before that in our study of living things has no name, but we may call it nascent biology. Nascent biology is incomplete, no better than partly true, and, lacking its first principles, cannot be set out as a structure of demonstrations. Biology as we practise it now is clearly nascent biology. In the same way, we should distinguish between ethics, an investigation that is in possession of its own first principles and argues from them, and nascent ethics, which involves a dialectical search for those first principles. The *Nicomachean Ethics* is largely an essay in nascent ethics. It is an argument to first principles, not from them. And what is true of the *Ethics* is true of Aristotle's other works, including his scientific treatises. They are largely essays in nascent biology, or nascent physics, or nascent politics. That is why they do not have the syllogistic structure Aristotle prescribes for a finished science, possessed of its first principles. The *Posterior Analytics*, on this view, outlines an ideal of scientific-knowledge, which only complete sciences can meet; it is not a characterization of how to do nascent science.[45]

Arguments to first principles in nascent biology or nascent ethics employ dialectical methods. But, if we are to be precise about it, these arguments belong to philosophy not to dialectic itself.[46] For

---

[45] See Barnes (1982, 38–9).

[46] And if we are to be ultra-precise we must question even that. *NE* 1181ᵇ14–15 (cf. 1152ᵇ1–2, *EE* 1216ᵇ26–39, *Pol.* 1279ᵇ11–15) implies that both ethics and politics are 'philosophy of human affairs'. *Top.* 104ᵇ1–2 is explicit that dialectic can be either practical or theoretical: 'A dialectical problem is a topic of inquiry that contributes either to choice and avoidance or to truth and knowledge.' But because *Metaph.* 993ᵇ19–23 suggests that philosophy must aim at theoretical not practical knowledge, Allan (1970, 123–5) denies that ethics is philosophy for Aristotle. Engberg-Pedersen (1985) counters that ethics is philosophy because it sets aside the practical aspect of its subject matter 'treating it *as if* it were concerned with a subject

dialectical methods can be used for other purposes than conducting philosophical investigations into first principles. The *Topics* mentions two of these. Dialectic is a form of mental gymnastics and a set of techniques enabling us to refute people from their own premises, revealing the 'ignorant pretender' to either knowledge or demonstration.[47] And to achieve these aims it can use either a proposition or its contrary, depending on what an opponent will concede, so that it sometimes argues from false premises.[48] But when dialectic serves philosophical purposes, it is restricted in its choice of premises in a way that otherwise it is not:

Our programme [in the *Topics*] was, then, to discover a capacity to construct deductions from the most reputable premises (*endoxotatōn*) on any topic put before us. For that is the function of dialectic by itself and of peirastic.[49] Inasmuch, however, as there is furnished along with it (*proskataskeuazetai*), because of its similarity to sophistry,[50] an ability to conduct its examinations not only dialectically but also with knowledge, we therefore proposed for our treatise not only the function of enabling us to produce an argument on any topic but also of enabling us to construct arguments in which we defend our thesis using the most reputable *endoxa* (*endoxotatōn*). (*SE* 183ᵃ37–ᵇ6)

When dialectic serves philosophy, when it argues 'with knowledge', it must argue, as we shall see in §5, from the most justified beliefs, from those most likely to be true. In one way, therefore, philosophy is more restricted in its choice of premises than dialectic, but in other ways it is less so. It can, for example, make use of premises that, 'lying too close to the conclusion', an opponent in a dialectical tussle might not grant.[51]

matter that naturally invites a theoretical inquiry'. Since 1103ᵇ27–9 gives us reason to doubt Engberg-Pedersen's proposal, it seems better to say that in *Metaph.* 993ᵇ19–23, Aristotle has first philosophy, not philosophy in general, primarily in view. See *Ph.* 192ᵃ35–6, 194ᵇ14–15; *Metaph.* 1061ᵇ4–11; Evans (1977, 7–52); §26.

[47] See *Top.* 101ᵃ25–ᵇ4, *SE* 171ᵇ3–6, *Rh.* 1355ᵇ16–17.

[48] See *APr.* 24ᵃ22–ᵇ15; *APo.* 72ᵃ8–11, 77ᵃ31–2, 81ᵇ18–23; *Top.* 161ᵃ24–33, 162ᵇ27–8; *SE* 169ᵇ25–9.

[49] Peirastic is a branch of dialectic (*SE* 169ᵇ25) that argues from premises 'accepted by the answerer and that anyone who claims to possess knowledge of the subject is bound to know' (*SE* 165ᵇ4–6) with the aim of unmasking the ignorant pretender to knowledge (*SE* 171ᵇ3–6).

[50] Sophistry 'is the semblance of wisdom without the reality' (*SE* 165ᵃ21); it is 'what appears to be philosophy but isn't' (*Metaph.* 1004ᵇ26). Hence dialectic together with the ability to conduct examinations with knowledge is philosophy.

[51] See *Top.* 105ᵇ30–1, 155ᵇ7–16; *APr.* 46ᵃ3–10.

But these differences aside, which are the result of their different aims, dialectic and philosophy have the very same scope and employ the very same methods: 'Dialectic does indeed deal with the same kind of things (*to auto genos*) as philosophy, but philosophy differs from dialectic in what it turns its capacity to (*tō(i) tropō(i) dunameōs*). . . . Dialectic tests (*peirastikē*) where philosophy seeks knowledge (*gnōristikē*)' (*Metaph.* 1004^{b}22–6). The methods of nascent ethics or biology are dialectical, then, but their aims are philosophical. (When I speak of dialectic, in what follows, I shall have in mind philosophical dialectic or dialectical methods adapted to the aims of philosophy.)

5 DIALECTIC

When he takes up the problem of *akrasia* or weakness of will in *NE* vii. 1, Aristotle gives one of his best brief accounts of what dialectic involves:

As in all other cases (*tōn allōn*)[52] we must set out the *phainomena* and first of all go through the *aporiai* (*diaporēsantas*). In this way we must prove (*deiknunai*)[53] the *endoxa* about these ways of being affected—ideally all the *endoxa*, but if not all, then most of them and the most compelling. For if the *aporiai* are solved and the *endoxa* are left, it will be an adequate proof. (1145^{b}2–7; see 1146^{b}6–8)

We set out the *phainomena*. We go through the *aporiai*. We prove the *endoxa*. But what are *phainomena*, *aporiai*, and *endoxa*?

Phainomena is the neuter plural of the present participle of the verb *phainesthai*, which means 'to appear' or 'to be plainly so'. Etymologically speaking, therefore, *phainomena* are things that appear, either veridically or non-veridically, to someone to be the case.[54] *Phainomena* include, in the first instance, empirical observations or perceptual evidence: 'This [that the earth is spherical] is

---

[52] The force of the unqualified *tōn allōn* is surely universal.

[53] The verb *deiknumi* has the primitive meaning of showing something forth or bringing it to light. And this may well be a less misleading way to render it here as we shall see. In order not to beg any questions, however, I have followed custom in translating *deiknumi* as 'prove'.

[54] Sometimes the *phainomena* and the facts (*gignomena, sumbainonta, huparchonta*) do not seem to be distinguished from one another. See *PN* 470^{b}5–10; *GA* 750^{a}21–3, 759^{a}11; 760^{b}28–32; *Metaph.* 1090^{b}19–20. Sometimes the *phainomena* are contrasted with the facts. See *Top.* 146^{b}36, 171^{b}27–30; *Metaph.* 1009^{a}38–1010^{a}3; *Rh.* 1402^{a}26–7, ^{b}23.

also shown by the sensory *phainomena*. For how else would lunar eclipses exhibit segments shaped as we see them to be?' (*Cael.* 297^{b}23–5).[55] But they also include things that we might not comfortably call observations at all, for example, things that strike people as true or that are commonly said (*legomena*) or believed (*doxa*) by them. So, for example, the following is a *phainomenon* or *legomenon*: 'The akratic or weak-willed person knows that his actions are base, but does them because of his feelings, while the enkratic or self-controlled person knows that his appetites are base, but because of reason does not follow them' (1145^{b}12–14; see 1145^{b}26–7). *Phainomena* are usually neither proved nor supported by something else. Indeed, they are usually contrasted with things that are supported by proof or evidence (*PN* 462^{a}23–9, *EE* 1216^{b}26–8). But there is no *a priori* limit on the degree of conceptualization or theory-ladenness manifest in them. They need not be—and in Aristotle seem rarely if ever to be—devoid of interpretative content; they are not Baconian observations, raw feels, sense data, or the like.[56]

The *endoxa*, or putative *endoxa*, are defined in the following passage from the *Topics*:

Endoxa are those opinions accepted by everyone or by the majority or by the wise—either by all of them or by most or by the most notable and reputable (*endoxois*). . . . For not every *phainomenon* is an *endoxon*. (100^{b}21–6)

A little later, however, Aristotle makes an important but frequently neglected clarificatory comment about it:

Clearly also, all opinions expressed by the crafts (*kata technas*) are dialectical premises. For people are likely to accept the views held by those who have made a study of these things, for example on a question of medicine they will agree with the doctor, and on a question of geometry with the geometer; and the same in all the other cases. (104^{a}12–37)

This comment suggests that the views of craftsmen, scientists, and other experts are *endoxa*, whether those experts have already

---

[55] See *APr.* 46^{a}17–27, *Cael.* 297^{a}2–6.
[56] Nussbaum (1986*a*, 240–63) is persuasive on this point. It follows that Aristotle's empiricism is rather different from that of (say) Locke, Ayer, or Quine.

gained reputations in their fields or not.[57] It follows that Aristotle's own views, in the many sciences he studied, are *endoxa*.[58]

It will not do, therefore, to identify *endoxa* with common beliefs or with reputable ones.[59] Some *endoxa* are common beliefs, namely, those that count as *endoxa* because they are believed by everyone: 'What seems to everyone, we say is' ($1172^{b}36$–$1173^{a}1$).[60] Others are believed by the majority of people but not by all; others still are believed by scarcely anyone: 'Some of these views are traditional, held by many, while others are held by a few reputable (*endoxoi*) men' ($1098^{b}27$–8). Plato's views about the good itself are certainly not commonplaces, indeed they conflict with common views. They are *endoxa* none the less because Plato is a notable and reputable philosopher whose views are supported by

---

[57] At *Top.* $104^{a}11$–12, Aristotle says that 'anyone would grant what is accepted by the wise *unless it is opposed to the views of the many*'. Does this mean that the beliefs of practitioners of 'recognized' crafts and sciences are only *endoxa* if they are not opposed to the views of the many? There is good reason to think that it does not. First, at $104^{a}33$–7, Aristotle makes this same point without any qualification at all. Second, *endoxa* do not have to be acceptable to the many or fail to conflict with their views. If they did, Aristotle's initial account of them ($100^{b}21$–6) would have to be much different. Third, Aristotle says that 'The opinion of the many accords with convention; the wise speak according to nature and truth' (*SE* $173^{a}29$–30). He would hardly say this and allow that the opinions of the wise, a group which includes the practitioners of the recognized crafts (*NE* $1141^{a}9$–12), are not *endoxa* unless they do not conflict with the views of the many. Finally, we need to distinguish between dialectical arguments in general and dialectical arguments used for philosophical purposes (§4). Philosophy can use *endoxa* as premises that an opponent in a dialectical wrestling match might not concede (*Top.* $155^{b}7$–16; §4). For a different, but for these reasons unsatisfactory, account of this passage, see Bolton (1987, 121–30).

[58] Hence arguments that begin from Aristotle's own views, such as those in *NE* i. 6, should not, for that reason alone, be characterized as not employing dialectical methods. Cf. Hardie (1968, 39).

[59] Nussbaum (1986*a*, 243) identifies *endoxa* with *phainomena* and with 'common conceptions or beliefs on the subject'. Irwin (1988*b*, 38) claims that *endoxa* are common beliefs 'held by fairly reflective people after some reflexion'. Both overlook or give insufficient weight to *Top.* $104^{a}14$–37. Barnes (1980, 498–502) identifies *endoxa* with reputable beliefs. However, he seems to think, on the basis of *Top.* $100^{b}21$–3, that a belief is reputable if everyone shares it. It seems more plausible to take the passage as saying that some beliefs are *endoxa* because they are reputable (i. e. believed by reputable people), while others are *endoxa* because they are believed by many people or by everyone. Plato's views on *eudaimonia* merit careful treatment precisely because they are reputable; the views of the many can be dismissed, because on this topic their views are disreputable. Compare *NE* $1095^{a}28$–30 (*EE* $1214^{b}28$–$1215^{a}4$) with *NE* 1. 6. See *NE* $1176^{b}16$–21, §28.

[60] *Ha gar pasi dokei, taut' einai phamen.* Alternatively: 'What seems [good] to everyone, we say is [good]'. See *Top.* $100^{b}22$, *PN* $462^{b}14$–18.

argument as well as by the weight of his reputation as a thinker (1095ª26–8, 1096ª11–1097ª14). Socrates' view that *akrasia* is impossible is almost universally rejected, but it counts as an *endoxon* for similar reasons (1145ᵇ21–31, below). Expert opinions, whether widely shared or not, are *endoxa* because experts have and are recognized as having superior knowledge. Finally, other opinions—though perhaps not widely shared or expert in the same way as a craftsman's or scientist's—are *endoxa* because they have the weight of experience behind them: 'We must attend, then, to the undemonstrated remarks and beliefs of experienced and older people or of people with *phronēsis* . . . For these people see correctly because experience has given them their eye' (1143ᵇ11–14). Universal acceptance, argument, experience, and having a reputable or expert source are all factors, then, that can add sufficient epistemic weight to a *phainomenon* to turn it into an *endoxon*. And 'the most reputable *endoxa*', which Aristotle recommends as premises of philosophical arguments, will presumably be those *phainomena* that have the most such weight (see *SE* 183ª37–ᵇ6).

Roughly speaking, then, an *edoxon* is a *phainomenon* with some additional epistemic weight, weight it can acquire from a variety of sources. Everything else being equal, then, an *endoxon* must be more likely to be true than a bare *phainomenon*. But to see why this is so, we need more than we have been given so far. We need some reason to think that there is some truth in bare *phainomena*, and more truth in those *phainomena* that turn out to be *endoxa*. Is there any such reason? In §§6–8 we shall see that there is.

Endoxa are not, then, generally the same as *phainomena*, but Aristotle seems not to be always concerned to distinguish the two. In the discussion of *akrasia*, for example, the *endoxa* to be proved are also referred to as *legomena* (1145ᵇ20), which seem not to be distinguished from *phainomena*.⁶¹ And in the *Eudemian Ethics*, the goal of dialectic is characterized in terms not of proving *endoxa* but of according with the *phainomena*:

We must accept the reasoning that will both best explain to us the views (*ta dokounta*) held about these matters and will loosen the *aporiai* and contradictions; and we will achieve this if we show that the conflicting views are held with good reason. For such reasoning will most closely

⁶¹ See 1098ᵇ9–12, 1152ᵇ23–4, 1174ª11–12.

accord with the *phainomena*; and it will allow the conflicting views to be retained if analysis can show that each is partly true and partly false. (*EE* 1235^{b}13–18) Thus it seems that proving the *endoxa* and reasoning in a way that will 'most closely accord with the *phainomena*' come to much the same thing here.[62]

Aristotle often uses the term *aporia* to refer to problems whose solution seems simply to lie in further observations, in acquiring knowledge of more facts. Thus the following are *aporiai*: 'What is wind and how does it arise? What is its efficient cause and what its origin?' (*Mete.* 349^{a}33–4). Moreover he sometimes describes his scientific researches into such problems in ways that make them sound dialectical: 'Let us explain the nature of the winds and all windy vapours, also of rivers and of the sea. But here again we must first go through the *aporiai* (*diaporēsantes*)' (*Mete.* 349^{a}12–14). This should not surprise us. Scientific problems are yet problems— *aporiai*—that science itself identifies and tries to solve. But some of the *aporiai* Aristotle wrestles with in his own philosophical works —his discussion of *akrasia* in Book VII of the *Ethics* is often cited as an example—seem not to be empirical. It is not more facts we need to solve them, it seems, but more conceptual sophistication or greater subtlety. And occasionally, indeed, Aristotle actually contrasts scientific research and (non-philosophical) dialectical inquiry:

Those who dwell in intimate association with the natural facts are better able to lay down principles that can be coherently conjoined and are broadly applicable. Those, on the other hand, who engage in lengthy discussions without taking the facts into account are more easily revealed as people of narrow scope. One can see, too, from this the great difference that exists between those whose researches are based on the facts of nature and those who inquire [merely] dialectically (*logikōs*).[63] (*GC* 316^{a}5–11)

These apparent differences between types of *aporiai* and styles of approach to them suggest that there may be two dialectical

---

[62] It is possible, of course, that the switch from according with the *phainomena* in *EE* to proving the *endoxa* in *NE* represents a change of doctrine. But since it is hard to see any philosophical motive for the change, any real difference in dialectical practice between the two works, or any substantial difference in their conclusions about *eudaimonia*, this is not likely. See §28.

[63] *Logikōs* is a synonym for 'dialectical' at *Top.* 162^{b}27 and perhaps at *APo.* 88^{a}18–19, 93^{a}15. See Irwin (1988b, 558 n. 32) and Ross (1924, 2: 168) on *Metaph.* 1029^{b}13.

methods in Aristotle: one empirical and dealing with empirical *aporiai*; the other conceptual and dealing with conceptual *aporiai*.[64] But this suggestion is one that our discussion of the nature of dialectic itself will make clear we should resist.

Dialectical arguments are arguments to first principles. Does this mean that they are intended to prove or establish the truth of first principles or to justify us in believing them?[65] The answer to both questions is largely, no. It is the relations of *de re* necessity holding between universals that makes an epistemic first principle true, and it is experience that largely justifies us in believing it to be true:

Most first principles of a science are special to it. Hence it is the task of experience to supply the first principles in each science. I mean, for example that astronomical experience supplies the first principles of astronomy, for once the *phainomena* had been adequately grasped, astronomical demonstrations were soon discovered, and the same is true of any other craft or science. Consequently, if the facts are grasped in each, our next task will be to set out readily the demonstrations. For if our investigation leaves out none of the true facts, we will be able to discover and produce demonstrations of whatever can be demonstrated and to make that clear (*phaneron*) whose nature does not admit of proof. (*APr.* 46ª17–27)

But this seems to leave us with an *aporia* of its own. If dialectical arguments neither establish nor justify first principles, what is there left for them to do?

The answer is advertised in the final clause of our text. The role of dialectic is to make those propositions clear, which, not admitting of proof, must be first principles. In the very next sentence, Aristotle makes the allusion to dialectic explicit: 'Thus we have explained fairly well in general terms how we must select premises; we have discussed the matter precisely in the treatise on dialectic [the *Topics*]' (*APr.* 46ª29–30). Experience—experience that we may not be able to get unless we engage in careful professional investigation of the relevant things—provides us with obscurely grasped universals or inadequately worked out definitions. Dialectic enables us to grasp those universals clearly or to

---

[64] See Owen (1961) and Irwin (1987). Nussbaum (1986*a*, 240–63) is convincing that there is only one dialectical method. But her internal realist understanding of that method seems mistaken. See Cooper (1988*b*) and below.

[65] Cooper (1975, 68–9) sees clearly the importance of this question. But he thinks that the sharp distinction Aristotle draws 'between dialectical and scientific thinking prevents him from facing the question squarely'.

work out those definitions adequately. Dialectic takes us from things that are 'less clear in nature but clearer to us'—these being things we know through experience—to things that are 'by nature clearer and more knowable'—these being 'first principles, causes, and elements' (*Ph*. 184^{a}10–^{b}14). For clarity is the very hallmark of dialectic.^{66}

Dialectical arguments are not proofs of first principles, then. They do not have first principles as their conclusions. Instead, dialectic takes principles already justified by experience and made true by reality and 'clarifies' them. And this is as true in ethics, where the object of inquiry is the good, as it is in science (*APr*. 46^{a}16–17).

Dialectic clarifies first principles. But how does it do this? The answer is contained in the description of dialectic with which we began. Dialectic clarifies first principles by going through the *aporiai*. Through the empirical *aporiai* or the conceptual *aporiai*? The question is moot. Officially and paradigmatically, the *aporiai* that specifically dialectical arguments are intended to solve are problems that arise about first principles when all the facts—all the veridical *phainomena*—are already in, are already there to set out: 'If our investigation leaves out *none of the true facts*, we will be able to discover and produce demonstrations of whatever can be demonstrated and to make that clear whose nature does not admit of proof' (*APr*. 46^{a}24–7). Demonstration and dialectic, like the Owl of Minerva, do not appear on the scene until dusk.

It seems obvious to most people that *akrasia* occurs. At the same time, Socrates' argument that it is impossible proves difficult to refute. New facts seem not to be needed; all the relevant ones seem to lie to hand. Thus we are caught between a rock and a hard place: 'thought is tied up, for it does not want to stand still because the conclusion of the argument is displeasing, but it cannot advance because it cannot refute the argument' (1146^{a}24–7; see *Metaph*. 995^{a}29–33). This is an archetypal dialectical *aporia*—literally a problem that is aporous, one there seems to be no way out of. What dialectic does is to try to find a way out of such aporetic

---

^{66} See *DA* 413^{a}11–13, *NE* 1097^{b}22–4, *EE* 1216^{b}26–36. Another hallmark, or another way of expressing the same one, is that dialectic provides a *lusis* or loosing of aporetic knots. See e.g. *Ph*. 253^{a}31–3, 263^{a}15–18; *GC* 321^{b}11–13; *Mete*. 354^{b}22–4; *Metaph*. 995^{a}27–33, 1032^{a}6–11; *Po*. 1462^{b}16–19; Burnet (1900, xl–xliii).

predicaments by clarifying the *endoxa* about first principles that give rise to them. And clarification typically takes the form of detecting ambiguities, drawing distinctions, and reformulating principles and definitions in the light of those distinctions. We can see this vividly by examining Aristotle's discussion of *akrasia* itself, which is often acknowledged as a paradigm of dialectic.[67] Socrates argues that it is impossible to know what is best and not do it. The 'manifest *phainomena*' attest that it is possible to do just that (1145b21–31). Hence there is a conflict among the *endoxa* and an *aporia* to be solved. For what is widely believed is an *endoxon* and so is what is believed by a wise person who has investigated the matter. And to solve this *aporia*, to prove both *endoxa*, or to reason in a way that is as close to each as possible, Aristotle focuses on the notion of knowledge and begins to articulate it carefully. He first distinguishes between someone who has knowledge, but is not using it, and someone who is aware that he has it because he is presently using it. Then he distinguishes between knowing the universal premise (everything sweet must be tasted) in a piece of practical reasoning and knowing the particular premise (this, some one particular thing, is sweet) (1146^{b}31–1147^{a}5). Finally, he distinguishes between various ways of having, but not using knowledge. You know that Dublin is in Ireland, but you probably were not using that knowledge (or calling it explicitly to mind) until just now. Those who are mad or drunk or affected by strong feelings both have knowledge in a way and do not have it (1147^{a}10–17). Since it is an *endoxon* that akratics are affected by strong feelings (1145^{b}12–14), Aristotle concludes that, with respect to some of the things they know, they will be like people who are mad or drunk (1147^{a}17–18).

These three distinctions enable Aristotle to find the truth both in the Socratic *endoxon* about *akrasia* and in the apparently contrary one endorsed by common belief. A person with a strong desire for sweets might initially argue as follows:

Everything sweet ought to be tasted.

This particular thing is sweet.

If nothing interferes, Aristotle says, it is necessary that he tastes the sweet in question (1147^{a}30–1). But if the person is akratic in regard to sweets, something will interfere, namely, an argument developed

---

[67] See e. g. Cooper (1975, 69).

by reason. Since Aristotle refers only to the first or universal premise of this argument, there has been much controversy about how it should be reconstructed (1147ª31–2).[68] But for our purposes the details are irrelevant. So let us suppose it to go as follows:

> Nothing sweet ought to be tasted if it is unhealthy.
> This particular thing is sweet and unhealthy.

If nothing interferes with this argument, the person refrains from tasting. But, of course, something does interfere, namely, the initial argument engendered by his desire for sweets. And in the akratic, its interference is decisive: he will taste the sweet. How so? Aristotle's explanation is this. The akratic's strong desire to taste prevents him from using his knowledge of the minor premise of the argument produced by reason. He knows that tasting this particular sweet thing is unhealthy but, like a drunkard or a madman, he does not use his knowledge. His strong appetites prevent him from doing so (1147ª32–ᵇ12).

In one way, then, the common beliefs are right: *akrasia* is possible and it is caused by appetite overpowering reason. But Socrates is also right:

> Since the last premise [sc. this particular thing is sweet and unhealthy] does not seem to be universal or expressive of knowledge in the same way as the universal premise, even the result Socrates was looking for would seem to come about. For the knowledge that is present when someone is affected by *akrasia* and that is dragged about because he is affected is not the sort that seems to be knowledge to the full extent [i.e. knowledge of the universal] but only perceptual knowledge [i.e. knowledge based on perception of this particular thing]. (1147ᵇ13–17)

Thus, when the appropriate distinctions are drawn, when the *endoxa* are sufficiently refined and disambiguated, they are seen to be consistent with one another. In this way, the *endoxa* are proved and the *aporiai* are solved.[69] Proving the *endoxa* is not simply a

---

[68] The discussions in Charles (1984, 117–32) and Charlton (1988, 34–59) vividly convey the nature of the debate.

[69] Nussbaum (1986*a*, 240) is mistaken to suggest, therefore, that Aristotle rejects Socrates' account simply because it conflicts with the *phainomena* and 'sets himself to find an account of akratic behavior that will remain faithful to the "appearances" in a way that the rejected Socratic account does not'. It is rather the case that Aristotle saves both the *phainomena* and Socrates' account, clarifying or modifying both in the process.

matter, then, of showing them to be true as they originally stand. It is a matter of finding the truth in them by refining and articulating them; it is a matter of bringing the truth in them to light. But to reiterate: dialectic neither puts the truth in nor justifies us—or fully justifies us—in believing it to be there. The facts do the first; experience does the lion's share of the second.

Aristotle says that dialectic begins with the *hoti* and discovers the *dioti*—it begins with the facts and discovers their causal explanation (1095^b4–8). Does his discussion of *akrasia* do that? Yes, it does. Aristotle's refined Socratic principle tells us what *akrasia* really is and explains why it is true, as is commonly believed, that (certain sorts of) *akrasia* are possible and why it is also true, as Socrates believed, that (other sorts of) *akrasia* are impossible. It thereby explains the *endoxa*—the facts—with which the investigation began. It is a mistake, therefore, to think that Aristotle's dialectical investigation of place in the *Physics*, or parallel investigations in his other writings, are fundamentally different from his investigation of *akrasia*.[70] The *Physics* is explicit that dialectic seeks a causal explanation of the *endoxa*:

> It is from the things we take as true that inquiry must proceed. We must try to inquire in such a way that we uncover what the thing is, solve the *aporiai*, show that the *dokounta* [i.e the *endoxa*] about place are true of it, and, further, make clear what the causal explanation of the difficulty is and of the *aporiai* about it. (*Ph.* 211^a7–11)

The thumbnail sketch of dialectic in the *Ethics* is not so explicit, but what Aristotle actually does accords with the fuller description. None of the *endoxa* considered in the discussion of *akrasia* are dismissed as completely false, but, if they had been, Aristotle is clear that he would need to explain why they seemed true: 'We must, however, not only state the true view, but also give the causal explanation of the false one, since that promotes confidence. For when we have a clear and good account of why a false view appears true, that makes us more confident of the true view' (1154^a22–5). That is why he can allow that while dialectic should try to prove all the *endoxa*, it will succeed in its task, if it proves 'most of them and the most compelling' (1145^b5–6). For if it fails to prove all the *endoxa*, it will have to explain why the unproved ones, though they seem to be true, are actually false. In both the *Ethics* and the

[70] See Bolton (1987). Cf. Barnes (1980, 494–5).

Physics, then, the same dialectical method is involved and the search for causal explanations is part of that method in both works. Dialectic takes place when all the facts are in, but sometimes we think all or enough of the facts are in and start to do dialectic. If we are wrong, if what we have are not facts or not all of the facts, what we are practising is not dialectic proper but nascent dialectic. Because his 'facts' are mistaken or incomplete or both, many of Aristotle's dialectical discussions are clearly of this latter sort, even if he thought that they belonged to dialectic proper. We can often ignore the distinction between dialectic proper and nascent dialectic, but sometimes—as now—it is important to bear it in mind.

Because dialectic proper comes into play when all of the *phainomena* or *endoxa* are already in, there is a clear sense in which it is non-empirical. The sense is this: dialectic proper does not rely on any new empirical information to accomplish its goals. But there is another much more important sense in which it is empirical. It relies on *endoxa*, which are justified by experience and made true—even necessarily true—by reality. If Aristotle's discussion of *akrasia* belongs to dialectic proper, his refined Socratic principle will be an empirically justified *de re* necessary truth, although it will have been discovered in part by non-empirical methods. Almost every major theoretical discovery in science is like this.

In fact, however, it is much more likely that Aristotle's discussion belongs only to nascent dialectic. And if that is so, it is empirical in yet a further way: its findings could be falsified by the discovery of new facts or the empirical falsification of old *phainomena* or *endoxa*. The principles that Aristotle takes as *endoxa* or *phainomena* for his discussion of *akrasia*, for example, are not conceptual truths, they are, or include, empirical psychological principles, which could turn out to be false.[71] Indeed, they presuppose a whole way of looking at the psyche, belief/desire psychology or folk psychology, which could itself turn out to be false. Some argue, indeed, that it has already been falsified by more professional psychological theorizing. So Aristotle's modified Socratic principle about *akrasia* is not a conceptual truth either. It is an empirical claim, which future empirical research in psychology could well undermine. Because of this, nascent dialectic is obviously not con-

[71] See Cooper (1988*a*).

servative. It is as radical as our capacity to discover new facts. But, then, dialectic proper is not correctly characterizable as conservative either. It is as conservative or non-conservative as the truth turns out to be.[72]

6 THE TRUTH IN *PHAINOMENA*

The end of the dialectical process, which begins with *phainomena*, is to discover the truth about first principles by solving the *aporiai* to which *endoxa* about them give rise. But how do we reach the truth by solving these *aporiai*? How is it that we do not—or cannot —end up with nothing better than puzzle-free or euporetic false opinions?

The most natural answer to these questions is that truth must enter the picture from the bottom, that it must be transmitted from the relevant bit of reality to *phainomena* and from them to *endoxa*. And this natural answer seems to be Aristotle's. Having surveyed the relevant *phainomena*, the opinions of the many and the wise about what *eudaimonia* is, for example, Aristotle has this to say about them: 'Some of these views are traditional, held by many, while others are held by a few reputable men; and it is reasonable for each group to be not entirely in error but correct on one point at least or even on most points' (1098^{b}27–9). It is clear, therefore, that he believes that *phainomena* have truth in them. But why does he believe this?

A famous text from the *Metaphysics* suggests a blunt answer. The truth is (in one way at least) so easy to know that *phainomena* need little further defence:

Studying the truth is in one way hard, in another easy. An indication of this is found in the fact that no one is able to attain the truth adequately, while on the other hand, we do not collectively fail but everyone says something true about the nature of things and while individually we contribute little or nothing to the truth, by the union of all a considerable amount is amassed. Therefore, since the truth seems to be like the proverbial door, which no one can fail to hit, in this respect it must be easy. But the fact that we can have a whole truth and not the particular part we aim at shows the difficulty of it. Perhaps, too, as difficulties are of two kinds, the cause of the present difficulty is not in the facts but in us. For as the eyes of bats are to

---

[72] Other accounts of dialectic worth comparing to this one are Barnes (1981); Irwin (1987), (1988*b*, 26–72); Nussbaum (1986*a*, 240–63); and Owen (1961).

the blaze of day, so is the *nous* in our psyches to the things that are by nature clearest of all. (*Metaph.* 993ª30–ᵇ11)

In the *Rhetoric*, the other side of the coin is succinctly characterized. The truth is (in one way) easy for us to know because we are adapted by nature to know it: 'human beings are naturally adequate as regards the truth and for the most part (*pleiō*) they happen upon the truth' (*Rh.* 1355ª15–17). Essentially the same idea seems to be presupposed in the *Eudemian Ethics*: 'each person has something of his own to contribute to the truth' (1216ᵇ30–1). But this blunt answer, though certainly revealing, is not explanatory bedrock. Underlying it is an elaborate psychological theory, a naturalized epistemology, which attempts to explain how the senses provide (largely accurate) information about reality.[73]

And underlying this theory, in turn, and partly based on it, there is a teleological theory according to which we are by nature adapted to get on well in the world and achieve our purposes in it:

Each animal as such must possess perception. For it is by this that we distinguish being an animal from not being an animal. As for the various particular senses, taste and touch are necessarily present in all animals— touch for the reason we gave in *De Anima* and taste because of nutrition. . . . The senses that depend on an external medium, on the other hand, such as smell, hearing, and sight, belong to animals with the power of locomotion only. All who possess these senses have them for the sake of survival, in order that they may perceive in advance what is nutritious and so avoid what is bad or destructive. In animals that enjoy *phronēsis*, they are also for the sake of doing well. For they inform us of many distinctions from which arise *phronēsis* about the concerns both of *nous* (*tōn noētōn*) and of the practicable (*praktōn*). (*PN* 436ᵇ10–437ª3; see *DA* 434ª30–ᵇ2)

This theory may not explain why perceptions in general must be largely veridical: information that promotes survival may not coincide across the board with information that accurately reports the facts about the world; illusions sometimes have more survival value than the awful truth. 'Human kind', the poet reminds us, 'cannot bear very much reality.' But the theory does seem to succeed somewhat better with the particular perceptions it refers to. If our senses did not generally distinguish the nutritious from the

---

[73] Modrak (1987) is a philosophically perceptive account of the theory as a whole. On naturalized epistemology see Quine (1969, 69–90).

destructive, the good for us from the bad for us, we would none of us survive for very long.[74]

It is true, of course, that this entire edifice of theory, which includes both first-order beliefs about mind-independent reality and second-order beliefs about how those beliefs are veridically formed, rests ultimately on experience, on the sensory *phainomena* themselves: 'it is the business of experience to give the first principles of each subject' (*APr.* 46ª17–18; see *APo.* 81ª38–ᵇ9); 'lack of experience diminishes our capacity to comprehend the admitted facts' (*GC* 316ª5–6); 'without sensation a man would not learn or understand anything' (*DA* 432ª7–8). But it is not a theory that simply assumes that experience is veridical; it contains the materials for an experience-based critique or justification of experience.

And what is true about knowledge of reality in general is equally true of that part of reality that is the subject matter of ethics. The ground-floor ethical data are the ethical *phainomena*, the deliverances of ethical experience, of lived life:

> The truth, however, in questions about action is judged from the facts (*tōn ergōn*) and how we live, since these are what control the answers to such questions. Hence we ought to examine what has been said by applying it to what we do and how we live; and if it harmonizes with what we do, we should accept it, but if it conflicts we should count it mere words. (1179ª17–22)

> For arguments about actions and feelings are less credible than the facts; hence any conflicts between arguments and perceptible facts arouses contempt for the arguments and undermines the truth as well as the arguments. . . . True arguments, then, would seem to be the most useful, not only for knowledge but also for the conduct of life. For since they harmonize with the facts they are credible and so encourage those who comprehend them to live by them. (1172ª34–ᵇ7)[75]

Since experience is, *ceteris paribus*, reliable, it is, *ceteris paribus*, reliable about what pleases us and pains us, what satisfies and frustrates, what is worthwhile and what is not, what helps us flourish and what causes us to languish, and about 'the actions in life that politics argues from and about' (1095ª2–4). And these discriminations are the raw data for our knowledge of *eudaimonia*, of what 'all by itself makes a life choiceworthy and lacking in nothing' (1097ᵇ14–

---

[74] See Barnes (1987) and Stich (1990, 55–74) for further discussion.
[75] See *Cael.* 293ª25–30; *GC* 316ª5–11; *GA* 760ᵇ30–4; *NE* 1098ᵇ11–12, 1143ᵇ11–14; *EE* 1216ᵇ40–1217ª19.

16). For, as Aristotle puts it, 'it would seem that people not unreasonably reach their conception of the good, that is of *eudaimonia*, from the lives they lead' (1095^{b}14–16). The discriminations of experience are also the raw data for our knowledge of ethical principles other than the' first principle. The *phainomena* about *akrasia*, for example, are also based on experience, although their familiarity may tend to make us forget that fact.

7 FROM ETHICAL *PHAINOMENA* TO ETHICAL *ENDOXA*

There is truth in *phainomena* generally, then, and more particularly in ethical *phainomena*, truth in them about the first principle of ethics. But because they are inconsistent not all such *phainomena* can be true—hence the need for *ceteris paribus* clauses in characterizing the reliability of the senses. So how are we to filter out the true ones? The first step is to find the *endoxa*, the *phainomena* that have something more to be said for them. But how are we to take the first step? How are we to get from *phainomena* about *eudaimonia* to *endoxa* about it?

The following passage from the *Eudemian Ethics*, which parallels *NE* 1095^{a}28–30 but elaborates on it, suggests an answer:

Many opinions are held by children and by the diseased and mentally unbalanced and no sensible man would concern himself with *aporiai* about them. The holders of such views are in need not of arguments but of maturity in which to change their opinions or else of correction of a civil or medical kind (for medical treatment is no less a form of correction than flogging is). Similarly, neither need we examine the views of the many; they speak in an unreflective way on almost any topic, most of all when they speak about this. Only the opinions of decent people should be examined.[76] For it would be strange to present arguments to those who need not argument but experience. (*EE* 1214^{b}28–1215^{a}3)[77]

Only the opinions of the sane, mature, and (appropriately) experienced are relevant *endoxa*; only the *aporiai* to which those *endoxa* give rise need to be considered. Unfortunately, this answer about how to select the relevant *endoxa* and *aporiai* does not as yet explain very much. It does not tell us why sanity, maturity, and experience lend credibility to opinions about *eudaimonia*. More

---

[76] Following Woods (1982, 200) I have translated *kai malista peri tautēs, alla tas tōn epieikōn monas*.
[77] See *Top.* 105^{a}3–6, 170^{b}6–8.

important, it does not tell us what the relevant kinds of sanity, maturity, and experience are. It suggests, however, that these might be useful questions to pursue. People form their opinions about *eudaimonia* from the kinds of lives they lead. But not all lives result in the formation of true or reliable opinions. Only those whose upbringing have given them 'fine habits' have the true opinions that are the appropriate starting points of ethical inquiry; only what seems so to them is a relevant *endoxon*:

We need to have been brought up in fine habits if we are to be adequate students of what is fine and just and of political questions generally. For the first principle we begin from is the belief that something is true and if this is apparent enough to us, we will not, at this stage, need the reason why it is true in addition; and if we have this good upbringing, we have the first principles to begin from, or can easily acquire them. (1095^{b}4–8; see 1098^{a}33–^{b}8)

What we need, therefore, is an explanation of what fine habits are and of why it is that only those brought up in them are sources of *endoxa* in ethics.

Aristotle mentions three major ways to gain access to first principles and implies that there are others: 'Some first principles are studied by means of induction (*epagōgē(i)*), some by means of perception, some by means of some sort of habituation (*ethismō (i)*), and others by other means' (1098^{b}3–4). And he is explicit that it is the third of these ways—habituation—that enables us to form true opinions about the first principle of ethics: 'It is virtue, either natural or habituated, that teaches true opinion about the first principle' (1151^{a}17–19).[78] Since the first principle of ethics is *eudaimonia*, the habits that will enable us to form true opinions about *eudaimonia* must be just those habits that will result in our having habituated virtue: 'Inferences about the practicable have a first principle: "Since the end, i.e. the best good, is this sort of thing", whatever it is—let it be any old thing for the sake of argument. And this is apparent only to the good person. For vice perverts us and produces false beliefs about the ends of actions' (1144^{a}29–36). And these habits are the fine ones. For habits are fine if they lead to the formation of fine states of character and the virtues are such states (*EE* 1248^{b}36–7). Only those whose fine

---

[78] See 1104^{b}9–13 with 1140^{b}16–19, 1179^{b}23–9. Natural virtue is further discussed in §14.

habits have resulted in their possession of habituated virtue, then, are sources of *endoxa* in ethics. Hence Aristotle can dismiss whole classes of ethical *phainomena*, such as the views of the many about what *eudaimonia* is (1096ª5–10), as having no weight.

But the claim that only those with fine habits are reliable sources of ethical *endoxa* is an extraordinary one, of course. It entails that the first principle of ethics and so, presumably, many of the things demonstrable from it are somehow epistemically inaccessible to the less than virtuous. We are not used to thinking about epistemic access in that way. Modern epistemology has little room for the idea that the good can know things that the bad cannot.[79] Clearly, then, we need to probe further if we are not to lose touch with Aristotle at the beginning.

8 ETHICAL *ENDOXA*

In *NE* vi. 2, Aristotle distinguishes between theoretical knowledge and truth, on the one hand, and practical knowledge and truth, on the other:

As assertion and denial are to thought, so pursuit and avoidance are to desire. Now virtue of character is a state that decides; and decision is a deliberative desire. If, then, the decision is to be excellent, the reason must be true and the desire correct, so that what reason asserts is what desire pursues. This, then, is practical thought and practical truth. By contrast, when thought is theoretical, not practical or productive, its good or bad state consists in being true or false. For truth is the function of whatever thinks; and that of practical thought is truth agreeing with correct desire. (1139ª21–31)

Practical knowledge requires both correct desire and true reason. Since ethics is a practical matter, the truth that only those brought up in fine habits are said to grasp (1095ᵇ1–9, 1098ª33–ᵇ3) is surely practical truth. But to recognize something as a practical truth—to have practical knowledge of it—it is not enough to believe it with justification (or whatever), desire must enter the picture. More than that, the desire that enters the picture must be correct; it must be for the correct end. But what makes desire be for the correct end? Since habituated virtue ensures the truth of practical opinion about *eudaimonia* and *eudaimonia* is the correct end (1102ª2–3), the

---

[79] The Platonic origins of this idea are explored in Reeve (1988, 43–117).

answer must be: habituated virtue. Habituated virtue is required for true opinion about *eudaimonia*, on this showing, because the opinion in question, being practical not theoretical, requires correct desire, and it is habituated virtue that ensures desire is correct.

But why does Aristotle think that habituated virtue makes desire be for the correct end? There is little doubt that part of the answer lies in the controversial function argument (see §22). For the conclusion of that argument is that 'the human good turns out to be an activity of the psyche that expresses virtue' (1098ᵃ16–17). And given this conclusion and the identification of the human good with *eudaimonia*, we can understand why Aristotle thinks that *eudaimonia* is an activity of the psyche expressing virtue (1102ᵃ5–7). Now virtue is a state of the psyche that decides (1106ᵇ36). And decision, which is the cause of psychic activity expressing reason or virtue, is a desire of a certain sort (1139ᵃ3–ᵇ5, §15). Hence a desire will be 'correct'—it will result in *eudaimonia* or activity expressing virtue —if and only if it is appropriately controlled by virtue (see §§30, 32). It follows that it is virtue that ensures that desire is correct.

We have not yet reached the appointed conclusion, however, because our story so far has been about full virtue not about habituated virtue. When we discuss the relations between *phronēsis* and virtue in §14, however, we shall see that habituated virtue, too, ensures that desire is for the correct end.

The effect of drawing on Aristotle's distinction between practical and theoretical belief and knowledge should be to restore us to comprehending contact with his thought. For while we may have doubts about how virtue could affect epistemic access, we surely find it at least intelligible that it affects our conative apparatus, our will and desires. The vicious may in our epistemology be as knowing as the virtuous, but the will of the latter differs from that of the former in the ends it pursues. The virtuous pursue the ethically correct end; the vicious do not.

Aristotle's argument that habituated virtue is the guarantee of truth in practical beliefs about *eudaimonia* is, of course, rather abstract. It is important to remember, therefore, that its authority rests on its harmony with ethical experience, with the appropriate *phainomena* or *endoxa*. At the end of the function argument, Aristotle reminds us of this requirement: 'We should examine the first principle not only from the conclusion and premises of a deductive argument, but from the *legomena* about it. For all the facts (*ta huparchonta*)[80] harmonize with a true account, whereas the truth soon clashes with a false one' (1098^{b}9–11). And elsewhere he is at pains to point out that his conclusions accord with the judgements of those whose ethical authority the conclusions underwrite: 'Actions [that express the virtues] are good and fine as well as pleasant; indeed, they are good, fine, and pleasant more than anything else, since on these questions the decent person has good judgement and his judgement agrees with our conclusions' (1099^{a}22–4).[81] If the function argument most closely accords with the *phainomena*, *legomena*, or *endoxa* about *eudaimonia*, it can help explain and justify them, but if it fails to closely accord with them, it fails altogether (see §25).

If habituated virtue makes desire right, and in that way, and in that way only, plays a role in practical knowledge or belief, it is surely possible for someone to have true theoretical opinion about *eudaimonia* even if his vice, or lack of habituated virtue, makes it impossible for him to have true practical opinion about it. Aristotle seems to deny this, however. Those who have not been brought up in fine habits have the wrong desires; they desire the wrong end. But this conative defect sometimes gives rise to a further more strictly cognitive one. Someone who has not been brought up in fine habits, who has not acquired habituated virtue, may not even *understand* arguments that try to get him to pursue some end other than the wrong one with which his bad upbringing has left him:

Arguments and teaching surely do not influence everyone but the psyche of the student needs to have been prepared by habits for enjoying and hating finely like ground that is to nourish seed. For someone whose life follows his feelings would not listen to an argument turning him away or even understand (*suneiē*) it. (1179^{b}23–7)

How are we to explain this further claim?

A natural thought is this. To recognize something as *eudaimonia* is to recognize it as something that 'all by itself makes a life choiceworthy and lacking in nothing' (1097^{b}14–16). It follows that, if one cannot see how something could make a life choiceworthy or desirable in this way, one will not be able to understand it as being *eudaimonia*. Now it is certainly not true that

---

[80] The *huparchonta* and the *phainomena* are clearly one and the same here. See *Rh*. 1396^{a}23–^{b}10.
[81] See 1113^{a}31–3, 1176^{a}15–19.

failure to desire something prevents one from understanding it to be valuable or worth going after, but none the less it can pose a barrier —a variably permeable barrier—to understanding. This is especially true where experience is crucially involved. Witness the following passage in which Aristotle seems to be making just this sort of point: 'Since they (the many) live by their feelings, they pursue their proper pleasures and the sources of them, avoid the opposed pains, and have no conception (*oud' ennoian echousin*) of what is fine and truly pleasant, since they have had no taste of it (*ageustoi ontes*)' (1179^b13–16; see 1176^b16–21). The many have had no taste of the fine, which is an essential end of truly virtuous action (1120^a23–4, 1122^b6–7), because their actual desire structure ensures that they pursue only their proper pleasures. If such people were to do a fine action, in other words, they would do it only as a means to something other than the fine (see *EE* 1247^b37–1249^a3). Hence they would not experience what it is to act for the sake of the fine considered as an end desirable because of itself, as an intrinsic good. Since on Aristotle's view we gain access to universals from experience of the particulars that instantiate them (see §9), it follows that the many can have 'no conception of what is fine'. And this will remain true of them until their desire structure is altered by something sterner than argument (1179^b28–9).

If this is Aristotle's thought here, it is one with which we can sympathize. For we agree that we cannot judge or evaluate certain things adequately until we have actually experienced them. The proof of the pudding, as we say, is in the eating. And we also allow that we may need lengthy training in order to have those experiences: the uninitiated are deaf to Messiaen and blind to Pollock. Aristotle's point is a cognate one: to have a conception of the fine, we need to be able to experience it, and such experience is possible only for those whose desire structure has been appropriately shaped by habituation and upbringing. But it is also, of course, an expression of his empiricism. Without experience of the relevant phenomena, our knowledge and understanding of them is bound to be limited (*APo.* 81^a38–$^b9$).

One way in which desire structure can affect our capacity to understand, then, is by limiting our access to essential experience. But desire structure can also affect our understanding in another way. A person's desire structure may be such that, though he does the fine thing, he must frustrate some of his other desires in doing it:

the enkratic or self-controlled person, who does the fine thing because his rational wish (*boulēsis*) is stronger than his opposing appetites, is of this sort (1151^{b}35–1152^{a}3). Such a person will not find unalloyed pleasure in acting finely because of the frustration involved in doing it. And because he does not find pleasure in it, his capacity to fully understand the fine, to discriminate its shades and nuances—his capacity to be ethically creative—is compromised:

Each pleasure is proper to the activity it completes. For the proper pleasure increases the activity. For we judge each thing better and more exactly when our activity is associated with pleasure. If, for example, we enjoy doing geometry, we become better geometers and understand each question better; and similarly lovers of music, building, and so on improve at their proper function when they enjoy it. (1175^{a}29–35)

To grow in the fine, to be ethically subtle and discriminating, to be ethically alive, we must take pleasure in doing fine things. If we do not enjoy being ethical, we will never be anything much better than blunt instruments, sticking doggedly to principles because we cannot altogether trust our judgement and perception (see §11).

Given the role of desire structure in practical—and to a lesser extent in theoretical—cognition, we can understand why Aristotle emphasizes the importance of proper upbringing and habituation for ethics. And emphasize it he certainly does. A few examples must stand for many: 'it makes no small difference, then, whether we form habits of one kind or of another from our very youth; it makes a very great difference, or rather all the difference (*mallon de to pan*)' (1103^{b}23–5); 'the right habituation is what makes the difference between a good political system and a bad one' (1103^{b}6).[82] Even for adults, indeed, habit remains as a crucial bulwark against slipping into vice: 'Presumably, however, it is not enough to get the correct upbringing and attention when they are young; rather they must continue the same practices and be habituated to them when they become men. Hence we need laws concerned with these things also and in general with all of life' (1180^{a}1–4). It is important to be clear, however, especially in the face of these somewhat strident statements, that habituation is seldom either watertight or singleminded. The akratic and the enkratic, the weak-willed and the self-controlled, are testimony to that (1151^{a}11–28). Both have been sufficiently well habituated to

---

[82] See 1095^{b}7–8, 1104^{b}9–13.

have true beliefs about *eudaimonia*. However, the akratic's habituation has not been good enough to rid him of strong appetites that cause him to act against those beliefs, and the enkratic, though he does act in accordance with his true beliefs about *eudaimonia*, frustrates his insufficiently moderated appetites in doing so.[83]

But though habituation is neither watertight nor singleminded, reason typically has its work cut out for it if habituation has failed to do its share:

> There are three things that make someone good and excellent. The three are nature, habit, and reason . . . Man has reason and man alone. Therefore, because of this, they [nature, habit, reason] must be in harmony [for a man to be good or virtuous], for they do not always agree; men do many things against habit and nature because of reason, if haply (*ean*) it persuades them to be better. (*Pol.* 1332ᵃ38–ᵇ8)

Reason sometimes wins out even against the habits resulting from bad upbringing, though usually it needs good luck—note the 'haply' in Aristotle's formulation—if it is to succeed. It is not impossible, but it is 'not easy' either, for argument to alter 'what has long been absorbed by habit' (1179ᵇ16–18).

The move from *phainomena* to *endoxa*, then, is mediated or underwritten by a naturalized empiricist epistemology and by a theory of reliability in specifically ethical evidence (the function argument), these theories being in turn underwritten by the *endoxa* and *phainomena* they help underwrite (see §25). The move is not based simply on an intuitive judgement about which *phainomena* to credit. This important but insufficiently appreciated fact greatly increases the subtlety and credibility of Aristotle's ethical epistemology.

We are now in a position to explain why *endoxa* must be proved and *aporiai* solved. In ethics, our aim is practical knowledge and hence practical truth, just as in a science our aim is theoretical knowledge and theoretical truth. Since there is good reason, provided in part by the theory we have just been scouting, to think that *endoxa* are true, it follows that we cannot achieve our aim of knowing the truth unless our theory proves the *endoxa*. The same interest in knowledge and truth explains why the *aporiai* must be solved. Conflicts among the *endoxa* are perplexing, first, because

---

[83] See Burnyeat (1980, 83–8), §15.

each *endoxon* has a claim to truth, and second, because the Law of Non-Contradiction—itself the subject of a justly celebrated dialectic defence in *Metaphysics* iv $(1005^b35-1009^a5)$[84]—rules out the possibility that conflicting *endoxa* can all be true. Until we see our way through such conflicts, therefore, we cannot be fully clear about where the truth lies.

9 NOUS OF FIRST PRINCIPLES IN SCIENCE AND ETHICS

APo. ii. 19 tells us the following story about our knowledge of first principles. Cognitive access to first principles begins with (1) perception of particulars (99^b34-5), perception being a critical or discerning capacity (*kritikon*). In some animals, perception of particulars gives rise to (2) retention of the perceptual content in the psyche $(99^b39-100^a1)$.[85] When many such perceptual contents have been retained, some animals (3) 'come to have an account from the perception of such things' (100^a1-3). The retention of perceptual contents is memory and a collection of remembered or retained perceptual contents, or the account generated from them, is an experience (100^a3-6). (4) From such experiences the universals are reached that are the first principles we are seeking: 'And out of experience or out of the whole universal resting in the psyche—the one beside the many, one and the same in all of these [retained perceptual contents]—comes the first principle of a craft or science; of a craft if it concerns coming to be, of a science if it concerns being' (*APo.* 100^a6-9). This entire process, from perception of particulars to grasp of universals, is induction (*epagōgē*) (100^b3-5).[86]

In the brief concluding section of ii. 19, Aristotle tells us how *nous* fits together with induction. It is because we are capable of *nous*, as other animals are not, that the process just described leads in our case to universals and first principles. That is why Aristotle says that our scientific-knowledge of first principles itself has a first

[84] Good recent discussions of this argument include Code (1986), Dancy (1975), and Irwin (1988b, 179–88).

[85] See Barnes (1975, 252–3).

[86] Engberg-Pedersen (1979, 301–7) is persuasive that *epagōgē* means something like attending to particular cases with the consequence that insight into some universal point is acquired, and that, unlike what we call induction, it does not involve inference. Cf. Greenwood (1909, 29–32).

principle (by which he clearly means an ontological first principle), namely, *nous* (88ᵇ35–6, 100ᵇ15). For without *nous* scientific-knowledge of first principles would be impossible (see *DA* 430ᵃ25; §27). The *Nicomachean Ethics* gives a parallel account of our knowledge of *eudaimonia*, which it is convenient to treat in two phases. The first exhibits the close analogies between the two accounts. The second brings out the one really significant difference between them. The following passage of the *Ethics* parallels *APo*. ii. 19:

[A] *Nous* is also concerned with the last things (*tōn eschatōn*) and in both directions. For about the first definitions (*horōn*) and the last things (*tōn eschatōn*) there is *nous* but no argument (*logos*). [B] In demonstrations *nous* is about the unchanging definitions (*horōn*) that are first principles. [C] In practical reasoning, *nous* is about the last thing, the one that admits of being otherwise (*endechomenou*), and hence about the other premise (*tēs heteras protaseōs*). For these last things are the first principles of the end to be aimed at, since universals are reached from particulars. We must, then, have perception (*aisthēsin*) of these particulars and this perception is *nous*. (1143ᵃ35–ᵇ5; see 1139ᵇ28–9)⁸⁷

(B) deals with the role of *nous* in demonstrations. It reflects the doctrine of the *Posterior Analytics* and needs no further comment. (C) deals with the role of *nous* in practical reasoning. (A) makes a proleptic claim about *nous* based on (B) and (C): in demonstrations, we have *nous* of the unchanging indemonstrable definitions or first principles; in practical reasoning we have *nous* of 'the last things'. The immediately preceding passage (1143ᵃ25–9) and the concluding sentences of (C) tell us that the last things in question are particulars, *kath' hekasta*.

---

⁸⁷ To understand this passage, it is important to avoid some translations that it invites, but does not mandate. *Horos* can mean 'term' (e. g. *APr*. 24ᵇ16) or 'definition' (e. g. *Top*. 101ᵇ38); *logos* can mean 'account', 'definition', 'argument', and other things as well. But we should not translate *horos* as 'term' or *logos* as 'account'. For what the universals that are first principles lack is not an account—they have definitions—but arguments that prove them. Hence *logos* must mean 'argument'. But then *horos* must mean 'definition', because terms, unlike definitions, cannot be supported by arguments. Greenwood (1909, 197) comes close to recognizing this. Neither should we translate *eschaton* as 'last term'. For, first, the only reason to do so is that we have already mistranslated *horos* as 'term', and, second, *eschaton* clearly does not mean 'term' in the immediately preceding passage (1143ᵃ25–35)—actions (*prakta*) are *eschata* (ᵃ34–5) but they are not terms. Rackham (1934) is better here, therefore, than Irwin (1985b) or Ross (1980).

Aristotle's claim in (A) and (C) that there is *nous* of particulars has caused much controversy, but it is hardly likely to represent a departure from oft-repeated doctrine: perception is of particulars; *nous* of universals.[88] In the *De Anima*, however, Aristotle allows that perception, which discerns (*krinō*) a particular, may be either distinct from *nous*, which discerns the universal that is the essence of that particular, or it may be 'the same capacity differently disposed' (429^b10–14; see 429^b18–21).[89] The perception of particulars is presumably *nous*, therefore, just in so far as it is an awareness of a particular as instantiating a relevant universal or of the universal in the particular.

(C) is difficult, but the following simplified sketch conveys what Aristotle seems to have in mind. It is more easily drawn in terms not of *eudaimonia*, but of its equivalent *eupraxia* or acting well (1095^a18–20, 1139^b1–4). John is told what to do—what kinds of actions to perform—in order to act well in a variety of different circumstances. As a result, he comes to grasp a general action-guiding principle, which we may represent as follows: 'Always act well'. Simultaneously, and by a psychological process analogous to the four-stage one described in *APo*. ii. 19, John gains a partial grasp or understanding of a certain universal, namely, acting well: to act well in these circumstances is to do an act of type F1; to act well in those other circumstances is to do an act of type F2; and so on. When he employs this action-guiding principle together with his partial understanding of acting well in order to determine how to act in a particular situation, it appears as the major premise in a practical argument, which we can think of him as addressing to himself:

Always act well.
Doing an action of type F3 here now would be acting well.
[If nothing interferes, he does an act of type F3].[90]

The second or minor premise of this argument, since it is the one that deals with last things, is the one referred to as 'the other premise' at 1143^b3. And the last thing is the particular action John does, which is a token of the type F3. This action will involve John's

---

[88] See *APo*. 81^a38–$^b9$, 87^b28–88^a17, 88^b30–89^a10, 100^a13–$^b17$; *NE* 1112^b34–1113^a2, 1126^b3–4, 1147^a25–6; §§1–2.

[89] See Modrak (1987, 113–32) for further discussion.

[90] Aristotle often seems to suggest that the conclusion of a practical syllogism of this sort is the action itself. See *NE* 1147^a35–41, *MA* 701^a22.

bringing about a change in his will and his body, and typically in some other part of the world as well, which is guided both by his knowledge of F3 and his perception of the particular changes he is bringing about. That is why Aristotle refers to what John does as an *endechomenon*, as something that could be otherwise. He means that the particular action John does will be (or involve) a change in what could be otherwise (see §§13–14).

It is by doing actions, such as actions of type F3, which he thinks will be cases of acting well, that John comes to understand more fully what acting well actually is or consists in. So what (C) is saying—in terms now of *eudaimonia*—about the first principles of ends is just this. We acquire our (more filled-out) conception of *eudaimonia*, our knowledge of the universal *eudaimonia* is, by doing actions of types that we think will exemplify (our more schematic conception of) *eudaimonia*. For the effects of those actions on ourselves or on others will help us to determine whether or not acting like that makes life choiceworthy and lacking in nothing. Hence it is that these actions are the first principles—the epistemic first principles—of the end to be aimed at.

We can now understand why (A) says that *nous* is concerned with last things or particulars in 'both directions'. Perception of particulars leads by induction to *nous* of the universals from which demonstration begins. In practical reasoning, *phronēsis* or practical wisdom uses perception to apply a universal—F3 in our sketch—supplied by *nous* to guide a particular action. Demonstrations begin with a universal abstracted from particulars; practical reasoning ends with a universal being applied to a particular. Hence the two directions (see *APo.* 82ª21–4).[91]

In science, which consists entirely of demonstrations, *nous* is involved in only the first of these ways. In ethics, which is part demonstration and part practical reasoning, *nous* is also involved in the second way. *Nous* grasps *eudaimonia* from the experiences of particular actions. But when someone recognizes that to achieve *eudaimonia* in these circumstances he must act in such and such a

---

[91] It is a mistake, therefore, to think that (A) involves two kinds of *nous*, theoretical *nous*, which is of universal first premises, and practical *nous*, which is of particulars. See e. g. Greenwood (1909, 71–2). Practical *nous*, as this notion is understood in the *De Anima*, is practical because it is the ultimate teleological cause of action—indeed, of everything. See §§18, 27 for further discussion.

way, *nous* is involved again. This time in applying a universal to a
particular (see §§11–12).[92]

Nous plays two roles in ethics, then, but only one in science. This
is a difference, to be sure, but not a really significant one. For it is
explained by the fact that scientific-knowledge is exclusively
concerned with universals. And where universals alone are concerned, *nous* plays exactly the same role in ethics as it does in
science. The really significant difference lies in the different
processes by which *nous* of first principles is achieved in science and
ethics. In science, it is achieved by induction or *epagōgē*; in ethics it
is achieved by habituation or *ethismos*.

Now our analysis of (C) makes it quite clear that habituation is a
type of induction. It is a process that leads to *nous* of a universal, a
first principle. Hence, it is a mistake to treat habituation as a
mechanical process divorced from intellect or cognition. Habituation is just as unmechanical and intellectual, just as much a
cognitive process, as induction itself. The difference between
induction and habituation is that habituation involves more, not
less, than induction. A simplified sketch will again help us to see to
the heart of the matter.

John is taught to do actions of types F1 and F2 as fine, just, right,
or examples of acting well, and to avoid actions of type G1 and G2
as shameful, unjust, wrong, or examples of acting badly. He is
rewarded with something pleasant for doing F1 or F2 or for
avoiding G1 or G2; he is punished with something painful for
avoiding F1 or F2 or for doing G1 or G2. This training, coupled
with further experience of the sort described in our earlier sketch,
has two inseparable but distinguishable results. First, it leads by the
familiar four-stage process of induction to *nous* of the appropriate
ethical universals, of the fine, the just, the right, and their opposites,
and of the first principle of ethics, acting well or *eudaimonia*.
Second, it leads to habits, to structures of desire and revulsion,
which are appropriately correlated with those ethical universals. As
a result of being encouraged and discouraged, rewarded and
punished, John comes to be disposed to do acts of type F1 and F2

---

[92] Dahl (1984, 227–36), Greenwood (1909, 69–72), and Stewart (1892, 2: 92–3)
agree that *nous* is involved in the first of these ways. Irwin (1978, 266 n. 6) disagrees:
'1143ᵃ35–ᵇ5 does not say, but denies that *nous* grasps the first principles which are
the basis of deliberation'. He overlooks the fact that the 'last things are the first
principles of the end to be aimed at', and that the end to be aimed at is the first
principle of ethics, *eudaimonia*.

and to avoid acts of type G1 and G2, and so on. It is this second result that marks the difference between induction and habituation. But what requires that difference is that in ethics we must acquire practically true beliefs whereas in science we need acquire only theoretically true ones. And practical truth involves not just correct belief but correct desire.[93]

It is the involvement of our will and desires in practical belief, then, that explains why it is habituation and not just induction that is involved in ethics. But is that explanation bedrock? Is the philosophical spade turned here or is there more to be said? My own view—and I think Aristotle's—is that though our schematic story can be filled out and made more realistic it cannot really be much deepened. We can get beneath the fine, the just, the right, and their opposites, we can get beneath *eudaimonia*, to whatever is the ethical equivalent of the dainty and the dumpy—the nice and the nasty, perhaps.[94] We can talk about how primitive pleasures can be exchanged for less primitive ones as things first pursued for adventitious ends (pleasing Mum and Dad) come to be enjoyed for their own sakes. We can talk about pathological development where primitive pleasures are exchanged for less primitive ones, which are never really enjoyed, but are persisted in none the less out of duty (or because Mum and Dad did a very thorough job)—the akratic and enkratic have no doubt developed in some such ways. We can explain how experience leads to discrimination, maturity, and what I earlier called ethical creativity. What we cannot do is explain why it is that changing desires, our own or other people's, typically involves a lot of repetition and really hard work. We face an analogous problem in explaining why it typically takes hard work and much repetition to acquire a skill. There is an explanation of these facts, no doubt, but 'we must hear it from the natural scientists' (1147^b8–9), not from philosophers.

---

[93] The role of intellect in habituation receives interesting discussion in Burnyeat (1980) and Sherman (1989, 157–99). But none of these accounts brings *nous*, induction, and practical belief into the picture in the right way.

[94] See Hursthouse (1988, 213): 'Suppose we considered training for the virtue of temperance (*sophrosunē*) in just that area which is concerned with having the right attitude to the pleasure of food. Surely this starts at least as far back as saying to toddlers "You don't want that nasty dirty thing".'

10 DIALECTIC AND *NOUS*

A *normative* account of our knowledge of first principles explains how our claims to know them are justified. A *non-normative* account describes the psychological mechanisms involved in acquiring knowledge of first principles but does not necessarily explain how our claims to know them are justified. Is the account discussed in §9 intended to be normative or non-normative? The traditional answer is that it is normative. For *nous*, on this view, is a form of intuitive reason that simply enables us to detect indemonstrable first principles in a way that justifies us in believing them to be intrinsically necessary.[95] If Aristotle thought of *nous* in this way, his account of it would, indeed, be normative.

Let us suppose for a moment, therefore, that some such normative account is what Aristotle has in mind. How satisfactory an account would it be? If the first principles of biology (say) were fairly simple analytic truths, it might be plausible to believe that we know them to be intrinsically necessary by something like intuition or mental vision. It seems certain, however, that biological first principles are not going to be like that. Instead they are going to be very complex propositions indeed. As one recent writer has put it 'a *good* definition of Man might be a million pages long, perhaps a length of the order of that of the program by which Nature *constructs* a man; briefly it would have to be the cash to meet . . . the enormous paper draft on such a definition contained in the words "organized body potentially having (human) life in it".'[96] Moreover, they are going to be very complex propositions that, on Aristotle's view, are necessary not *de dicto*, but *de re*. And, clearly, it is not reasonable to think that we could know such complex propositions to be intrinsically necessary *de re* in something like the way that we know that bachelors are unmarried men. When we discover what Aristotle thinks *eudaimonia* actually is, and the kinds of arguments he uses to show what it is, we will see that what is true of biological first principles is equally true of ethical ones (see §§19–28). It is just not plausible to believe that we could come to know them in the way we know simple analytic truths.

But did Aristotle really think of *nous* in the way we have been exploring? Did he intend, in *APo.* ii. 19 and *NE* 1143ᵃ35–ᵇ5, to be

---

[95] See e. g. Ross (1923, 41–55), Scholz (1930), Irwin (1977).
[96] Furth (1988, 105).

offering a normative account of our knowledge of first principles? The answer is that he did not. Aristotle's normative account of our knowledge of first principles is his account of how dialectic enables us to argue to them.

But if dialectic enables us to argue to first principles, what exactly does *nous* do? How are *nous* and dialectic related? The most reasonable answer is that *nous* must follow upon a successful dialectical clarification of first principles and so must occur not at the beginning of research but at the end. For dialectic itself must wait on science to do its empirical work. And this seems to be what Aristotle has in mind. For, first, he says that nothing could be more exact or truer than scientific-knowledge except *nous* (*APo*. 100^{b}5– 12).[97] But this would not be true if dialectic clarified the very first principles that *nous* had already fully grasped. Second, he refers to *nous* as the *kephalē*, the crown or coping stone or completion, of scientific-knowledge (*NE* 1141^{a}18–20). And this clearly suggests that full-blown *nous* of first principles is the very last move in the game.

The overall picture might, then, look something like this. Someone who has had the relevant experience and done the appropriate inducing of concepts or universals from it, will in time be able to identify many different principles, some of which, because they can be 'coherently conjoined and are broadly applicable' (*GC* 316^{a}7–8), will be candidate first principles. Some of these principles will be syllogistically deducible from others, perhaps, but there is no presumption that all lower-level principles are discovered by being deduced from more primitive ones (although some may be discovered in that way). Syllogistic structure, if it can be imposed on the emerging theory at all, will come later, and not primarily for the purposes of discovering new principles, but to gain insight into the explanatory relations between principles already discovered and, thereby, into the systematic structure of the reality that the theory as a whole reflects.

Someone who has acquired principles in this way—'through intimate association with natural facts' (*GC* 316^{a}6–7)—will have a good understanding of those principles and of why they are true. He will have a good mastery of a fragment of his nascent subject,

<hr>

[97] The conditions under which one science is more exact than another are discussed in §26.

whether it is biology or ethics or theology. As yet, however, he has no unconditional scientific-knowledge.

Much further on in the development of his subject, we may imagine that an empirically adequate theory is developed, one whose principles persuasively explain all the true *phainomena* or *endoxa* with which the subject in question is concerned. Someone who has scientific-knowledge of that theory, who has arrived by successful dialectical argument at a clear grasp of its essentially matterless first principles, and who has demonstrated all the other principles from them, has unconditional scientific-knowledge of the principles he has thus demonstrated and—for the first time—*nous* of the first principles he has demonstrated them from.[98]

If this is the place of *nous* in ethics or biology, is it reasonable to think of it as a kind of intuition, a kind of seeing? The answer may be more a matter of taste than of argument. But we can well imagine that someone who has mastered ethics or biology in the way we have been describing will simply be able to *see* that first principles—however complex and impenetrable they may seem to someone less experienced—are intrinsic necessities, that they could not be otherwise. When Aristotle describes first principles as 'knowable through themselves' (*APr.* 64^{b}34–6), as 'convincing on the strength not of anything else but of themselves' (*Top.* 100^{a}30–^{b}21), when he suggests that they are self-explanatory (*APo.* 85^{b}24–5), he is surely thinking of them in relation to such a person, to someone in 'good intellectual condition' (*Top.* 142^{a}9–11), and not to just anyone who happens upon them. Otherwise it would not be as difficult as it is 'to know whether we know from the first principles of a thing or not' (*APo.* 76^{a}26–8). *Nous* may be a kind of intuition, then, a kind of seeing, but it is one based on empirical research and dialectic, not one on which they are based.[99]

So much seems to be Aristotelian doctrine. But is it credible doctrine? Is it reasonable to believe that empirical research aided by dialectic can yield knowledge of intrinsically necessary first principles? A challenge will help us to find our way by reminding us of the road we have already travelled.[100] Dialectic proves first

---

[98] It may well be, of course, though we may ignore the fact for present purposes, that the first principles of biology, like those of physics, are all essentially enmattered. If this is so, unconditional scientific knowledge is impossible in biology.

[99] Cf. Burnyeat (1981, 131–32) and Kosman (1973).

[100] This challenge is pressed in Irwin (1977, 210–17).

principles by means of arguments whose premises are *endoxa*. Those arguments are our justification for believing first principles as such. But *endoxa* are just widely shared or reputable beliefs. Surely, it follows that dialectic cannot accomplish the tasks Aristotle has set it. For how can an argument based on mere beliefs establish something as an intrinsic necessity or enable us to know it to be one?

This challenge looks compelling, but our earlier investigations show it to involve three different misconceptions. The first is about the nature of *endoxa*. *Endoxa* are not just beliefs people happen to have. They are beliefs that have a real claim on truth, a claim underwritten by a naturalized epistemology and, in the case of ethical *endoxa*, by other theories as well. They may, for that matter, represent the most authoritative expert judgement on the topic.

The second misconception is about what makes first principles necessary. On Aristotle's view, scientific first principles are unconditionally necessary, but they are not analytic or necessary *de dicto*; they are necessary *de re*. An epistemic first principle is a definition that articulates the essence of a universal or ontological first principle. It is intrinsically necessary—if it is—because of the relations holding among the universals that constitute the real essence it articulates. But if epistemic first principles are necessary *de re*, we obviously do not need dialectic to confer necessity on them. That is done by nature.

The third misconception is about our knowledge of first principles. We are justified in believing first principles to be intrinsically necessary by the fact that the theory of which they are a part, and which offers the best explanation of the relevant phenomena, represents them as being intrinsically necessary *de re*. Dialectic's role is to clarify first principles underwritten by experience and empirical research. Dialectic may partly justify our belief in first principles, then, but most of the work is done by empirical research itself.

Can we conclude that empirical research coupled with dialectic is a sufficiently potent combination to yield scientific-knowledge of first principles? Obviously, we cannot. Epistemological scepticism remains to be answered. What empirical research and dialectic give us is knowledge of first principles conditional upon the sceptic's possibilities—that we are victims of an evil genius or brains in vats —not in fact being realized. If those possibilities are realized, empirical research and dialectic yield no knowledge of mind independent reality at all. But if those possibilities are not realized, empirical research and dialectic do seem to have what it takes to yield knowledge of intrinsically necessary first principles. Many would allow, indeed, that empirical research can accomplish that task all by itself.

If ethics is realist, it too will feel the sting of the sceptic's argument just like biology and the other natural sciences.[101] But realism in ethics has its own special problems in addition; problems familiar to any reader of recent work in ethics. Aristotle does not explicitly engage these problems. But if ethical realism is, as I think, a plausible doctrine, then discovering the ethical truths should not be all that different, from the epistemological point of view, from discovering the biological ones. If empirical research and dialectic are adequate for the latter task, they should also be adequate for the former.[102]

[101] Irwin (1988*b*) argues resourcefully that Aristotle has a general answer to the sceptic about metaphysical realism whether in ethics or in epistemology generally. Some *endoxa*, such as the Principle of Non-Contradiction, are justified, he claims, in ways that are *to some degree* independent (see pp. 274–6) of the experience whose veracity the sceptic has put into question (see *Metaph.* 1005^{b}35–1009^{a}5). 'Strong dialectic', which is the method of first philosophy (pp. 18–21, 153–276), uses such *endoxa* to work out the 'features of reality that are necessary for it to be an object of scientific study at all' (p. 19). The quasi-transcendental argument that results underwrites the view that reality must consist of 'subjects with essences' (p. 19) and, hence, the function argument (pp. 153–469). The function argument is, thus, part of the experience-independent metaphysical foundations of Aristotle's *Ethics* and *Politics*. I am unpersuaded by Irwin's argument for two reasons. First, *endoxa* are not just reflectively acceptable common beliefs (pp. 26–50), they are the sort of expert opinions on which a metaphysical realist theory can be reasonably and appropriately based. This theory will, however, be dogmatic or precritical—to use Kantian terminology—unless it can answer the sceptic. Second, strong dialectic may be part of an answer to the sceptic. But the answer cannot extend through the function argument to ethics and politics. For the function argument is answerable to experience and so cannot underwrite it in a way that will answer the sceptic's question (see §§1–9, 22–5). My own views on first philosophy, which accord a more central role to *Metaph.* xii. 6–10 than Irwin's, will be clear from the discussion in §26.

[102] Ethical realism is defended against many of the objections commonly brought against it in Brink (1989).

2
PHRONĒSIS

The good is what . . . everyone would choose if he could
acquire *nous* and *phronēsis*.

(*Rh.* 1363ᵇ12–15)

IN Book VI of the *Ethics*, Aristotle tries to explain the precise
nature of *phronēsis* by locating it in a complex conceptual network
consisting of perception, scientific-knowledge, craft-knowledge
(*technē*), politics, deliberation (*bouleusis*), decision (*proairesis*),
nous, the virtues of character, wisdom (*sophia*), and other less
prominent psychological capacities, such as cleverness (*deinotēs*),
comprehension (*sunesis*), and natural virtue (*phusikē aretē*). We
shall explore this network in eight stages (§§11–18) beginning with
the involvement of *phronēsis* with a sort of perception and ending
with its involvement with wisdom. In Chapter 1, we focused on
knowledge of ethical universals. In the present chapter, we shall be
considering the ways in which we utilize that knowledge in
particular situations in order to best promote *eudaimonia*.

11 PRACTICAL PERCEPTION

Phronēsis has cognitive access to or knowledge of both universals
and particulars: '*Phronēsis* is not about universals only. It must also
come to know (*gnōrizein*) particulars, since it is concerned with
action and action is concerned with particulars' (1141ᵇ14–16; see
1143ᵃ28–35). For in order to guide action in particular circumstances, *phronēsis* needs knowledge of both universal ethical
principles and the particular circumstances themselves. But perception 'controls' particulars (1147ᵃ25–6). Hence *phronēsis* must
include a kind of perception, which we may call *practical*
perception.

Aristotle's brief account of the nature of practical perception is
contained in the following difficult text:

[A] *Phronēsis* is evidently not scientific-knowledge. For, as we said, it concerns the last thing (*tou eschatou*), since that is the practicable (*ton prakton*). [B] Hence it is opposed (*antikeitai*) to *nous*. For *nous* is about the definitions (*tōn horōn*) for which there is no argument (*logos*), but *phronēsis* is about the last thing (*tou eschatou*), an object of perception, not of scientific-knowledge.[1] [C] This is not the perception of proper objects but like that by which we perceive that the last among mathematical objects is a triangle. For there, too, there will be a stop. [D] And it is more (*mallon*) this perception that is *phronēsis*,[2] but it is of a different kind than the other. (1142ᵃ23–30)

(A) *Phronēsis* is concerned with particulars (last things); scientific-knowledge with universals only; therefore, *phronēsis* is not scientific-knowledge. (B) *Nous* in science is 'opposed' to *phronēsis* because the one is concerned with universals, the other with particulars, and universals and particulars are opposed: 'what is most universal is furthest away (from perception), the particulars nearest; and these are opposed (*antikeitai*) to one another' (*APo.* 72ᵃ1–5).[3]

(C) Practical perception is not perception of colours, which are the proper objects of the sense of sight, or of sounds, which are the proper objects of hearing, or of any other such things (see *DA* 418ᵃ7–25, 425ᵃ14–24). Instead, it is like what we may call *geometrical* perception, but what sort of perception is that? A passage in Book III provides a clue: 'A deliberator would seem to inquire and analyse . . . as though analysing a diagram. For apparently all deliberation is inquiry, but not all inquiry, for example in mathematics, is deliberation. And the last thing (*to eschaton*) found in the analysis is the first that comes to be' (1112ᵇ20–4). The picture seems to be this. A geometer is searching

---

[1] On the translation of *horos, eschaton,* and *logos* see Ch. 1 n. 87.

[2] Some MSS have (1) *hē phronēsis*, which I have translated. Some have (2) *ē phronēsis*. Burnet (1900, 274) suggests (3) *ē hē phronēsis*. If (2) is adopted, as it is by Bywater (1894), Rackham (1934), Stewart (1892, 2: 77–78), and others, we should translate: 'But this perception is perception more than *phronēsis*'. If (3) is adopted, as it is by Gauthier and Jolif (1970, ii. 2: 506–7), Engberg-Pedersen (1983, 205), Irwin (1985*b*, xxvii), we should translate: 'And this is perception more than *phronēsis* is'. Neither (2) nor (3) bring out the crucial point that knowledge of particulars is more what *phronēsis* is because *phronēsis* is more concerned with particulars than with universals (see below). Hence, (1) must be the correct text. The passage as a whole is discussed in Cooper (1975, 33–45), Engberg-Pedersen (1983, 205–7), and Greenwood (1909, 196–203).

[3] *Nous* in practical reasoning is, of course, not opposed to *phronēsis*. See 1143ᵇ5 and §9.

for a way to solve a problem involving the construction of a complex figure. He finds the solution by actually performing the construction: 'It is evident . . . that the potentially existing constructions are discovered by actually being drawn' (*Metaph.* 1051ª21–30). But performing the construction—which in (C) Aristotle specifies as being based on triangles—takes both knowledge of universals (the type of triangle to be drawn to effect the construction) and perception of particulars (the particular triangle I am drawing is of the required type). Particulars of this type are the last things to be discovered in the analysis and the first things to come to be in the construction.

In the same way, the *phronimos* is trying to solve a problem. He is searching for a way to act well or achieve *eudaimonia* in this particular situation (1144ª29–36). When he hits on a type of action that is within his power to do in the situation, he has partly solved his problem (1112ᵇ15–1113ª7). But to solve it completely, he must actually do an action of that type: 'Someone does not have *phronēsis* simply by knowing; he must also act on his knowledge' (1152ª8–9).[4] And such action takes both knowledge of universals (the type of action to be done to achieve *eudaimonia*) and of particulars (the particular act I am doing is of the required type).[5]

The perception involved in *phronēsis* is like that involved in the geometrical example in three respects, then. First, it is not perception of proper objects. Second, it is a search, partly perceptual, for the solution to a problem. Third, it involves finding the right universals and bringing them together with a particular in the way that solves that problem.

The first clause of (D) is obscure, but light is thrown on it by 1140ᵇ14–23. There Aristotle says that someone who knows that bird meats are healthy will 'more (*mallon*) produce health' than someone who knows that light meats are healthy but not 'what sorts of meats are light' (ᵇ18–21). His point, as *mallon* suggests, is that the closer one comes to knowledge of which particular things

---

[4] See 1143ª6–10, 1146ª7–9.

[5] I agree only in part with Cooper (1975, 33–41, 183–6), therefore, that the *eschaton* or last thing that *phronēsis* discovers is a type (see 1112ᵇ34–1113ª2). Deliberation does stop when a type is reached that is sufficiently specific that perception can recognize tokens of it. But *phronēsis* does not stop there. It must correctly recognize a particular token of that type and then produce appropriate action. What *phronēsis* 'sees' is not a type—perception is of particulars (1147ª25–6) —but that a particular is a token of the right type.

produce health the better. To know that bird meats are healthy is better than to know that light meats are healthy. But to know that *this* meat is healthy is best of all since by acting on that knowledge one is guaranteed to eat healthily. That is why Aristotle concludes the passage by saying that *phronēsis* 'must possess both [knowledge of universals and particulars] or the [latter] more (*mallon*)' ([b]21–2). We can now understand why it is more practical perception that is *phronēsis*. It is because *phronēsis* is more the knowledge of particulars that such perception makes possible than it is knowledge of universals.[6]

The second clause of (D) is now of little importance. Aristotle could just be saying that practical perception is different from the perception of special objects, but since he has already told us that in (C), it is more likely that he is saying that practical perception is different from geometrical perception. And the relevant differences are patent. Practical perception plays a role in deliberation; geometrical perception does not (1112[b]20–4). Practical perception is seeking a way to *eudaimonia* or *eupraxia*; geometrical perception is not (see 1142[a]31–2).

Practical perception plays a role in deliberation. More precisely, it comes into its own when deliberation has done its work: 'Nor do we deliberate about particulars, for example about whether this is a loaf or is cooked the right amount. For these are questions for perception and if we keep on deliberating at each stage we shall go on without end' (1112[b]34–1113[a]2). Deliberation finds a universal of the right sort for perception to use. And bird meat is such. For we can learn to recognize birds by sight and their meat is bird meat. Similarly, we can learn to tell by the sound it makes when we knock on it whether a loaf is sufficiently cooked. Practical perception uses such universals to guide action in accordance with deliberation and with the wish that originates it (see §15).

But practical perception, or something analogous to it, has another role to play besides this.[7] Before we begin to deliberate at all we have to be presented with a practical problem to deliberate about. Now sometimes it is our appetites (*epithumiai*) that

---

[6] Cooper (1975, 27–36) seems mistaken, therefore, that 1140[b]14–23 gives us reason to belive that *kath' hekasta* are types. Bird meat is a type of meat, to be sure, but it is not a *kath' hekaston*.

[7] My appreciation of this fact was heightened by Nussbaum (1986*b*) and Sherman (1989, 12–55).

inaugurate deliberation. We are hungry; we desire to eat; we wish for the good. Hence, we begin to deliberate about what to eat: light meats are good; bird meats are light; here—practical perception tells us—is some bird meat ready and available for eating. If nothing prevents us, we eat it (1147^a30–1).

Often, however, it is not our appetites that inaugurate deliberation but the situation in which we find ourselves, in which we perceive ourselves to be. And the way in which the situation brings itself to our attention is often, though not always, through our feelings, our *pathēmata*.[8] The situation rouses our anger or our fear or our sympathy and these emotions, having motivational force, set us deliberating much as our appetites do.

It is not bare, unconceptualized situations, however, that affect us in these ways. Our emotions are engaged by situations conceived of as insults or threats or examples of unmerited suffering. Indeed, they help to interpret or compose the very situations to which they are responses. A fearful person tends to see situations as threatening; an angry person sees insults in every harmless utterance:

> We are easily deceived by our sense perceptions when we are in an emotional state, some when in one state, others in others, for example the coward when afraid, the lover when aroused, so that even from a very slight resemblance the coward thinks that he sees his enemy and the lover his beloved, and the more emotional he is, the smaller is the similarity required to produce this effect. (*PN* 460^b3–11)[9]

But these non-normal cases dramatize what is true of all of us: it is partly because we are capable of anger or fear that we see situations as insults or as threats.[10]

Our emotions are, therefore, modes of practical perception. They are ways we perceive situations as problematic, as requiring deliberation and action. And this is how Aristotle himself conceives of them. He recognizes, first of all, that though emotions typically involve sensations and somatic disturbations, they also essentially involve beliefs and desires. Anger is 'boiling of the blood around the heart' ($DA403^a27$–$^b2$), but it also involves complex beliefs and

---

[8] Aristotle sometimes includes both appetites (hunger, thirst, sexual desire) and emotions (see *NE* 1105^b21–3), in the class of *pathēmata*, but sometimes appetites are excluded (see *Rh.* 1378^a20–3). I shall refer to the more inclusive class as *feelings* and the narrower class as *emotions*. See Leighton (1982) for discussion.

[9] I am grateful to Richard Kraut for drawing this passage to my attention.

[10] See DeSousa (1979).

desires about such ethically salient things as insults and revenge: 'Anger is a desire (*orexis*), accompanied by pain, to take what is believed to be revenge because of what is believed to be an insult' (*Rh.* 1378ª30–2).[11] Second, Aristotle argues that *phronēsis* and the virtues of character require one another, that we cannot have the virtues without *phronēsis* or *phronēsis* without them (see §14). And he defines the virtues of character as states or dispositions regarding feelings (see §30). Thus someone who possesses *phronēsis* will have emotions that correctly interpret a situation, that are appropriately responsive to it, and so will have veridical practical perception of it.

What exactly do 'correctly', 'appropriately', and 'veridically' mean here? Are they terms of cognitive approbation or something else? They are the former, but the cognition is practical. Emotions involve beliefs. Hence they are rational and educable. A fearful person can become less fearful through learning that the things he fears really pose no threat to him. But emotions also involve somatic disturbances, and these are less easily changed by cognitive means: we need time and experience with garden snakes to overcome our fear of them even after we know coldly in the head that they are harmless.[12] That is why habituation is typically needed to acquire the virtues. But habituation is an inductive intellectual process not a merely mechanical one. In learning to fear the right things in the right way at the right time, we are gaining practical knowledge of the threatening or dangerous as well as control of our trembling limbs and fast-beating hearts.

But what makes this practical knowledge, what makes our fear right in all these ways, is its relation to *eudaimonia* (see §30). Our fear is right, we possess the virtue related to it (courage), if it best promotes *eudaimonia*. If this were not so, *eudaimonia* would neither be 'the activity of the psyche that expresses virtue' (1138ª17–18) nor the first principle of ethics.

Our analysis has uncovered two crucial facts about *phronēsis*, then. First, *phronēsis* is more a kind of perception than it is a kind of knowledge of universals. Second, the kind of perception it is

---

[11] Aristotle's theory of emotion is discussed in Fortenbaugh (1975) and Leighton (1982; 1988).

[12] 'We are often unable to act on our certainties; our objection to a contrary issue (were it possible) is so strong that it rises like a spectral illusion between us and our certainty: we are rationally sure that the blind-worm cannot bite us mortally, but it would be so intolerable to be bitten, and the creature has a biting look—we decline to handle it' (George Eliot, *Daniel Deronda*).

none the less crucially involves knowledge of universals and of how to bring them to bear appropriately in particular situations.

12 SCIENTIFIC-KNOWLEDGE, CRAFT-KNOWLEDGE, AND POLITICS

The major difference between *phronēsis* and scientific-knowledge— to reiterate—is that scientific-knowledge is concerned exclusively with universals while *phronēsis* is concerned with particulars and universals both. But while *phronēsis* is concerned with both, it studies only particulars. That is the message encoded in the following text:

> Let us assume that there are two parts of the psyche that have reason; one with which we study beings whose first principles do not admit of being otherwise and one with which we study beings whose first principles do admit of being otherwise (*endechomena*). For when the beings are of different kinds, the parts of the psyche naturally suited to each of them are also of different kinds, since the parts possess knowledge (*gnōsis*) by being somehow similar and proper to their objects. Let us call one of these the scientific part (*epistēmonikon*) and the other the rationally calculating part (*logistikon*), since deliberating is the same as rationally calculating and no one deliberates about what cannot be otherwise. (1139ª6–14; see *Metaph.* 993ᵇ19–23)

The scientific part and the calculating part must study completely different, non-overlapping things, otherwise they would not be two distinct psychic parts. The scientific part is clearly the locus of scientific-knowledge. The calculating part is the locus of *phronēsis*. For it is the part that deliberates and the *phronimos* is a good deliberator (1140ª25–8). Now the things that do not admit of being otherwise, since they are studied by scientific-knowledge, must be universals and the necessary relations between them. Presumably, then, *phronēsis* must study only particulars; for only they admit of being otherwise.[13]

Phronēsis is concerned with universals. For it must have access to universals in order to bring them appropriately to bear in particular

---

[13] Aristotle usually uses the phrase *kath' hekasta* to refer to particular things but he also uses it to refer to types (more fully specified universals). Cooper (1975, 27–36), who cites examples of both usages, argues powerfully that in the *Ethics kath' hekasta* are types. But since these *kath' hekasta* are *endechomena*, this must be mistaken. For types, being universals, do not admit of being otherwise.

circumstances. It must know, for example, that 'all sorts of heavy water are bad' (1142^a20–3). But since *phronēsis* does not study universals, where does it get its knowledge of them from? Only one answer has any plausibility: *phronēsis* must get its knowledge of universals generally, as it gets its knowledge of *eudaimonia*, from the only source that can provide it, namely, the amalgam of scientific-knowledge, dialectic, and *nous* that gives rise to an Aristotelian science.[14]

Phronēsis studies *endechomena*, things that admit of being otherwise. But craft-knowledge, too, is concerned with such things: 'what admits of being otherwise includes what is produced (*poiēton*) as well as what is practicable (*prakton*)' (1140^a1–2; see 1140^b3–4). Moreover, just as *phronēsis* is able to bring its knowledge of universals to bear in particular cases, craft-knowledge, too, involves a similar ability:

From craft come the things whose form is in the psyche of the producer— and by form I mean the essence of each thing and the primary substance. . . . For example, health is the account in the psyche, the knowledge [of the form]. So the healthy thing comes to be when the physician reasons as follows: Since health is this, necessarily if the thing is to be healthy this must be present—for example a uniform state—and if the latter is to be present, then there must be heat, and he goes on, always thinking like this, until he is led to a final this that he himself is able to make. Then the process from this point onward, toward health, is called production. (*Metaph.* 1032^a32–$^b10$; see 1025^b22–4)

The craftsman must know the form and be guided by his knowledge of it in making a particular that instantiates it. And for this he needs a type of perception akin to practical or geometrical perception, he needs a trained eye.

But for all their similarities, *phronēsis* is not craft-knowledge. For *phronēsis* is concerned with acting and craft-knowledge with producing and these are different (1140^a2). The following terse sentence explains how: 'Producing is different from (*heteron*) its end, but acting (*praxeōs*) isn't, since its end is acting well (*eupraxia*)' (1140^b6–7). When X produces a chair, his end (the chair) is different from his production of it. For example, the chair comes into existence only when the production of it ceases. But when X performs an action, his unconditional end just is acting

[14] Cf. Greenwood (1909, 44).

well, and that is not different from his performance of the action in the same way as the chair is different from the production of it. For example, the action ceases to exist when the performance of it ceases. Actions are for their own sakes or because of themselves; productions are for the sake of or because of their products.[15] Phronēsis studies things that admit of being otherwise with an eye to action, then. Craft-knowledge studies them with an eye to production. But do they study the same things or different ones? Aristotle is clear that they study different ones: 'Questions about actions and expediency, like questions about health, have no fixed answers. And when our universal account is like that, the account of particular cases is all the more inexact. For these fall under no craft or profession and the agents themselves must consider in each case what the opportune action is' (1104ª3–9). If something is studied by a craft, that craft tells us how to deal with it in order to achieve our end. But if no craft deals with it, it is a matter for phronēsis. Hence the endechomena studied by phronēsis are those that are not studied by craft-knowledge.[16]

But craft-knowledge and phronēsis are not simply separate endeavours having nothing to do with one another; craft-knowledge is subordinate to phronēsis:

> Reasoning of its own accord, however, moves nothing, but the kind that is for the sake of something and practical. For this is the sort that is also the first principle of production. For every producer produces for the sake of something and the unconditional end is not the product—which is only an end in relation to something else—but the practicable. (1139ª35–b3; see §15)

This does not mean that phronēsis studies through the crafts under it the very things that they study; that is ruled out. It simply means that among the things that admit of being otherwise that phronēsis studies are the various ways in which craft-knowledge might be used to promote eudaimonia or eupraxia. For that does not fall under any craft. But phronēsis does study such things. For

---

[15] A glance at 1112b32–3, 1177b2–4, 12–18 will reveal some of the difficulties lurking behind these apparently straightforward claims. See §19.

[16] If we include what holds for the most part among the endechomena (APr. 25b14–15, 32b4–13), phronēsis studies those endechomena that are not studied by a craft and that do not hold for the most part (see §13).

phronēsis is the same state as politics and—as we are about to see —
politics studies them.[17]

Politics and *phronēsis* are 'the same state [*hexis*], but their being
[*einai*] is not the same' (1141^{b}23–4). They are the same state
because the abilities, skills, and virtues an individual needs to
promote his own *eudaimonia* reliably are the same as those that a
good ruler of a polis needs (*Pol.* 1277^{b}25–30, §32). For 'human
beings are by nature political' (1094^{b}8–9) and 'one's own doing
well (*to hautou eu*) requires household management and a political
system' (1142^{a}9–10). But *phronēsis* and politics yet differ in their
being or essence:

> *Phronēsis* concerned with the individual himself seems most of all (*malist'*)
> to be *phronēsis*; and this part of *phronēsis* often monopolizes the name
> *phronēsis*, a name that applies in common to all the parts. Of the other
> parts, one is household management, another legislation, another political,
> one part of the latter is deliberative another judicial. (1141^{b}29–33)[18]

Phronēsis is most of all *phronēsis* when it is concerned with the
individual's own good; politics is more concerned with acquiring
and preserving *eudaimonia* for 'a people and a polis' (1094^{b}7–11).

Now politics is an architectonic virtue to which all sciences,
crafts, and investigations are subordinate, and whose end or first
principle is both their ultimate end and the best good (see §20). It
follows that *phronēsis*, too, should be conceived of as an
architectonic virtue, which studies how best to use the other crafts,
sciences, and capacities in order most of all to promote the
individual's own *eudaimonia* (see §32). Given these facts, it is clear
that the contrasts between *phronēsis* and scientific-knowledge or
craft-knowledge will have to be drawn with great care and
circumspection.[19]

Many passages in the *Ethics* drive home the message that
phronēsis involves perception of ethically relevant particulars and

---

[17] Greenwood (1909, 37–8) argues that two different senses of *phronēsis* are
involved in the discussion of craft-knowledge. In one sense, *phronēsis* is distinguished from craft-knowledge as 'the *aretē* that leads to truth about *prakta* as
distinguished from *poiēta*'. In the other, '*phronēsis* is the *aretē* that leads to truth
about all human action whether *praxis* or *poiēsis*'. But these two senses collapse into
one once we see that the question of how best to use the crafts is itself a question
about *prakta* not about *poiēta*. See §§20, 32.

[18] See 1130^{a}12–13, MM 1181^{a}23–^{b}28, Gauthier and Jolif (1970, ii. 1: 10–12).

[19] They are somewhat overdrawn, in my view, by Nussbaum (1986a, 290–317;
1986b).

that ethically relevant particulars are hard to get an epistemic handle on. The following is typical:

> Still, we are not blamed if we more or less deviate from doing well but only if we deviate a long way, since then we are easily noticed. But how far and how much we must deviate to be blamed is not easily summed up in a formula. For indeed nothing perceptible is; and since these are particulars, discernment (*krisis*) of them depends on perception. (1109^{b}20–3)^{20}

But this is not a problem peculiar to ethically relevant particulars or to ethics. It is a problem that affects all particulars, whether they are studied by induction leading to scientific-knowledge, by *phronēsis*, or by craft-knowledge. It is because particulars are enmattered, after all, and not because they are ethically relevant, that there cannot be scientific-knowledge of them.

Phronēsis is practical. We seek knowledge of ethical universals in order that *phronēsis* can bring it to bear in particular situations. And such knowledge is essential for practical success. If we do not know what *eudaimonia* is, we will be like archers who do not know what target they are supposed to aim at (1094^{a}22–26). But the guidance that knowledge of universals can provide, though essential, is also limited. We see this vividly in the case of law:

> All law is universal, but in some areas no universal rule can be correct; and so where a universal rule has to be made, but cannot be correct, the law chooses the universal rule that holds for the most part (*hōs epi to pleon*), well aware of the error being made. And the law is no less correct on this account. For the source of the error is not in the law or the legislator but in the nature of the object itself, since that is what the matter of actions is bound to be like. (1137^{b}13–19; see *Pol.* 1287^{a}20–32)

Universal laws provide essential guidance in assessing individual cases. But the variation in such cases guarantees that the law will not fit all of them exactly. That is why equity (*epieikeia*) is needed to negotiate between universal law and the particular case (*Rh.* 1374^{a}26–34).^{21} That is why the Lesbian rule needs both a straight, invariant edge, and to be made of pliable material, if it is to do its work properly; one without the other is no good (1137^{b}29–32).

Scientific-knowledge is theoretical rather than practical. It is

^{20} See 1098^{a}26–33, 1107^{a}28–32, 1126^{b}2–4, 1137^{b}19–32, 1141^{b}14–16, 1142^{a}14–18, 1143^{a}25–^{b}5, 1164^{b}27–1165^{a}14.

^{21} Equity and the problems it is needed to solve are discussed in Sherman (1989, 13–28).

primarily interested in universal laws, in necessary relations among universals, not in particulars. Hence it does not involve any delicate negotiation between universals and particulars. It does not involve any analogue of equity. But in the development of a science, when universal laws or demonstrations are being discovered rather than used, there is such an analogue, namely, acumen: 'Acumen (*agchinoia*) is a kind of aiming well (*eustochia*) that hits instantly upon the middle term; for example if someone sees that the moon always holds its bright side towards the sun and quickly grasps that this is so because it gets light from the sun' (*APo.* 89^{b}10–13).[22] For, like equity or like *phronēsis* itself (1141^{b}14–16), acumen is an ability concerned with *stochazesthai*, with taking aim. But whereas equity finds the best match between the universal and the particular, acumen finds the explanatory universal in the particular. If (*per impossibile*) completed science needed to deal with particulars, as those who apply it in particular cases do (see *EE* 1216^{b}15–16), it would also surely involve something like acumen, equity, or *phronēsis*.

The analogies between *phronēsis* and scientific-knowledge are quite close, then. And the disanalogies can all be traced to a single cause that is in no way peculiarly ethical, namely, that the former deals with enmattered particulars, while the latter does not.

Turning, now, to craft-knowledge we find an even closer analogue to *phronēsis*. Unlike scientific-knowledge, craft-knowledge does have to do with particulars. Hence, like *phronēsis*, it cannot avoid the messiness inherent in them. But the crucial difference between *phronēsis* and craft-knowledge is signally not that *phronēsis* is less exact than craft-knowledge. On the contrary, Aristotle is explicit that 'virtue, like nature, is more exact and better than any craft' (1106^{b}14–16).[23] We are not worse off, therefore, because 'questions about actions and expediency . . . fall under no craft or profession' (1104^{a}3–9). Provided we are virtuous or possess *phronēsis*, we are actually better off. The crucial difference

---

[22] Acumen makes a brief appearance at *NE* 1142^{b}5–6 where it is again described as *eustochia tis*. See *HA* 587^{a}12 where cutting the umbilical cord is said to require acumen on the part of the midwife.

[23] The reason that virtue is more exact than any craft is this. Virtue makes our beliefs about *eudaimonia* correct. *Eudaimonia* is at once the final cause of action or *praxis* and of craft or *poiēsis* (1139^{b}1–4; §§15, 20, 31). Hence, virtue is concerned with its own final cause but craft is not. Hence, virtue is more exact than craft. See *APo.* 87^{a}31–7, §26.

between *phronēsis* and craft-knowledge is simply that *phronēsis* is concerned with action, craft-knowledge with production. And from the epistemological point of view, albeit not from the ethical one, that is not a terribly significant difference (see §19). There is good reason to believe, then, that *phronēsis* has at least two components. The first involves knowledge of ethical universals. This knowledge is scientific-knowledge of necessary principles that hold either universally or for the most part. It can, when complete, be set up as a structure of demonstrations from first principles. That, indeed, is just what it means to say that ethics or anything else has *first* principles. The second component involves the practical perception of particulars or the application of universal propositions to particular cases. This component of *phronēsis*, like the analogous component of craft-knowledge or like acumen in scientific-knowledge, cannot be set up as a structure of demonstrations. For in neither ethics nor craft nor science can we have exact scientific-knowledge of particulars. In scientific-knowledge, the first component is all important. In *phronēsis* and craft-knowledge, the second is at least as important as the first, if not more so. For *phronēsis* and craft-knowledge are practical, while scientific knowledge is theoretical. We need to know universals certainly; without knowledge of *eudaimonia* or health we will have no clear target to aim at. But unless we know what, particular course of action would promote *eudaimonia* or produce health, our knowledge of universals will be useless for practical purposes.

13 DELIBERATION

In §12, we discussed the relations between *phronēsis* and two types of cognition, scientific-knowledge and craft-knowledge, the one theoretical, the other productive. *Phronēsis* is neither theoretical nor productive, however, but practical, concerned with the practicable, with what is doable in action. How, then, is *phronēsis* related to other things concerned with action, to deliberation, for example, and to decision?

Aristotle's discussion of the relations between *phronēsis* and deliberation begins with a *phainomenon*. Someone is called a *phronimos*, or is said to possess *phronēsis*, if he is able to deliberate well about his own *eudaimonia*: 'It seems proper, then, to a *phronimos*, to be able to deliberate finely about what is good and

beneficial for himself, not about some restricted area—for example
about what promotes health or strength—but about what
promotes the whole of living well (*pros to eu zēn holōs*)' (1140^{a}25–
8; see 1141^{a}25–6). This suggests that there is a sharp divide
between one's own *eudaimonia*, one's own doing well, and that of
others. And this is not quite right. For an individual is by nature
political and needs a political system in order to be *eudaimōn*.
None the less, *phronēsis* is most of all *phronēsis* when it is
concerned with the good of the individual (1141^{b}29–30). That is
the core of truth in the original *phainomenon*. Hence we can
continue to think of *phronēsis* as being primarily concerned with
the individual's own *eudaimonia* provided that we no not conceive
of that concern as narrowly focused on himself to the exclusion of
others.[24]

The *phronimos* is a good deliberator about his *eudaimonia* as a
whole, and because he is, we can learn about *phronēsis* by
exploring the nature of good deliberation. Two related aspects of it
merit particularly close attention. First, 'no one deliberates about
what cannot be otherwise or about what cannot be achieved by his
action' (1140^{a}31–3; see 1111^{b}20–6). Second, we deliberate about
what promotes the end, what is *pros* the end, not about the end
itself.[25]

Because a person deliberates only about what is possible for him
to achieve in action, *phronēsis* is neither a craft nor a science:

If scientific-knowledge involves demonstration, but there is no demonstration of anything whose first principles admit of being otherwise, since every
such thing itself admits of being otherwise, and if we cannot deliberate
about what is by necessity, it follows that *phronēsis* is neither scientific-
knowledge nor craft-knowledge. It is not science, because what is
practicable admits of being otherwise, and it isn't craft-knowledge because
actions and productions belong to different kinds. (1140^{a}33–^{b}4)

Actions involve making changes in the world, beginning with
changes in the agent's own will and body. Hence only the part of
the world that is changeable is in the sphere of the practicable. Now
the subject matter of scientific-knowledge, comprising universals
and their necessary relations, is excluded from that sphere. The

---

[24] See Kraut (1989, 78–154) and §31.
[25] See 1111^{b}26–30, 1112^{b}11–12, ^{b}32–3, 1142^{b}28–31.

unconditionally necessary is clearly excluded, but so, though perhaps less clearly, is what holds for the most part. What holds for the most part admits of being otherwise (*APr.* 25ᵇ14–15, 32ᵇ4–13). But it is not an *endechomenon* of the sort that either *phronēsis* or craft-knowledge studies. For we can no more change the fact that for the most part all males have hair on their chins than we can change the unalterable human essence itself. After all, the explanation of why things that hold for the most part admit of being otherwise is 'the indeterminateness of matter' (*GA* 778ᵃ4–9), and that is something action is powerless to change. Aristotle acknowledges this when he writes: 'Craft is not concerned with things that are or that come about by necessity, or with things that are by nature, since these have their first principle in themselves' (1140ᵃ14–16). For the things that are or come to be by nature, as opposed to by (unconditional) necessity, are those that hold for the most part.²⁶ If craft is unconcerned with such things because they have their first principles in themselves, *phronēsis*, too, must be unconcerned with them for the same reason. Whether as actors or producers, we make changes that are allowed by the lawlike connections in nature; we do not change those connections themselves.

It follows that the first principles referred to at 1140ᵃ33–4 as admitting of being otherwise are not, as one might think, the first principles of ethics. The latter hold either always or for the most part. Rather they are the first principles of deliberation: 'Each of us stops inquiring how to act as soon as he traces the first principle to himself, and within himself to the dominant part, for it is the part that decides' (1113ᵃ5–7). When an agent, through deliberation, finds something that both promotes his end and is within his power to do, he has hit upon the first principle of his deliberation, this being his own capacity as a rational agent to initiate voluntary action.²⁷

The *phronimos* is a good deliberator. Hence he is good at finding ways to his end that begin with things in his power to do. But it is not because he is a good deliberator that his end is a good one. For

²⁶ '*Ta kata phusin* are not *poiēta*, for they grow of themselves: they are indeed not strictly *endechomena*, for they are *hōs epi to polu*, invariable except for the interference of chance, *to automaton*' (Greenwood 1909, 42–43).
²⁷ See 1111ᵃ22–4, 1112ᵇ31–2, 1139ᵇ4–5; Charles (1984, 57–108); and Sorabji (1980, 227–87).

Aristotle insists that deliberation is concerned with what promotes
the end, with what is *pros* or towards the end, and not with the end
itself: 'We deliberate not about ends, but about what promotes
ends (*peri tōn pros ta telē*)' (1112^b11-12). And he recognizes that
someone can be a good deliberator—albeit not an unconditionally
good one—in regard to any end whatever: 'Deliberation may be
unconditionally good or good only to the extent that it promotes
some end. Unconditionally good deliberation is the sort that
correctly promotes the unconditional end, while the other sort
promotes some other sort of end' (1142^b28-31; see §14). It is not
deliberation, then, that makes the end right. But why is it not? Why
does Aristotle insist that deliberation concerns only what is *pros* the
end, not the end itself?

We can deliberate about anything that is *pros* the end. The
formula is vague and therefore expansive. It gives us no reason to
think that we can deliberate only about external means to an end. It
is possible, so far as the formula goes, to deliberate also about an
end's constituents or components (*Metaph.* 1032^b18-29). And
deliberating about constituents is no doubt a kind of deliberation
about ends themselves. It is also possible to deliberate about ends in
another sense. For what is a means to an end in one piece of
deliberation can surely appear as an end in another piece of
deliberation: to reach the window I need a ladder; to get a ladder I
need to go to the hardware store; to get to the hardware store I need
my car; and so on. All of this is true. All of it is permitted by the
formula requiring that deliberation be *pros* the end. All of it is
philosophically heartening.[28] But it seems simply to make trouble
for the other part of the formula, the part that tells us that we do
not deliberate about ends. So let us turn to it.

We deliberate only about what can be otherwise. But there is an
end that cannot be otherwise, namely, *eudaimonia*. We do not
deliberate about what *eudaimonia* really is. We discover what it is,
as we discover what a crab is, by experience, empirical investigation, and dialectic. And if we have all the true facts and have solved
all the *aporiai*, what we discover will be a *de re* necessary truth. We
can wish, when that truth is in, that *eudaimonia* was something
else. We can wish, for example, that it was pleasure, or honour, or

---

[28] See Cooper (1975, 19–21), Greenwood (1909, 46–55), Sherman (1989, 56–
117), and Wiggins (1975, 221–40).

whatever it is we have built our lives around falsely believing it to be *eudaimonia*, but that will not change the truth (see §§19–28). We deliberate about what we can bring about in action. And the result of our deliberation is a decision, but we do not decide to be *eudaimōn*:

> We wish more for the end, but we decide to do what promotes the end. We wish, for example, to be healthy, but decide to do what will make us healthy; and we wish to be *eudaimōn* and say so, but it is inappropriate to say that we decide to be it, since in general what we decide to do would seem to be what is up to us (*eph' hēmin*). (1111ᵇ26–30)

And if we do not decide to be *eudaimōn*, we do not deliberate about whether to be *eudaimōn*. We do not deliberate, either, about whether to make *eudaimonia* our end. It is necessarily our end because it is our function or essence activated (see §§22–8). And it is not up to us to change our essence any more than it is up to us to change anything else that is unconditionally necessary or that holds for the most part. We can try not to activate our essence, certainly, but that will change what we do, not what we are.

Now *eudaimonia* is our unconditional end. So about our unconditional end we do not deliberate; about it Aristotle's formula about deliberation and ends holds.[29] But does he mean to extend that formula to other ends besides our unconditional end? To answer we must carefully consider the examples he gives in explanation of his formula:

> We deliberate not about ends, but about what promotes ends. For a doctor does not deliberate about whether he will cure, or an orator about whether he will persuade, or a politician about whether he will produce good order, or any other about the end. Rather, we first lay down the end and then examine how and by what means to achieve it. (1112ᵇ12–16)

Medicine is a craft that studies certain *endechomena* in order to produce a certain end, namely, health. Hence insofar as that craft dictates a person's actions he necessarily pursues that end—if he did not pursue it, he would not be practising the craft. A doctor, does not deliberate about whether or not he will cure, then, because *qua* doctor, *qua* practitioner of medicine, he necessarily tries to

---

[29] Nussbaum (1986b, 162) is mistaken, therefore, in claiming that Aristotle 'does not hold that ultimate ends cannot be objects of rational deliberation'. He holds precisely that. Rational argument can discover what our ultimate end necessarily is, as it can discover what our healthy state necessarily is, but such argument is not deliberation.

cure. If a question arises of whether to cure or whether, for example, to avoid curing in order to avoid the risk of contracting the disease, medicine will not answer it. For it belongs to those *endechomena* studied not by medicine but by *phronēsis*. In the same way, oratory, politics, or any other craft studies certain *endechomena* in order to produce its peculiar end. And what is true of the doctors, orators, politicians, and other craftsmen has its analogue in the case of human beings, in the case of ourselves. *Phronēsis* studies certain *endechomena* in order to achieve *eudaimonia*. Hence as *phronimoi* we do not deliberate about whether to pursue *eudaimonia*; as practically rational beings we necessarily pursue it. The point of the analogy, therefore, is not to show that *we* cannot deliberate about whether to cure or to persuade or to produce good order. Obviously, we can do that. The point is to show that, like the doctor *qua* doctor, the orator *qua* orator, and the politician *qua* politician, there is something we cannot deliberate about, to wit, the very thing that it is our essence to pursue.

When Aristotle says that deliberation is not about ends, then, all that follows is that we cannot deliberate about what is essentially an end and cannot be anything else: the unconditional end, *eudaimonia*. Aristotle's formula about deliberation and ends is much more restricted than one might think, therefore, and is intended to make a point very different from the one usually found in it. It is not a principle primarily of the logic of decision but rather one of natural teleology.[30]

14 PHRONĒSIS AND THE VIRTUES OF CHARACTER

The *phronimos* is a good deliberator. He is good at discovering things that conduce to his own *eudaimonia*. But it is not because he is a good deliberator that he has the right conception of *eudaimonia*. Deliberation concerns what promotes *eudaimonia* not

---

[30] Hence it is wrong to represent dialectic as a species of deliberation or as a deliberative method, as some recent writers do. See Irwin (1978, 257–9) and Sherman (1989, 56–117). Dialectic allows us to clarify first principles such as *eudaimonia* or its *de re* necessary definition. Deliberation, by contrast, helps us to achieve *eudaimonia*, when it has already been clarified. Cooper (1975, 14–18, 58–71) is much closer to the truth when he recognizes that the 'ultimate end itself is beyond deliberation and therefore beyond the kind of justification that deliberation can provide' (p. 18). Dialectic shows us what our ultimate end necessarily is. It does not, except coincidentally, tell us what end we should decide to adopt. For about the necessary we neither deliberate nor decide.

eudaimonia itself. What is it, then, that makes the *phronimos* aim at the right end, at *eudaimonia* correctly conceived? We will discover the answer by exploring the relationship between *phronēsis* and the virtues.

In one way, nothing could be easier than to say what the relationship in question is. For *phronēsis* and virtue are related by necessary equivalence: 'We cannot be fully good without *phronēsis*, or have *phronēsis* without virtue of character . . . as soon as someone has *phronēsis*, which is a single state, he has all the virtues as well' (1144^b30–1145^a2). But this does not explain very much. We need to see how and why it is that *phronēsis* and the virtues of character go together in this way. And to do this we need to make use of two notions, namely, cleverness (*deinotēs*) and natural virtue (*phusikē aretē*).

Cleverness is a capacity that enables us 'to do the actions that tend to promote whatever end is assumed and to achieve it' (1144^a23–6). Thus cleverness is like good deliberation coupled with an executive capacity like decision, which ensures that what will promote the end is actually done, so that the end will be achieved successfully. For good deliberation, in contradistinction to unconditionally good deliberation, finds what effectively and efficiently promotes whatever end one happens to have (1142^b28–31). But without decision deliberation alone is ineffective in producing or controlling action (1139^a31–3).

Now *phronēsis* requires cleverness but is not the same as it (1144^a28–9). And the reason for this is simple. Cleverness is not end-specific; *phronēsis* is. Cleverness enables us to achieve our end whatever it is. But, because it involves the virtues of character, *phronēsis* enables us to achieve only a single end, the correct one, *eudaimonia*:

> *Phronēsis*, that eye of the psyche, cannot reach its fully developed state without virtue, as we have said and is clear. For inferences about the practicable have a first principle: 'Since the end, that is, the best good, is this sort of thing', whatever it is—let it be any old thing for the sake of argument. And this is apparent only to the good person. For vice perverts us and produces false beliefs about the ends of actions. (1144^a29–36)

To see how virtue is involved with *phronēsis* we need the notion of natural virtue.

Natural virtue is full virtue from which *nous* has been, as it were, subtracted. That is the message of the following text:

Each of us seems to possess his type of character to some extent by nature, since we are just, prone to moderation, and courageous, or have another feature immediately from birth. However, we still search for some other condition as being full goodness (*to kuriōs agathon*) and expect to possess these features in another way. For these natural states belong to children and to beasts as well, but without *nous* (*aneu nou*) they are evidently harmful. At any rate this much would seem to be clear: just as a heavy body moving around unable to see suffers a heavy fall because it has no sight, so it is with [natural] virtue. But if someone acquires *nous*, he begins to act well; and the state he now has though still like the natural one, will be full virtue (*kuriōs aretē*). (1144^{b}4–14; see 1117^{a}4–5)

Now *nous* is of the first principle or unconditional end, *eudaimonia*. So what natural virtue lacks, as the analogy of the blind person makes clear, is grasp of the end, grasp of where it is going. Add that grasp to natural virtue and you get full virtue. That is why Aristotle can say: 'As *phronēsis* is to cleverness, not the same but similar, so natural virtue is to full virtue' (1144^{b}1–3). For what cleverness needs to become *phronēsis* is just what natural virtue needs to become full virtue, namely, *nous* of the right end, of *eudaimonia*. Indeed, what good deliberation needs to become unconditionally good deliberation is that same thing. For 'the unconditionally good deliberator is the one whose aim expresses rational calculation in pursuit of the best good for a human being that is achievable by action' (1141^{b}12–14).

But now it seems that what makes the end right is *nous*. And that seems to conflict with Aristotle's claim that it is virtue—natural, habituated, or full—that plays this role (1144^{a}29–36;, 1151^{a}17–19). In fact, however, there is no conflict here. If we lacked natural or habituated virtue, the experiences that formed the basis for the induction that terminates in our having *nous* of universals would be of the wrong sort to result in *nous* of *eudaimonia* as it really is. The vicious reach a first principle by induction from their experience (1139^{b}33–5). It is not *eudaimonia* they reach, however, but one of the many pretenders to that title. Hence all that those with natural or habituated virtue need to achieve full virtue is *nous*. Those without natural or habituated virtue need both proper habituation and *nous*. It is natural or habituated virtue, then, that 'teaches true opinion about the first principle' (1151^{a}17–19). *Nous* simply grasps the universal implicit in what they teach.

Aristotle contrasts *phronēsis* with good deliberation by saying that 'good deliberation is the type of correctness that expresses what is expedient for promoting the end of which *phronēsis* is true supposition (*alēthēs hupolepsin*)' (1142ᵇ31–3). At the same time, he contrasts *phronēsis* with virtue by saying that 'virtue makes the aim (*skopon*) correct; *phronēsis* what promotes it (*ta pros touton*)' (1144ᵃ8–9). Initially, these contrasts are confusing. They suggest that *phronēsis* grasps the truth about ends, not about what promotes them, and that it grasps the truth about what promotes ends, not about the ends themselves. Once cleverness and natural virtue are introduced, however, we can see clearly the truths expressed in these contrasts in just the way that we can see the truth in the seemingly conflicting *endoxa* about *akrasia* once we are made aware of the different ways in which we can know something. Unlike good deliberation, *phronēsis* does grasp the truth about ends, but it is natural or habituated virtue that enables it to do so. Unlike natural or habituated virtue, *phronēsis* can work out what promotes ends effectively, but it is cleverness that enables it to do so.

15 DECISION

The *phronimos* is a good deliberator, but he is more than that. He is also someone who decides. The *phronimos* is fully virtuous and 'virtue is a state that decides' (1106ᵇ36; see 1106ᵃ3–4). 'Someone is not a *phronimos* simply by knowing; he must also act on his knowledge' (1152ᵃ8–9; see 1146ᵃ7–9). And the cause of action is decision (1139ᵃ31–3). But what exactly is decision?

Aristotle's initial discussion of it in Book III culminates in the following definition:

What we decide to do is, then, something that is up to us that we deliberate about and desire. Hence decision is deliberative (*bouleutikē*) desire to do an action that is up to us. For when we have judged, our desire to do it expresses our wish (*kata tēn boulēsin*).[31] So much, then, for a sketch of decision and what it is about: it is about what promotes the end. (1113ᵃ9–14)

Two aspects of this definition require elaboration. First, decision is not just about what promotes the end to some extent; it is about what best promotes the end, about what better promotes it than

---

[31] Most MSS have *kata tēn bouleusin*, 'according to deliberation'. *Boulēsin* is supported by one MS, Gauthier and Jolif (1970, ii. 1: 205–6), Grant (1885, 2: 22), Irwin (1985*b*, xxvi), and below.

anything else available: 'what is decided is chosen *before* other things' (1112ª16–17).[32] Second, when we have judged, as a result of deliberation, that something best promotes the end 'our desire to do it expresses our wish'.[33] It follows that there must have been a wish there for desire to express. Now 'unconditionally and in truth, what is wished for is the good, but to each person what is wished for is the apparent good' (1113ª23–5). Hence what engenders a decision is not just any old desire, but a wish, a desire for the good or apparent good, for *eudaimonia* or what appears to be *eudaimonia*.

We wish for *eudaimonia*, then; we deliberate about what will promote it; we judge, as a result, that this thing that is up to us will do the trick better than any other available option; hence, we desire to do it, and that desire, which is a deliberative desire, is a decision. Decision is, therefore, like Hobbesian will, 'the last appetite in deliberation'. But it differs from Hobbesian will in that the last appetite must derive from an initial rational desire or wish (1111ᵇ26).[34]

In Book VI, Aristotle returns to decision and elaborates on his earlier account:

[A] Now the first principle of action—the source of the movement not the action's end—is decision and of decision desire and reasoning (*logos*) for the sake of something. [B] Hence decision requires *nous* and reasoning (*dianoias*) and also a state of character. [C] For acting well or its opposite in action requires both reasoning and character. [D] Reasoning of its own accord, however, moves nothing, but the kind that is for the sake of something and practical. [E] For this is the sort that is also the first principle of production. For every producer produces for the sake of something and the unconditional end is not the product—which is only an end in relation to something else—but the practicable. [F] For acting well is the [unconditional] end and the desire is for that. [G] Hence decision is either desiring *nous* or reasoning desire and such a first principle is a human being. (1139ª31–ᵇ5)

The line of inferential descent from (A) to (B) is extremely enthymematic, but the missing material lies ready to hand in §13.

---

[32] See Charles (1984, 137–8).

[33] If we are virtuous or enkratic. If we are akratic, our desire will not express our wish. See below.

[34] See Anscombe (1965, 148), Cooper (1975, 47 n. 59), Irwin (1988*b*, 337), Wiggins (1978, 252). Charles (1984, 151–5) is critical but not persuasive.

(F) tells us that the desire mentioned in (A) is for the unconditional end, *eupraxia* or *eudaimonia*. This pegs the desire as a *boulēsis* or wish (1113ª23–5), and underwrites our discussion of 1113ª9–14. It follows that the decision, of which that desire is a first principle, must aim to achieve *eudaimonia*. But if it is to achieve *eudaimonia*, it must have access to knowledge of what *eudaimonia* is. And this knowledge is provided only by *nous*. For *eudaimonia* is the first principle of ethics and the knowledge we have of first principles is *nous*. Therefore, decision requires *nous*. But *nous*, in turn, requires natural virtue. For without natural virtue we will not have the kind of experience from which the truth about *eudaimonia* can be reached by induction or habituation. *Nous* together with natural virtue is full virtue. And full virtue is a state of character (see §30). Therefore decision requires both *nous* and a state of character.[35] That it also requires reasoning follows trivially from (A).

But virtue is not the only state of character that will support a decision. (C) makes this explicit by telling us that acting well *or its opposite in action* requires both reasoning and character. Now the opposite of being *eudaimōn* is being *athlios* or wretched. And to be wretched is not simply not to be *eudaimōn*—to be neither gruntled nor disgruntled, so to speak—it is to be as far away from being *eudaimōn* as possible. Thus the fully virtuous person can cease to be *eudaimōn*, but he can never become wretched (1100ᵇ33–4, §29). Now as virtue is to *eudaimonia* so vice (*kakia, mochthēria, phaulia, ponēria*) is to wretchedness (1166ᵇ27–8). Like virtue, vice is voluntary (1113ᵇ16–17); like virtue, it 'expresses decision' (1151ª5–7);[36] like virtue, it is a state of character that is difficult, if not impossible, to alter;[37] like virtue, it determines how the best good appears to us. But while virtue ensures that the good appears veridically, 'vice perverts us and produces false beliefs about the first principles of action' (1144ª35–6; see 1151ª25–6). That is why the vicious person does not notice that he is vicious while the akratic does notice that he is akratic (1150ᵇ36). The latter knows what the good or *eudaimonia* is and knows that he does not do what promotes it. But the vicious person thinks that what he is promoting in his actions is *eudaimonia*. The incontinent is like a

---

[35] Anscombe (1965, 148) is wrong to claim, therefore, that Aristotle does not explain why one cannot have decision without character.
[36] See 1135ᵇ25, 1142ª18–20.
[37] See 1128ᵇ25–6, 1145ª36–ᵇ2, 1150ᵇ34–1151ª6.

polis 'that votes for all the right decrees and has good laws but does not apply them'; the vicious person 'is like a polis that applies vicious laws' (1152^{a}19–24).

Both vice and virtue support decision, then, but are they the only states that do so? No. The enkratic or self-controlled person also decides (1151^{a}29–^{b}4). For he wishes for *eudaimonia*, deliberates about what will promote it, judges as a result that this thing, which is up to him, will do the trick, forms a desire to do it, and—because his rational wish is stronger than his opposing appetites—actually does it.

Does the akratic or weak-willed person also decide? Let us see. He wishes for *eudaimonia* and has at least true belief about what it is (1151^{a}29–^{b}4). He deliberates about how to achieve it (1142^{b}18–20, 1150^{b}19–21). Hence he decides (1152^{a}15–17). But he does not act on his decision. Instead, what he actually does is what will promote the satisfaction of his wish-opposing appetites, not his wish. Thus his action does not express his wish in the way required for decision. It follows that the akratic does not decide to do what he does akratically. Like a child who has not yet formed his character, he acts voluntarily (1111^{b}6–9), but he does not decide to do what he does akratically (1151^{a}5–7).

The full message of (B) is, then, this. Decision requires both *nous* and a state of character. But the state in question can be either virtue, self-control, *akrasia*, or vice. If the state is virtue, self-control, or *akrasia*, *nous* will grasp *eudaimonia* as it really is. If it is vice, *nous* will grasp what is in fact wretchedness falsely believing it to be *eudaimonia*.[38]

The remaining sections of the text are now readily construed. (D) Reasoning by itself does not cause action, but practical reasoning (which is reasoning that takes place under the aegis of wish in order to discover what will promote its satisfaction) does. Such reasoning is, as (A) tells us, the first principle of decision and action. But it is also, (E) tells us, the first principle of production. For (F) what we produce, we produce for the sake of *eupraxia*—craft-knowledge, as we saw in §12, is subordinate to *phronēsis*. (H) simply sums up in

---

[38] It is also possible, though Aristotle has little to say about this, to be akratic or enkratic with respect not to *eudaimonia* itself but to what one falsely believes to be *eudaimonia*. No doubt he would categorize such people as relative (*pros ti*) akratics or enkratics, contrasting them with their unconditional (*haplōs*) analogues who have the correct conception of *eudaimonia*.

two equivalent formulae all that (A) through (G) have told us about decision.

With the exception of (B), this account of decision does not differ in any significant way from the earlier account in Book III. And even (B) is not cut from entirely whole cloth. For in Book III. Aristotle also connects decision with character: 'By deciding to do good things or bad things we are of a certain character, not by what we believe' (1112ª1–3). Our decisions express our beliefs about the good or *eudaimonia* and thereby reveal our character. For it is our character that determines our beliefs about *eudaimonia* and, hence, our decisions.

16 INSTANTANEOUS ACTION AND FUTURE PLANNING

A decision is a deliberative desire and deliberation takes time: 'Deliberation is not aiming well (*eustochia*); for aiming well involves no reasoning and is done quickly. But we deliberate for a long time. And it is said that we must act quickly on the outcome of our deliberation, but deliberate slowly' (1142ᵇ2–5; see 1135ᵇ8–11). It seems to follow that instantaneous actions cannot be decided upon. And in Book III, Aristotle cites a *legomenon* to that effect: 'instantaneous actions (*exaiphnēs*) are said to be (*legomen*) voluntary but not to express decision' (1111ᵇ9–10). In other texts, however, Aristotle seems to allow that such actions can be virtuous:

It is proper to the courageous person to stand firm against what is and what appears frightening to a human being, because it is fine to stand and shameful to fail. Indeed, that is why someone who is unafraid and unperturbed in a sudden alarm seems more courageous than someone who stands firm in dangers that are obvious in advance. For what he does is more the result of his state of character, since it is less the outcome of preparation. If an action is foreseen, we might decide to do it also by reason and rational calculation, but instantaneous action (*ta d'exaiphnēs*) expresses our state of character. (1117ª16–22)

He also claims, however, that virtuous actions must be decided upon, indeed, decided on 'because of themselves' (1105ª31–2). Thus we seem to have an *aporia*. But is it a genuine *aporia* or can dialectic find a way through?

The problematic notion is clearly decision, so let us focus on that. In contrasting deliberation with aiming well Aristotle says that 'we deliberate for a long time'. But the contrast would be just as effectively made if he said that we *often* deliberate for a long time. For aiming well is *always* instantaneous. And the following passage from *De Motu Animalium* suggests that this may indeed be what he intends:

> As for the premises in a practical argument, they are of two kinds—because of the good and because of the possible. And just as when we ask dialectical questions, so in this case also reasoning does not examine the second of these premises when it is obvious. For example, if walking is good for a man, reasoning does not waste time on the fact that he is a man. Hence whatever we do without calculation, we do quickly. (701ª23–9)

We could say, then, that instantaneous virtuous action involves instantaneous deliberation and decision. The courageous person just sees that he must stand firm right now, and straightaway, without explicitly going through what is obvious to him, he decides to stand firm and acts on his decision.

Instantaneous or compressed deliberation and decision offers us one way through our *aporia*. But there is another that underwrites the first and is instructive in its own right. Decision presupposes a state of character. But a state of character is not something we either have or lack by nature or chance. Our states of character are—except in cases of pathology—in part the results of our own voluntary actions: 'The virtues, as we say, are voluntary, since in fact we are ourselves in a way joint causes of our state of character, and by having the state of character we have we lay down the sort of end we do. Hence the vices will also be voluntary, since the same is true of them' (1114b21–25). Now we normally acquire a state of character through habituation not decision. By doing virtuous actions voluntarily—though not yet from the sort of stable state required for decision—we eventually acquire the virtuous state itself (1105ª17–b12). But we can also acquire such a state by deciding to do what will enable us to acquire it. This seems to be so, for example, in the case of the enkratic.

An enkratic has a state of character of the sort required for decision. But his state is not a virtuous state because his unruly appetites oppose his wish. Unlike the vicious person, however, his state need not be unchangeable or incurable.[39] Hence, he could decide to try to change his appetites, and if he succeeds and

---

[39] Aristotle says that the vicious are incurable, the akratic curable (1150b29–35). He does not explicitly say where the enkratic fall.

becomes virtuous, he will have his virtuous state in part because he has decided upon it. Spontaneous actions done from that state will then be—albeit indirectly—the result of prior deliberation and decision.

Now there are many different types of enkratic people. At one end of the spectrum, there are the very enkratic in whom wish is opposed by appetite on every type of occasion requiring decision and action. Such types are no doubt extremely rare. At the other end of the spectrum, there are the minimally enkratic in whom wish is opposed by appetite in only one type of occasion. The minimally enkratic have only one appetite that opposes wish—the desire for chocolate as it might be. Such types are also extremely rare. In between, there are the more common or garden variety enkratics in whom appetite opposes wish on some types of occasions but not on others. And surely all actual ethical agents, all fairly decent but non-saintly people, are in fact such common or garden enkratics (see 1179^{b}16–20). For their habituation has neither succeeded completely in making them virtuous nor failed completely. It is clear, therefore, that decent people can plan and decide to become less enkratic. And surely many of them do this successfully. It follows that most decent people have the states of character they have in part because they have deliberated about them and decided upon them. When they act spontaneously out of such states, their actions are—albeit indirectly—the result of deliberation and decision.

If we allow for the possibility of instantaneous deliberation and decision, then, or if we discern two roles for deliberation and decision, one concerned directly with what action to do right now and one concerned only indirectly with such actions, we can find a way through the *aporia* with which we began.

But is this second solution one that Aristotle could consistently have adopted? It may seem that it is not. For deliberation about how to change our state of character will almost certainly result not in a decision to act now but in a decision to put a plan for future action into effect. And Aristotle seems not to allow for this possibility. For he seems to think that action must follow at once upon decision:

I should make something good; a house is something good. At once (*euthus*) he makes a house. I need covering; a cloak is a covering; I need a cloak; what I need, I have to make; I need a cloak; I have to make a cloak.

The conclusion, 'I have to make a cloak', is an action. And he acts from a first principle. If there is to be a cloak, there must necessarily be this first, and if this, that. And that he does at once (*euthus*). That the action is the conclusion is now clear. (*MA* 701ᵃ16–23; see *NE* 1147ᵃ25–31)

And if action must follow at once upon decision, future planning seems to be ruled out.

In fact, however, Aristotle's commitment to the view that someone must act immediately on a decision includes an important conditional clause: he acts immediately 'if nothing interferes (*kōluē(i)*)' or compels him not to' (*MA* 701ᵃ16); he acts immediately if he is 'able and nothing interferes (*kōluomenon*)' (1147ᵃ30–1). And among the things that can interfere are his own practical beliefs (1147ᵃ31–2). So factors internal to the agent can prevent a decision from being effective in action.

Moreover, some purely mental activities count as actions (*praxeis*) for Aristotle. Thus, for example, he counts study as a kind of action: 'It is not necessary that an active life be in relation to others, as some people think, nor is that thought alone practical which is for the sake of the consequences of the action, but much more so are the studies (*theōrias*) and thoughts that are their own ends and for their own sakes' (*Pol.* 1325ᵇ16–21). There is no obvious obstacle, then, to allowing that some of the actions, which follow immediately upon a decision (provided, of course, that nothing interferes), are mental actions such as developing a plan or forming an intention.[40]

There is room in Aristotle's theory, then, both for instantaneous actions that are the results of decisions and for future planning, but Aristotle does not explicitly make that room for them. Hence the discussion of them is necessarily conjectural and should be viewed as such.

17 PHRONĒSIS AND WISDOM

In this section, we focus not on wisdom itself but on its relationship to *phronēsis*.[41] None the less, it is important to have some idea of what wisdom is even to discuss that more limited topic.

---

[40] Sherman (1989, 58–60) cites *Rh.* 1392ᵇ15–1393ᵃ4, which says that 'the thing will be done if the the individual is now setting about to do it or is going to do it later (*mellēsei*)', as evidence that Aristotle allowed for the possibility of future planning. The close relations between intentions and plans are elucidated in Bratman (1987).

[41] Wisdom is discussed in §§26–7.

Wisdom is the intellectual virtue that ensures the excellence of study (1177^a12–19); it is 'the most exact form of scientific-knowledge' (1141^a16–17); it is 'scientific-knowledge of the most valuable things with *nous* as its coping-stone' (1141^a17–20; see 1141^b2–4). Since human beings and their doings are not among these most valuable things (1141^a20–$^b2$), 'wisdom does not study any source of human *eudaimonia*, since it does not study any sort of coming into being' (1143^b19–20). But wisdom is very relevant to *eudaimonia* all the same. That is why *phronēsis*, which is most of all *phronēsis* when it is concerned with the *eudaimonia* of the individual, is concerned with wisdom.

Aristotle describes the relationship between *phronēsis*, wisdom, and *eudaimonia* in the following compressed passage:

[A] First, let us say that both *phronēsis* and wisdom must be choiceworthy by themselves, even if neither produces anything at all. For each is the virtue of one of the two rational parts of the psyche. Second, they do produce something. [B] Wisdom produces *eudaimonia*, not in the way that medicine produces health, but in the way that health does. [C] For since wisdom is a part of virtue as a whole, it makes us *eudaimōn* because it is a state that we possess and activate.[42] [D] Besides activity (*ergon*) expressing *phronēsis* and the virtues of character is complete.[43] For virtue makes the aim correct; *phronēsis* what promotes it. (1144^a1–9)

(A) is at least relatively intelligible: if *phronēsis* and wisdom really are choiceworthy by themselves, we can understand why they might be important for *eudaimonia*.

The problems begin with (B). Does it mean that wisdom produces *eudaimonia* in the way that health produces *eudaimonia* or in the way that health produces health? The issue is disputed but the evidence strongly favours the latter alternative.[44] First, (C) is obviously intended to explain (B). And the explanation it offers seems to be this: wisdom produces *eudaimonia* by being a state—namely, complete virtue—whose activation is identical to *eudaimonia* (1098^a16–18, 1178^a6–10).[45] But health cannot

---

[42] The meaning of the phrase 'virtue as a whole' is discussed in §23. States and their activations are discussed in §19.

[43] It is activities that are completed by the virtues proper to them (1098^a15). Hence *ergon* should be taken to refer—as it can refer (see *EE* 1219^a13–17 and §19) —simply to practical activity. It cannot refer to the human function because the human function is not practical activity and is not completed by *phronēsis*. See §23.

[44] See Burnet (1900, 283), Joachim (1951, 216–7), and Stewart (1892, 2: 98–9).

[45] See Gauthier and Jolif (1970, ii. 2: 542–7) and §§22–3.

produce *eudaimonia* in that way. For health, not being a virtue of the psyche (1102^a12–23), is neither complete virtue nor even a part of it. Hence it cannot produce *eudaimonia* by being a state whose activation just is *eudaimonia* itself.[46] Second, Aristotle uses the example of health producing health later in the *Ethics* in order to contrast the relationship between a state and its activation with that of a state and its producer: 'health and the doctor are not the cause of health in the same way' (1174^b25–6).[47] This makes it likely that he is using health in (B) to make the same sort of point. Wisdom produces *eudaimonia*, as health produces health, namely, by being the state or part of the state whose activation is *eudaimonia*.

Since *phronēsis* is concerned with *eudaimonia*, it is now obvious why it must also be concerned with wisdom. But what is the precise nature of that concern? Aristotle's answer is tantalizingly brief: '*Phronēsis* does not control wisdom or the better part of the psyche, just as medicine does not control health. For medicine does not use health, but only aims to bring health into being; hence it prescribes for the sake of health but does not prescribe to health' (1145^a6–9).[48] Despite its brevity we may, none the less, infer from it that *phronēsis* prescribes for the sake of wisdom and aims to bring it into being.

One way *phronēsis* produces *eudaimonia*, then, is by bringing wisdom, whose activation is *eudaimonia*, into being. But that is not the only way *phronēsis* produces *eudaimonia*. According to (D), *phronēsis*, which involves the virtues of character as a whole, completes practical activity. Now when this activity is completed well it is *eudaimonia* or a kind of *eudaimonia* (1098^a15–17, 1178^a6–10). Consequently, *phronēsis* is both a state whose activation is *eudaimonia* and a state that prescribes for the sake of a different state whose activation is also *eudaimonia*.

But how can *phronēsis* be related to *eudaimonia* in both these ways? There is only one possible answer. There must be two kinds of *eudaimonia*, one being the activation of *phronēsis* and the other the activation of wisdom. Moreover, these two kinds must be so

---

[46] Greenwood (1909, 47) is mistaken, therefore, when he writes: '*iatrikē*, the meaning will then be, is an external means to *hugieia*, but *hugieia* a component means to *eudaimonia*, and *sophia* and *phronēsis* are component means in the same way.'

[47] Carrie Swanson reminded me of this.

[48] See *EE* 1249^a22–$^b25$; *MM* 1198^b9–20, 1208^a9–21; *Pol.* 1334^b17–28.

related that the first is for the sake of the second. For *phronēsis* prescribes for the sake of wisdom.

Consistency and philosophical scrutability require, then, that there be two kinds of *eudaimonia* appropriately related. But did Aristotle recognize this requirement? We shall see that he did. Study expressing wisdom is primary *eudaimonia*; practical activity expressing *phronēsis* is secondary *eudaimonia*; and the latter is for the sake of the former.[49]

18 PHRONĒSIS AS A VIRTUE

The *phronimos*, being naturally virtuous, has *nous* of what *eudaimonia* really is. Hence he is fully virtuous. He is a good deliberator, able to determine what type of action will promote *eudaimonia* in different types of circumstances. He has the practical perception needed to determine what type of circumstances he is in and what type of action he is actually doing. He decides in accordance with his wish to do a type of action that will best promote *eudaimonia* in those circumstances (it might be the action of forming a plan or intention to act in the future). And he acts on his decision correctly performing an action of that type. Hence the *phronimos* will act well and achieve *eudaimonia* and a *eudaimōn* life if any human being does. And because all that is true, because *phronēsis* is able to do all that, it is the intellectual virtue of the calculating part of the rational part of the psyche. For the virtue of anything is what enables it to perform its function well and the function of the calculating part is to do what best promotes *eudaimonia*. But it is no part of the function of *phronēsis* to discover what *eudaimonia* is. That function belongs to scientific-knowledge, dialectic, and *nous*.

Nous thus plays two different but related roles in relation to *phronēsis*. First, it provides *phronēsis* with the knowledge of ethical universals it needs in order to achieve *eudaimonia* reliably. But, second, it—or rather its activation, study—is the teleological cause of practical activity, of activity expressing *phronēsis*. For activity

---

[49] See §§26–32. It follows that the doctrines of *NE* x. 7–8 are required by those of vi. 12–13. They are also, as we shall see, required by the arguments in i. 7 (see §§19–24). The *Ethics* is not inconsistent, then, as Cooper (1975, 155–77) has argued, and there is no need to excise x. 7–8 to restore it to consistency, as Nussbaum (1986a, 373–7) has proposed.

expressing *phronēsis* is for the sake of study. That is why, indeed, the first principles of *nous* and of desire are the same (*Metaph.* 1072^{a}27). For *nous* conceived of as primary *eudaimonia* is the first principle, or final end, of desire, and *nous* conceived of as study, as the most exact form of scientific-knowledge, being identical to god, is its own first principle or final cause (see §26).

3
ACTIONS, ENDS, AND FUNCTIONS

The function is in a way the producer activated.

(*NE* 1168^a7)

BOOK I of the *Ethics* is filled with complex arguments about *eudaimonia* and with important methodological remarks that vividly remind us of the limits of those arguments and of the power of the ethical *endoxa* and *phainomena* to which they are ultimately answerable. The argument in i. 1–2 identifies *eudaimonia* with the end of politics and politics with the most architectonic virtue. The argument from completeness, self-sufficiency, and choiceworthiness, which shares i. 7 with the function argument, introduces new conceptual apparatus crucial to the remainder of the discussion. The function argument itself establishes the relevance of virtue to *eudaimonia* thereby setting the agenda for much of the rest of the *Ethics* (1102^a5–7). Having already discussed method, the arguments are our present topic. When we have properly understood them, our grip on *phronēsis* and its relationship to *nous* and *eudaimonia* will be immeasurably tightened. But before we can hope to reach such an understanding, we need to probe Aristotle's views on different types of ends and on the different kinds of things we do to achieve them.

19 ACTIONS, PRODUCTIONS, AND ENDS

Doings have ends; they are for the sake of something, but there are different kinds of doings and different kinds of ends. *Eudaimonia* is desirable and choiceworthy 'because of itself (*di' autēn*) never because of something other (*di' allo*)' (1097^b1). And it is the only thing that has this feature: 'in a word, we choose everything for the sake of some other thing (*heterou heneka*) except for *eudaimonia*' (1176^b30–1). *Eudaimonia* is, therefore, the one unconditional end (1139^b1–4).

Because *eudaimonia* is an unconditional end it is also a *kath' hauto* end, one choiceworthy by itself. For 'when we speak of something unconditionally, we speak of it by itself *(kath' hauto)*' (1151ᵇ1–2). Moreover, *eudaimonia* is choiceworthy because of itself. And for this reason, too, it is choiceworthy by itself: 'what belongs to something because of itself *(di' hauto)* belongs to it by itself *(kath' hauto)*' (*APo.* 73ᵇ10–11).

All *di' hauto* ends are *kath' hauto* ends, then, but are all *kath' hauto* ends choiceworthy *di' hauto*? We would expect the answer to be: yes. For it is hard to see how something could be choiceworthy by itself, if it were not choiceworthy because of itself. But there is an obstacle to attributing this answer to Aristotle. Wealth, he claims, is choiceworthy by itself: 'Some sources of pleasure are necessary; others are choiceworthy by themselves *(kath' hauta)*, but can be taken to excess . . . for example victory, honour, wealth *(plouton)*, and similar good and pleasant things' (1147ᵇ23–31). But he denies that wealth is choiceworthy because of itself: 'Though apparently there are many ends, we choose some of them, for example wealth *(plouton)*, flutes, and, in general, instruments, [solely] because of something else *(di' heteron)*' (1097ᵃ25–7). It seems to follow that he did not identify *kath' hauto* with *di' hauto* ends.[1]

But this conclusion must be resisted. For if it is allowed to stand, Aristotle's account of the relative completeness of ends at 1097ᵃ30–4, in which *kath' hauto* ends are clearly treated as being choiceworthy because of themselves, is rendered unintelligible (see §20). But how are we to resist it? In the *Politics* (1256ᵃ11–1258ᵇ8), Aristotle distinguishes two kinds of wealth, natural wealth and artificial wealth or money. The first consists of 'those goods, capable of accumulation, which are necessary for life and useful to the community of polis or household' (1256ᵇ28–30; see 1257ᵇ18–22). 'It is of these goods', he says, 'that true wealth *(alēthinos ploutos)* seems to consist' (1256ᵇ30–1). Natural wealth, we may infer, is choiceworthy both by and because of itself (and also, though this is not now relevant, for the sake of other things). Artificial wealth or money, on the other hand, has exchange value only. It is choiceworthy neither by nor because of itself, but solely because of something else (1257ᵇ8–22). Presumably, then, Aristotle has natural wealth in mind at 1147ᵇ23–31; and money or artificial

---

[1] This problem is unremarked in the standard commentaries.

wealth in mind at 1097ᵃ25–7. *Kath' hauto* and *di' hauto* ends are thus the same as one another, and something is choiceworthy by itself if and only if it is choiceworthy because of itself. Not all ends are *kath' hauto* ends, however. Some are *allo* ends: 'Actions (*praxeis*) are for the sake of other things (*allōn*)' (1112ᵇ32–3). And some are *para* ends: 'However, there is an apparent difference among ends aimed at. For the end is sometimes an activity (*energeiai*), sometimes a product over and above (*para*) the activity' (1094ᵃ3–5). Are these different kinds of ends or, like *kath' hauto* and *di' hauto*, is the difference between them merely nominal? The answer is that they must be different. For actions and activities are distinguished from productions by reference to the kinds of ends they have (see 1140ᵇ6–7, §12). But if *allo* and *para* ends were the same, all these doings would have precisely the same kinds of ends.

Even *para* ends do not quite complete the list, however. For there are some ends that seem to be different from any already on it: 'Honour, pleasure, understanding, and every virtue we certainly choose because of themselves (*di' auta*) (for even if they had no consequences, we would still choose each of them), but we also choose them for the sake of *eudaimonia*, supposing that through them we shall be *eudaimōn*' (1097ᵇ2–5). This suggests that some things, being choiceworthy because of themselves and because of *eudaimonia*, are some kind of hybrid of *kath' hauto* and either *allo* or *para* ends.

So far, then, we have uncovered what seem to be four types of ends: *kath' hauto* or *di' hauto* ends; *allo* ends; *para* ends; and hybrid ends.

Kath' hauto or *di' hauto* ends are sufficiently intelligible for present purposes, so let us turn to *allo* and *para* ends. Aristotle gives actions as examples of things that have *allo* ends and crafts or productions as things that have *para* ends. This suggests that the difference between *allo* and *para* ends will be illuminated by the distinction between action (*praxis*) and production (*poiēsis*).

Aristotle sometimes uses the term *praxis* and the cognate verb *prattein* to refer to any intentional action. Thus he allows that children and beasts 'act (*praxei*) voluntarily' (1111ᵃ25–6). But he also uses the term in a stricter, canonical sense to refer only to what results from decision. And he then excludes children and beasts from having a share in *praxis*: 'We do not say that a child acts (*prattein*) or a beast either' (*EE* 1224ᵃ28–9).² For children and beasts lack the capacity to deliberate and decide. In the looser sense of the term, productions are actions, but they are not real or canonical actions. The following passage explains why:

Since of the actions (*praxeōn*) that have a limit (*peras*) none is an end (*telos*) but all are in relation to the end (*peri to telos*)—as, for example slimming is to slimness. For the bodily parts themselves, when they are slimming, in that respect are in motion (*en kinesei*), but those things the motion is for the sake of do not yet belong to them—and such things are not actions or at least not complete ones (*teleia*) (for they are not an end). But the sort in which its end is contained is a (real) action. For example, in the same moment one is seeing and has seen, is exercising *phronēsis* (*phronei*) and has exercised it (*pephronēke*), is exercising *nous* (*noei*) and has exercised it (*nenoēken*). But if you are learning, it is not the case that in the same moment you have learned, nor if you are being cured, that in the same moment you have been cured. However, someone who is living well (*eu zē(i)*) at the same time has lived well and someone who is *eudaimōn* at the same moment has been *eudaimōn*. If that were not so, these things [living well, being *eudaimōn*] would have to come to an end at some time, as is the case with slimming. Of these, then, one group should be called movements (*kinēseis*) and the other activities (*energeias*). For every movement is incomplete (*atelēs*). For example, slimming, learning, walk-taking, house-building; these are movements and are incomplete. For one cannot in the same moment be taking a walk and have taken it, nor be house-building and have built a house, nor be coming to be and have come to be, nor be moving and have been moved; they're different, as [in general] are moving (*kinei*) and having moved (*kekinēken*). (*Metaph.* 1048ᵇ18–33)³

Canonical actions are activities or *energeiai*, then, whereas productions are movements or *kinēseis*.

Why do activities and actions, so conceived, interest Aristotle? The question is a deep one and we must content ourselves, for the moment, with a somewhat schematic answer. Actions are caused by decisions; decisions are caused in part by wish; wish is a type of desire. And if desire is not to be empty, we cannot desire X for the sake of Y and Y for the sake of Z and Z for the sake of . . . without

---

² See *NE* 1099ᵇ32–1100ᵃ3, 1139ᵃ20; *EE* 1222ᵇ20.
³ My translation is indebted to Furth (1985, 68–9). See *PN* 446ᵇ2; *NE* 1173ᵃ29–ᵇ4, 1174ᵃ14–ᵇ6. Kosman (1984) is a particularly good discussion of this passage. Some of the difficulties Ackrill (1965) raises for the distinction between activities and movements are answered in Charles (1985) and Penner (1970). Ackrill (1980) and Charles (1986) critically discuss Aristotle's notion of an action.

end (1094^a18–22). But emptiness is not the only threat to desire; there is also termination. When some desires are satisfied, they are terminated as sources of motivation and have to be replaced by other ones. A third threat to desire is frustration. We can be frustrated in achieving a desired end by factors outside our control. Now actions are tailor-made to circumvent all three of these threats as far as possible. Actions are complete at every moment: if Øing is an action, one both is Øing and has (successfully) Øed simultaneously. Hence, everything else being equal, a desire to Ø is less liable to frustration than a desire to (say) build a house or run a marathon. And because activities are complete at every moment they contain their ends. A desire to Ø will thus be satisfied at every moment of Øing. A desire for the end of house-building, by contrast, will not be satisfied until the house-building has successfully terminated in a house. Moreover, activities have no built in limit: if Øing is an activity there is nothing built into the very notion of Øing that necessitates its coming to an end. Hence a desire to Ø can go on being satisfied by Øing without end. The threat of termination is thus avoided. With house-building, on the other hand, things are different. We desire a house and set about building one, but when the house is completed our desire is satisfied and gone and we do need to find another desire.

Actions and activities are made to be ends, therefore, in a way that productions are not, and they interest Aristotle for that reason. For he believes that a satisfactory explanation of natural phenomena must be teleological. Hence, he is interested in anything that, like an action or activity, is a potential terminator of a teleological explanation.

But activities and actions interest Aristotle for a deeper and more theoretical reason, which stems from his investigation of substance in the *Metaphysics*. Substance, he argues, must be both ontologically and epistemically prior to all the other categories—their being and their being known must depend on its being and being known, but not vice versa. It follows, for reasons we shall explore in greater detail in §§26–7, that primary substance must be an essentially matterless activity that is the teleological cause of all the other beings. This activity is god. But god is also *eudaimonia* or the unconditional end of action. Hence, the metaphysical investigation of being and substance ends in the same place as the ethical investigation of the human good, and *nous* and desire have the same first principles (*Metaph.* 1072^a27; see 982^b5–10).

Now the end of the process of production is the product. And the product is certainly *para* or over and above the production of it. It lasts longer, for one thing, and comes into existence only when the process of production is over. We now know what *para* ends are. They are *ends* that are over and above. But what are *allo* ends? What is the end of an activity?

In the following passage, Aristotle seems to be trying to tell us: 'The result (*ergon*)[4] is the end, the activity is the result, and this is why the term activity (*energeia*) is said with relation to the result (*kata to ergon*) and is extended to the activation (*entelecheian*)' (*Metaph.* 1050ᵃ21–3). But to grasp what he has in mind, we need to delve a bit behind the scenes. The activation to which Aristotle is referring is the activation of a second potential or state. And a second potential is the activation of a first potential. So: John has a first potential to be virtuous if he is naturally fitted to acquire the virtues. If he actually does acquire them, through habituation and the rest, he has activated his first potential. He now possesses a virtuous state or second potential. If he activates that second potential by engaging in virtuous action, his activation is an activity (*DA* 412ᵃ1–28, 417ᵃ21–ᵇ2).[5] The activation of a potential must be distinguished, however, from the result of activating it. Consider the following example:

John laughed a hollow laugh.

The hollow laugh is the result of John's activating his potential to laugh such laughs. It is an activity in the primary or non-extended sense of the term. His laughing is an activity in a secondary or extended sense because what he is doing would not be called laughing if it did not result in a laugh.

But what is the nature of the relation between the hollow laugh and the laughing of it? It is this: the hollow laugh is the internal and logically necessary result of laughing. This relation is difficult to grasp because we almost always use the same word for both the activation and its result. And the word then becomes act/result ambiguous. But sometimes we have different words for the act and its internal result. For example, we strike blows and sing notes. And we distinguish the blow from the striking of it and the note from the

---

[4] *Ergon* is usually translated as 'function'. But here 'result' makes Aristotle's thought a little easier to follow. See §22.

[5] Irwin (1988*b*, 223–47) is a good recent discussion of the varieties of activation and potentiality.

singing of it. Likewise we need to distinguish the act from the doing of it, the activity as result from the activity as activation of a state.

It is this distinction between act and result that Aristotle seems to mark by *allo*, so that the result of activating a state is the *allo* end of the activation. And he contrasts this with a *para* end because, while a *para* end is over and above the doing whose end it is, an *allo* end is not over and above the activation of the state whose end it is. The note is not something over and above the singing of it; it lasts only as long as it is sung. The blow is not over and above the striking of it; it lasts only while being struck. Likewise an action or a thought is not over and above the doing or thinking of it. But the internal end is not the same as the activation of the state. It is the *allo* but not the *para* end of activating it.[6]

We may say, then, that *allo* and *para* ends differ as follows. *Allo* ends are other than, but not over and above, the doings whose ends they are; *para* ends are other than, because over and above, the doings whose ends they are.

The ends of processes are paradigmatic *para* ends. But there are *para* ends that are not the ends of processes. For some actions or activities, too, have *para* ends:

But from the virtues concerned with action we try to a greater or lesser extent to gain something over and above the action itself (*para tēn praxin*). . . . But the actions of the politicians are unleisured also. Over and above (*par'*) political activities themselves these actions seek positions of power and honours; or at least they seek *eudaimonia* for the politician himself and his fellow citizens, which is something different (*heteran*) from politics itself and clearly is sought on the assumption that it is different. Hence among actions expressing the virtues those in politics and war are preeminently fine and great; but they require trouble, aim at some [further] end, and are not choiceworthy [simply] because of themselves (*di' hautas*). (1177[b]2–18)[7]

---

[6] I have benefited in this and the preceding paragraph from Charles (1986, 132–9).

[7] Charles (1986, 129 n. 15) is mistaken in claiming, therefore, that *praxeis* are a 'subset of activities . . . which are not chosen for a further goal over and above (*para*) the activity'. At 1140[b]6–7 Aristotle says: 'production is different (*heteron*) from its end, but action isn't; since its end is acting well.' This seems to contradict 1177[b]2–18. But in fact it does not. For what it means is presumably this: Production's end is different from (because over and above) production. But action's end is not always different from (because over and above) action, since it can be an *allo* end, namely, acting well.

But how can this be? How can actions expressing *phronēsis* and the virtues of character, which are non-productive, possibly have *para* ends? An answer will begin to emerge in §20 and will emerge fully in §32. For the present we must rest content with identifying the various ends of the virtues and getting clear about their inter-relations.

The virtues are states choiceworthy both because of themselves and for the sake of *eudaimonia*. Is *eudaimonia* their *allo* end or their *para* end? It can only be the latter. For only activities have *allo* ends. Now the function argument establishes that *eudaimonia* is activity expressing virtue (1098ª17–18). This suggests that *eudaimonia* is the *allo* end of activating virtue. But if the virtue in question is *phronēsis*, then, as we have just seen, it also has a *para* end, which must, in the limit, also be *eudaimonia*. For *eudaimonia* is the best good, the end for the sake of which we do everything else. Hence all chains of ends finally terminate in *eudaimonia*. It seems to follow that *eudaimonia* is at once the *allo* and the *para* end of activating *phronēsis*. But, given the definitions of *allo* and *para* ends, that is obviously impossible, unless there are, in fact, two kinds of *eudaimonia*, one of which is the *allo* end of *phronēsis*, the other its *para* end. But did Aristotle think that *eudaimonia* was so structured? In §17, we saw evidence that he did: study is primary *eudaimonia*; practical activity is secondary *eudaimonia* and is for the sake of primary *eudaimonia*. In other words, secondary *eudaimonia* is the *allo* end of activating *phronēsis* and primary *eudaimonia* is its *para* end.[8]

20 THE ARGUMENT FROM POLITICS

Politics is the same state as *phronēsis*; *phronēsis* is a virtue of thought; therefore, politics must also be a virtue of thought.[9] But what exactly is politics? The opening argument of the *Ethics* will tell us part of the answer. It begins as follows:

---

[8] It might also be said that the fine is the *allo* end of activating *phronēsis*. See *EE* 1248ᵇ36–8.

[9] See 1141ᵇ23, §12. Aristotle refers to politics as a capacity or science (1094ª25–6). Presumably, it does not matter at this stage of the game just what sort of thing it is. But a virtue is neither a science nor a capacity since they can be used to produce either good or bad results while a virtue can only be used to produce good ones. See §29.

[A] Every craft and every investigation and likewise every action and decision seems (*dokei*) to aim at some good; [B] hence the good has been well described as that at which everything aims. (1094ᵃ1–3)

The operative contrast in (A)—which *dokei* identifies as an *endoxon*—seems to be between things that have only *para* ends and things that also have *allo* ends. And this is borne out by the fact that Aristotle later expresses the contrast as being between 'action and craft' (1097ᵃ15–16). For crafts have only *para* ends whereas actions also have *allo* ends. The things (A) refers to, then, are crafts and the like, which aim only at *para* ends, and actions and the like, which do not. Both of these, Aristotle claims, *seem* to aim at some good. Is he right?

Action is caused by decision and decision by wish. And wish is a rational desire for the good or *eudaimonia*. Hence all actions— remember Aristotelian actions form a narrower class than what we call actions—aim at a good. And what is true of actions is true also of crafts. For crafts and actions both have decision as a first principle (1139ᵇ1).

Aristotle concludes that (B) 'the good has been well described as that at which everything aims'. By whom has it been so described? A likely answer is Plato himself: 'we all seek what is really good' (*R.* 505d5–9); 'the good is the for sake of which (*agathon to hautou heneka*)' (*Def.* 413a3; cf. *Rh.* 1363ᵇ12–13). An *endoxon* endorsed by so reputable an authority no doubt has admirable bona fides, but should Aristotle have accepted it on the basis of (A)? It may seem that he should not. One must always sneeze into a handkerchief; but it does not follow that there is a handkerchief into which one must always sneeze. Likewise, from the fact that everything aims at some good, it does not follow that there is something—the good—at which everything aims. Does the opening argument of the *Ethics* commit an elementary logical fallacy, then? We shall see that it does not.

Immediately following the argument under consideration, Aristotle begins a defence and clarification of it:

[C] Since there are many actions, crafts, and sciences, the ends turn out to be many as well. For health is the end of medicine, a boat of boat building, victory of generalship, and [natural] wealth of household management.¹⁰ But whenever any of these sciences is subordinate to some one capacity

¹⁰ See *Pol.* 1256ᵃ1–1258ᵇ8.

(*dunamin*)—as, for example, bridlemaking and every other science producing equipment for horses are subordinate to horsemanship, while this and every action in warfare are in turn subordinate to generalship, and in the same way other sciences are subordinate to further ones—in each of these the end of the ruling science is more choiceworthy than all the ends subordinate to it, since it is the end for which those ends are also pursued. And here it does not matter whether the ends of the actions are the activities themselves, or some product over and above (*para*) them, as in the sciences we have mentioned. (1094ª6–18)

Crafts and actions have different ends, but when a number of different crafts 'are subordinate to some one capacity', then, in addition to its own peculiar ends, the subordinate crafts also have the end of the superordinate or ruling craft as their common end. Thus the bridlemaker makes the kinds of bridles that the general tells him are best in warfare; the horseman learns to ride in the way that will make him most useful as a cavalry member; and so on.

In the case of crafts this phenomenon of subordination is readily intelligible. The product of one craft is the raw material for a higher craft, which dictates to it what sort of raw material it most needs. But is the phenomenon equally intelligible when applied to activities, which have no products? Surely, it is. Suppose that I engage in the activity of playing the cello for its own sake, so that the end for which I play is the playing itself. At the same time, I am part of a string quartet, so that my playing is also subordinated to the end of the quartet, which may also be playing simply for the sake of it. Here my activity is both for its own sake and for the sake of the end of the quartet. In this example, my activity is a component of the higher activity for the sake of which I also engage in it; my playing is part of the quartet's playing, but activities do not have to be related in this way to exhibit the kind of subordination in question. A courageous soldier stands firm in battle in part for its own sake or to express courage in his actions, but he also fights for the sake of peace and for the study that peace makes possible (see §32 and below). His activity is not, however, a component of those peaceful activities for the sake of which he also fights (see §23).

So much, then, for the first part of Aristotle's defence of his opening argument. Now for the second part:

[D] If, then, there is some end of the practicable that we wish for because of itself and because of which we wish for the other things; and [E] we do not choose everything for the sake of something else, [F] since if we do, it will go on without limit, making desire empty and futile; [G] then clearly this end will be the good, that is the best good. (1094ª18–22)

The argument might seem to go as follows: Aristotle believes that (D) and (E) are exclusive possibilities; he uses (F) to establish that (E) is false; he concludes that (D) must therefore be true. But (D) and (E) are not exclusive possibilities. Desire would not be vain or empty if there were two or more distinct things we desired for their own sakes, and if we desired some things for the sake of one of them and the rest for the sake of the other. Hence if the argument is of this form, it involves the very fallacy that seemed to plague (A)–(B).

We might try to rescue Aristotle from this fallacy by offering him the following additional premise: 'Where there are two or more separate ends each desired for itself we can say that there is just one (compound) end such that each of those separate ends is desired not only for itself but also for *it*'.[11] But this proposal is unattractive. First, it makes Aristotle's discussion of subordination among crafts and actions unnecessary. For the new premise itself entails that there is a single compound end of all crafts and actions having ends wanted for their own sakes, no matter how these crafts and actions are related to one another. Second, it makes the argument unattractively enthymematic. For Aristotle nowhere expresses, what, on this proposal, turns out to be his argument's key premise and crucial principle. Finally, the proposal makes Aristotle's argument overly controversial. For the additional premise presupposes that all things desired for their own sakes combine to form a single thing desired for its own sake. But this is very hard to swallow without argument (see §23).

If (D)–(G) is intended to be an argument for the existence of the best good, then, it is an unprepossessing argument. But what else could it be? Taken at face value, it is just two things: a definition of the best good and an argument about rational choice and desire. The argument is as follows. It is not impossible to choose everything for the sake of something else: to choose money in order to buy property in order to make more money in order to buy more property is an example of that. But it would be silly or irrational to choose everything for the sake of something else, since it would make desire empty and futile.

[11] Ackrill (1974, 26).

But if that is all (D)–(G) is intended to do, how does it further Aristotle's defence of his opening argument? The answer will emerge when we see the next step in that defence. This is provided by the argument (1094ª28–ᵇ11) that there is in fact a capacity— actually, a virtue—to which all crafts and actions are subordinated, namely, politics. Politics prescribes which crafts and sciences should be studied in a polis, which ones each class should learn, and how far they should go with them (1094ª27–ᵇ1). The most honoured capacities, such as generalship, household management, and rhetoric are subordinated to politics (1094ᵇ2–3). It uses the other 'sciences concerned with action', and legislates about what is to be done and what not (1094ᵇ4–6). But if this is so, the facts about subordination introduced earlier entail that the end of politics is the end for the sake of which all the other crafts and actions are pursued. Given that we do not choose everything for the sake of something else, it follows that the end of politics is the best good defined in (G). For every other end will be pursued for its sake; and it, being pursued for no other end, will be pursued solely for its own sake.

One problem with this way of interpreting (D)–(G) is that it makes it hard to understand the fact that before he introduces politics, Aristotle seems to write as if he has already proved that there is a best good: 'Will not the knowledge of it [the best good], then, be of great importance for the conduct of our lives and if, like archers, we have a target to aim at, are we not more likely to hit the right mark?' (1094ª22–4).[12] But this problem is not pressing. For we can take these remarks as both hypothetical and proleptic. The best good is defined in (G). Aristotle is then able to ask (rhetorical) questions about it, on the hypothesis that there is something that fits the definition.

The structure of Aristotle's overall argument, then, is as follows:

1. Every action or craft seems to aim at some good; hence, the good has been well described as that at which everything aims.

2. You might wonder about (1) reflecting that different crafts have different ends, but you should recall that when crafts are subordinate to a single capacity, their ends are for the sake of its end. And this is just as true of activities as it is of crafts.

---

[12] See Ackrill (1974, 25–6).

4. So if we do not choose everything for the sake of something else (which would be irrational), and if there is an X for the sake of which we choose everything else, and we choose X for itself, then X will be the best good.
5. Knowledge of such a (still hypothetical) best good will clearly be very important for the conduct of our lives.
6. If (1)–(5) is so, we should try to discover what this (still hypothetical) best good is and what capacity is concerned with it.
7. And, indeed, there does seem to be a capacity—actually a virtue—to which all crafts and activities are subordinate, namely, politics.
8. Hence, its end is the human good or the best good.

This argument is neither invalid nor lacking in crucial premises. These are obvious points in its favour and in favour of attributing it to Aristotle. But it remains a controversial argument none the less.

The most likely focus of controversy is premise (6). Aristotle is prepared to accept that politics is in fact the virtue to which all crafts and actions are subordinate in the requisite sense. He is not alone in this. Plato countenances such a virtue in the *Republic*, as does Socrates in the *Euthydemus*.[13] But we might reasonably doubt whether politics is a virtue of this sort or whether such a virtue is even possible. Aristotle, himself, shows some hesitation: 'And so if there is some end of everything that is pursued in action, this will be the good pursued in action; and if there are more ends than one, these will be the goods pursued in action. Our argument has progressed, then, to the same conclusion [as the argument from politics]' (1097ᵃ22–4). This is very cautious. Appropriately so, given the controversial presuppositions of the argument.[14]

In any case, Aristotle is persuaded, that politics is the architectonic virtue whose end is the best good. He is sometimes thought to infer from this—and to be correct in doing so—that the best good must include the ends of all the subordinate capacities, crafts, and sciences.[15] The text containing the alleged inference is this:

[13] See Reeve (1988; 1989, 124–44).

[14] We are probably a little more prepared to accept the possibility of the intrapersonal analogue of politics, namely, *phronēsis* (§§12, 32, and below). *Phronēsis* is akin to rational prudence: it exhorts us 'correctly and towards what is best' (1102ᵇ15–16). The question, which we will not now pursue, is whether the existence of *phronēsis* is sufficient for Aristotle's purposes here.

[15] See Grant (1885, 425–6) and Irwin (1988b, 605 n. 25).

[H] It [politics] prescribes which of the sciences ought to be studied in poleis, and which ones each class in the polis should study and to what extent they should study it. [I] Again, we see that even the most honoured capacities, for example, generalship, household management, and rhetoric, are subordinate to it. [J] Further, it uses the other sciences concerned with action (*praktikais*),[16] and legislates what must be done and what avoided. [K] Hence its end *periechoi* the ends of the other sciences and so will be the human good. (1094^{a}28–^{b}7; see *Pol.* 1252^{a}1–6)

Everything, it is readily apparent, hinges on (K) and on the interpretation of the verb *periechō*. This verb can mean 'encompass', 'embrace', or 'include' and most translations so render it.[17] But it can also mean 'be superior to', 'surpass', or 'excel'.[18] Hence (K) is potentially ambiguous and cannot by itself establish what Aristotle had in mind. In context, however, matters are somewhat clearer.

Aristotle has earlier established that the end of an architectonic or ruling virtue 'is more choiceworthy than all the ends subordinate to it' (1094^{a}14–15). And from this, together with (H), (I), and (J), which establish that all other capacities, crafts, and sciences are subordinate to politics, it follows directly that the end of politics is superior to, surpasses, or excels all other ends, and is the best good. Aristotle has not said anything at all, however, about whether the ends of an architectonic virtue must include the ends of its subordinates. Hence, if he did believe this, he has not explained

---

[16] Bywater (1894) brackets *praktikais*.

[17] See Gauthier and Jolif (1970, i.2: 2), Irwin (1985*b*, 3), Rackham (1934, 7), and Ross (1980, 2).

[18] See Liddell, Scott, and Jones (1966) s.v. *periechō*. Aristotle uses the verb in this sense at *Phys.* 259^{a}3–4, where he says that the unmoved mover '*periechei* all the other movers, and exists apart from each of them'. The unmoved mover is certainly superior to all the other movers (*Metaph.* 1074^{b}33–5), but there is no sense in which he literally contains them. For he exists apart from each of them. See §§26–7. But Aristotle also uses *periechō*, understood in the first of the senses we distinguished, to express a number of very different relationships, e.g. between an end or limit and the things whose end or limit it is (*Metaph.* 1055^{a}15), between a universal and its instances (*GC* 317^{b}7, *Metaph.* 1023^{b}30, *NE* 1129^{b}10, *Pol.* 1252^{a}6), between form and matter (*Cael.* 310^{b}10, 312^{a}12; *Ph.* 207^{b}1, 211^{b}12), between a spatial container and its contents (*GA* 753^{b}22, 758^{b}4), between a genus and its species (*Top.* 121^{b}25, *HA* 534^{b}13), between what surrounds something and the thing it surrounds (*Mete.* 339^{b}7, 369^{a}6), between the environment and the thing whose environment it is (*Ph.* 253^{a}16, 259^{b}11; *DA* 411^{a}19; *PN* 465^{b}27). This fact, which has obvious bearing on (K), is unremarked in any of the standard commentaries. An interesting alternative interpretation of *periechō*, which also avoids the conclusion that the end of politics is inclusive of all the other ends, is developed by Kraut (1989, 220–5).

how it is supposed to follow from what he has already established. Nor has he established that the most inclusive good is the best one. And neither omission is trivial. It is not obvious that the end of an architectonic virtue must be inclusive. And it is not obvious that the more inclusive an end is the better it is (see §§21–4). So, if (K) is about the inclusivity of the end of politics, Aristotle's argument is again troublingly enthymematic. If, on the other hand, (K) is simply about the superiority of that end, it follows from what he has already explicitly said. This is surely a compelling reason to take (K) as no more than a conclusion about the surpassing excellence of the best good.

The best good is the end of politics, then, and it is superior to all others. But what is that end? Politics is the same state as *phronēsis*. Hence its activation and that of *phronēsis* must be the same. The activation of *phronēsis* is practical activity or secondary *eudaimonia*. Hence the activation of *politics* is also practical activity. But *phronēsis* is for the sake of study; study is its *para* end. Hence politics should also be for the sake of study. But does Aristotle think this? And what exactly does it mean?

That he thinks it is clear from the following account in the *Politics*:

Since the end of individuals is the same as that of the community, the aim (*horon*) of the best man and of the best constitution must also be the same; it is evident, therefore, that the virtues of leisure ought to exist in both of them. For peace, as we have said many times, is the end of war and leisure of unleisure. But leisure and amusements may be promoted not only by those virtues that are practised in leisure, but also by some of those that are useful in unleisure. For many necessities have to be supplied before we can have leisure. Therefore a polis must be moderate and courageous and able to endure. For truly, as the proverb says, 'there is no leisure for slaves', and those who cannot face danger like men are the slaves of any invader. Courage and endurance are required for unleisure, philosophy for leisure, moderation and justice for both, but more especially in times of peace and leisure. For war compels men to be just and moderate, whereas the enjoyment of good fortune and the leisure that comes with peace tend to make them insolent . . . There is no difficulty in seeing why the polis that would be *eudaimōn* and excellent ought to share in these virtues. It is shameful in men not to be able to use good things, it is particularly shameful not to be able to use them in time of leisure, to manifest good qualities in unleisure and war and when they have peace and leisure to be no better than men sold into slavery. (1334ª11–40)

Politics aims, first, to provide the peace and necessities—the external goods—that are essential for leisure and for study, which is the only truly leisured activity (*NE* 1177^{b}1–26). Second, it aims to provide the civic virtues that guarantee the stability and harmony of the polis.[19]

But politics is a virtue, practical not productive. How, then, can it provide these things? The answer is there in (A)–(K). Politics rules the capacities, productive crafts, and sciences—including the theoretical sciences, which are 'incidentally useful to us for many of the things we need' (*EE* 1216^{b}15–16). It is not directly productive itself. For the *endechomena*—the things that admit of being otherwise—studied by the productive crafts are not studied by politics. But the use of those crafts to ensure *eudaimonia* is among the *endechomena* studied by politics. Politics has study as its *para* end, then, not by being directly productive of it, but by ensuring that the other capacities, crafts, and sciences are exercised so to promote it best (see §§29–32).

21 COMPLETENESS, SELF-SUFFICIENCY, AND CHOICEWORTHINESS OF ENDS

'The many and the wise' agree that the best good, the end of politics, is called *eudaimonia* and they 'suppose that living well (*to d' eu zēn*) or acting well (*to eu prattein*) are the same as being *eudaimōn*' (1095^{a}17–22). They also agree that *eudaimonia* is the most complete, self-sufficient, and choiceworthy of ends (1097^{a}25–^{b}22). They totally disagree, however, about what *eudaimonia* actually is. The many think it is pleasure or wealth (1095^{a}22–3; with 1096^{a}5–7); the more cultivated, 'those active in politics', think it is honour (1095^{b}22–3); the wise think it is the good itself, which causes 'all these goods to be goods' (1095^{a}27–8; see 1102^{a}2–4). The question is, how can the many and the wise agree that the best good is called *eudaimonia* and that *eudaimonia* is complete, self-sufficient, and most choiceworthy, if they disagree so fundamentally about what *eudaimonia* is?

The answer to this question must surely lie in the meaning or nominal essence that the many and the wise attach in common to the term *eudaimonia*. But what is that nominal essence? One

---

[19] See 1103^{b}2–6, 1179^{b}31–1180^{a}32; §30.

important clue to its identity is provided by the following exchange between Socrates and Diotima in the *Symposium*:

'Tell me, Socrates, a lover of good things has a desire; what does he desire?'
'That they become his own,' I said.
'And what will he have when the good things he wants become his own?'
'This time it is easier to come up with the answer,' I said. 'He'll have *eudaimonia*.'
'That's what makes *eudaimōn* people *eudaimōn*, isn't it—possessing good things? There's no need to ask further, "What's the point of wanting *eudaimonia*?" The answer you gave seems to be final (*telos*).'
'True,' I said. (204e2–205a4)

It is pointless to ask people why they want *eudaimonia*. Hence the very meaning of the term must rule the question out of court. Clearly, then, its meaning must be something like 'what everyone desires solely because of itself or for its own sake'. For it is pointless to ask, Why to you want what everyone desires solely for its own sake?

That *eudaimonia* is commonly understood in this way is further established by Aristotle's account in the *Rhetoric*: 'We may define *eudaimonia* as acting well with virtue, or as self-sufficiency of life, or as a life secure and most pleasant, or as a body and property in good condition together with the capacity to protect them and to use them in action' (1360ᵇ14–17). For everything mentioned here is something people desire because of itself.

Now if what is desirable solely because of itself is the meaning or nominal essence the many and the wise attach to *eudaimonia*, completeness, consistency, and choiceworthiness are presumably to be understood as measures of intrinsic value or intrinsic choice-worthiness, and disputes about what *eudaimonia* really is are to be understood as disputes about what is really choiceworthy solely because of itself according to those measures: the many think that it is pleasure; the more cultivated think that it is honour; the wise think that it is the good itself. But can completeness, self-sufficiency, and choiceworthiness be understood in this way? If they can, our hypothesis about the meaning of *eudaimonia* will have proved its worth; if they cannot, we shall have to think again.

An early text in the *Ethics* connects completeness of ends to choice or desire: 'Though apparently there are many ends, we choose some of them, for example money, flutes, and, in general, instruments, [solely] because of something else; hence it is clear that not all ends are complete (*teleia*)' (1097ª25–8; see 1096ª5–10). An end is incomplete if we choose it solely because of something else. Why? The obvious answer is that if X is an incomplete end, getting it by itself, without the thing to which it is a means, will not satisfy our X-related desire at all. Our money-related desire, for example, will not be satisfied by getting money by itself, since we desire the money solely in order to use it to achieve other ends (*Pol.* 1257ᵇ8–22).

Aristotle's subsequent discussion bears out this idea of completeness:

[A] An end pursued by itself (*kath' hauto*), we say, is more complete than an end pursued because of something else (*di' heteron*); [B] and an end that is never choiceworthy because of something else (*di' allo*) is more complete than ends that are choiceworthy both by themselves (*kath' hauta*) and because of this end (*di' auto*); [C] and hence an end that is always choiceworthy by itself (*kath' hauto*), never because of something else, is unconditionally complete (*haplōs*). (1097ª30–4)

(A) distinguishes an end like virtue, which is partly chosen by or because of itself, from an end like money, which is chosen solely because of something else. Desire is, therefore, better satisfied by virtue than by money. For money by itself does not satisfy our money-related desire at all. But virtue does partly satisfy our virtue-related desire since it is choiceworthy, in part, because of itself.

In explanation of (B), Aristotle has this to say: 'Honour, pleasure, and understanding, and every virtue we certainly choose because of themselves (*di' auta*) (for even if they had no consequences, we would still choose each of them), but we also choose them for the sake of *eudaimonia*, supposing that through them we shall be *eudaimōn*' (1097ᵇ2–5). Thus (B) is concerned with things we never choose *solely* because of their consequences or *para* ends, not with things we never choose even *in part* because of their *para* ends. For the virtues are ends of the former not the latter sort. The test provided in (B) applies, then, only to ends X and Y where X is never chosen solely because of a *para* end, and Y is chosen both by or because of itself and because of X. In such cases, (B) says, X is more complete than Y.[20]

---

[20] Keyt (1978, 365) suggests that the division between (A), (B), and (C) is as follows: 'First, there are ends such as wealth, flutes, and instruments in general that are chosen only for the sake of other things [subservient ends]. Secondly, there are

Our hypothesis about completeness explains why this is so. Desire is better satisfied by *eudaimonia* than by virtue because, when we are virtuous, part of our virtue-related desire—the part that is for the *para* end of virtue—remains unsatisfied. But when we possess *eudaimonia* our *eudaimonia*-related desire is completely satisfied. For *eudaimonia* is choiceworthy solely because of itself, never because of a *para* or *allo* end.

(C) distinguishes primary *eudaimonia* from all other ends. Since it alone is pursued solely because of itself, it is unconditionally complete. For we desire all other ends in part for the sake of something else, so that by themselves they fail to fully satisfy our desire for them. But *eudaimonia* does fully satisfy our *eudaimonia*-related desire.[21]

Our investigation of completeness has yielded three results. First, *eudaimonia* is unconditionally complete. Second, *eudaimonia* is, therefore, the best good. For the best good is complete, indeed, most complete (1097[a]28–30). Third, completeness can be understood as a measure of intrinsic value or choiceworthiness.

We turn, now, to self-sufficiency (*autarkeia*):

[A] The same conclusion [that *eudaimonia* is the best good] also appears to follow from self-sufficiency, since the complete good seems to be self-sufficient . . . [B] Anyhow, we regard something as self-sufficient when all by itself it makes a life (*bion*) choiceworthy and lacking nothing; and this is what we think *eudaimonia* does. (1097[b]6–16)

(B) is clearly a definition (or partial definition) of self-sufficiency. But it admits of two different interpretations. It could mean

X is self-sufficient if and only if a life *of a certain sort* that has X added to it is choiceworthy and lacking in nothing

or it could mean

ends such as honour, pleasure, and reason that are chosen both for their own sake and for the sake of other things [subordinate ends]. And, finally, there are ends such as happiness that are always chosen for their own sake and never for the sake of anything else [ultimate ends].' But this is mistaken. For on this understanding of (B), all the virtues, being subordinate ends, are equally complete. But this is not so. For wisdom is more complete than *phronēsis*. See §23.

[21] Irwin (1988*b*, 605–6 n. 30) argues that (C) must mean 'in all our choices, we choose *eudaimonia* and choose it because of itself'. But this would commit Aristotle to the view that choice (*hairesis*) aims at *eudaimonia* and this is ruled out because it would collapse the distinction between actions that are decided upon and those that are merely chosen.

X is self-sufficient if and only if a life *of any sort* that has X added to it is choiceworthy and lacking in nothing.

Which of these interpretations of self-sufficiency is correct? *Eudaimonia* is an activity expressing complete virtue (1098ª16–18). It is also self-sufficient (1097ᵇ14–16). But it is not enough by itself to make someone *eudaimōn*. For to be *eudaimōn* a person also needs both external goods and a life of sufficient length: 'why not say that the person is *eudaimōn* whose activity expresses complete virtue, and who is adequately supplied with external goods, not just for any chance period but for a complete life?' (1101ª14–16). *Eudaimonia* is not sufficient by itself, therefore, to make someone *eudaimōn*. But if his life already includes an adequate supply of external goods, and has enough *eudaimonia* added over a long enough time, it will be choiceworthy and lacking in nothing. A self-sufficient end need not be one that would make just any sort of life choiceworthy and lacking in nothing, then, it is enough that it confers these features on a life of a certain sort, one suitably equipped with food, health, other essential services, friends, and able co-workers.[22]

Between (A) and (B), Aristotle makes another claim about self-sufficiency:

Now what we count as self-sufficient is not what suffices for a solitary person by himself, living an isolated life, but what suffices also for parents, children, wife, and, in general, for friends and fellow citizens, since a human being is naturally a political animal. Here, however, we must impose some limit. For if we extend the good to parents' parents and children's children and to friends of friends, we shall go on without limit; but we must examine this another time. (1097ᵇ8–14)

This claim is best understood as follows. We are by nature political animals, animals who live and want to live in a family and a polis (*Pol.* 1253ª1–3). Hence a life would not be choiceworthy and lacking in nothing for us if it did not include parents, children, friends, and fellow citizens. Neither would it be choiceworthy and lacking in nothing if the parents, children, friends, and fellow citizens were not themselves *eudaimōn*. Hence we must extend the good to them: 'We do not altogether have the character of

---

[22] See 1100ᵇ22–1101ª13, 1177ª27–ᵇ1, 1178ª33–5; §§28–32. *Rh.* 1360ᵇ19–26, which might be cited in this regard, is discussed below. 1177ª27–ᵇ1, which offers particularly compelling evidence for this view of self-sufficiency, is discussed in §28.

eudaimonia if we look utterly repulsive or are ill-born, solitary or childless, and have it even less, presumably, if our children or friends are totally bad, or were good but have died' (1099^b3-6).[23] A self-sufficient end must, then, be something that makes a life of the right sort both choiceworthy and lacking in nothing to someone who naturally possesses needs and desires of certain sorts. It is not enough that it be choiceworthy to someone who lacks, or thinks he lacks, those needs and desires.[24]

But this does not mean, to reiterate, that *eudaimonia* itself provides the family, friends, and polis that a *eudaimōn* life needs. These external goods must be provided, to be sure, but an end is self-sufficient if, when added to a life that already contains them, it makes that life choiceworthy and lacking in nothing.[25]

Turning back, now, to completeness, we can see why the unconditionally complete good 'seems to be self-sufficient' (1097^b8-9). *Eudaimonia* is the best good and is unconditionally complete. Hence we choose everything else at least in part because of it, and choose it solely because of itself. Added to a life, equipped in the manner we have been discussing with external goods and the rest, therefore, it must make it choiceworthy and lacking in nothing. For the life in question lacks nothing that is a means to *eudaimonia* and *eudaimonia* is a means to nothing further. It follows that self-sufficiency, like completeness, can be understood as a measure of intrinsic value or choiceworthiness.

---

[23] See 1157^b2-23, 1169^b16-22, 1170^a5-7. These texts show that the suggestion by Clark (1975, 183) that (C) means only 'that a man's *eudaimonia* benefits his associates: he is a good man to have around', is mistaken. Cf. Joachim (1951, 47).

[24] Irwin (1988*b*, 362–3) distinguishes between a 'conative conception' of the best good, and a 'normative conception' of it. On the first conception, the best good is determined by our initial desires, whatever they happen to be. On the second, 'if some of our desires are mistaken, and there are some goods that we neither desire nor achieve, our rational aims cannot achieve a complete good'. Since self-sufficiency refers to the fact that we are by nature political animals, Irwin rightly concludes that Aristotle's conception of self-sufficiency and, hence, of unconditional completeness, which entails it, must be normative: 'Aristotle must reject a purely conative account of the final good. For we have no reason to suppose that all rational agents want to realize their political nature.' The good is not what everyone happens to want, it is what everyone 'would choose if they could acquire *nous* and *phronēsis*' (*Rh.* 1363^b12-15).

[25] It is important to note that only *eudaimonia* is self-sufficient in this way. For any other good thing, such as a virtue, is a means to *eudaimonia*. Hence adding it to a life already suitably equipped with external goods does not ensure that that life will be choiceworthy and lacking in nothing, since it can still lack *eudaimonia* itself.

The final feature of the best good is that of being the most choiceworthy of ends or goods:

[A] Moreover, we think *eudaimonia* is most choiceworthy (*hairetōtatēn*) of all goods, since it is not counted as one good among many. If it were counted as one good among many, then, clearly, we think that the addition of the smallest of goods would make it more choiceworthy. (Or: [A*] Moreover, we think *eudaimonia* is most choiceworthy of all goods, when it is not counted with other goods. When it is so counted, then, clearly we think that the addition of the smallest good to it makes it more choiceworthy.) [B] For [the smallest good] that is added becomes an extra quantity of goods [so creating a good larger than the original good], and the larger of two goods is always more choiceworthy. (1097^b16-20)

This text is difficult because (A) and (A*) are both possible translations of its opening sentence.[26] Hence our first task is to decide which of them is correct.

The following argument from *NE* x. 2 seems to favour (A):

Indeed Plato uses this sort of argument when he undermines the claim of pleasure to be the good.[27] For, he argues, the pleasant life is more choiceworthy when combined with intelligence than without it; and if the mixed [good] is better, pleasure is not the good, since nothing can be added to the good to make it more choiceworthy. (1172^b28-32)

Here the good or *eudaimonia* is something that cannot be made more choiceworthy by the addition of something else. Hence it seems that Aristotle cannot be claiming, as (A*) requires, that *eudaimonia* does become more choiceworthy by the addition of some good.[28] This is an important point, which greatly increases the likelihood that (A) is the premise Aristotle intends.

Many commentators who defend (A), however, argue that it entails that *eudaimonia* is an inclusive end that embraces all intrinsically good or desirable things, all things that we want because of themselves.[29] But there is good reason—beyond that uncovered in §20—to believe that this is not so. The first has to do with the pleasant amusements discussed in *NE* x. 6: 'But pleasant amusements also [seem to be choiceworthy because of themselves].

---

[26] Most scholars favour (A). But some, e.g. Kenny (1978, 204) and Clark (1975, 154), favour (A*).

[27] See *Phlb.* 60a–61a.

[28] See Devereux (1981, 248–50).

[29] See Ackrill (1974, 21), Burnet (1900, 33), Devereux (1981, 250), Gauthier and Jolif (1970, ii. 1: 53–4), Irwin (1985b, 304).

For they are not chosen because of other things' (1176^b9–10). Pleasant amusements are choiceworthy because of themselves. They are not parts of *eudaimonia*, however, because we choose them in order to relax, so that we can achieve *eudaimonia* in the future (1176^b30–1177^a1, §28). It follows that pleasant amusements are not included in *eudaimonia*, which is no more than one of their *para* ends, and that *eudaimonia* is not an end that includes all intrinsically good or desirable things.

Second, *eudaimonia* is an activity, the activation of the state that is the best and most complete virtue. Presumably, then, whatever is included in it must be the sort of thing that such an activity can contain. It is not clear, however, that all intrinsic goods have this feature. Honour is an intrinsic good (1097^b2), for example, but it is not clear how activity expressing complete virtue can contain honour. Pleasures, too, are intrinsic goods (1097^b2–3). But no activity can contain more than a single pleasure; for distinct pleasures impede one another resulting in unpleasure (1154^b20–8, 1175^a29–$^b24$).

Eudaimonia is not, then, an end composed of all the things we want because of themselves. But if it is not, how are we to explain the fact—crucial to the argument from (A) or (A*) to (B)—that *eudaimonia* together with some other intrinsic good is not more choiceworthy than *eudaimonia* alone?

In the following passages Aristotle introduces the notion of *eudaimonia* as a limit or measure in relation to which things are either unconditionally good or bad:

And because *eudaimonia* needs fortune added, good fortune seems to some people to be the same as *eudaimonia*. But it is not. For when it is excessive, it actually impedes *eudaimonia*; and then, presumably, it is no longer rightly called 'good' fortune, since the limit (*horos*) [up to which it is good] is defined in relation to *eudaimonia*. (1153^b21–5)

It is proper to the political philosopher to study pleasure and pain, since he is the architect of the end (*telous*) by relation to which we call anything unconditionally bad or good. (1152^b1–3)[30]

And it is this notion that is the nerve of the problematic argument. If some amount of some good is required for *eudaimonia*, any

---

[30] See 1138^b18–25 with 1094^a22–6, *EE* 1249^a22–$^b25$. Since ends are limits (*Pol.* 1257^b28), we could substitute 'limit' for 'end' in this passage, making its bearing on the point at issue even clearer.

further amount of that good would not in fact be a good at all, since the limit up to which it is a good is defined in relation to *eudaimonia*. Therefore, *eudaimonia* together with that further amount is not more choiceworthy then *eudaimonia* alone. For *eudaimonia* together with that further amount is not in fact a bigger good than *eudaimonia*.

In some texts, Aristotle speaks of *eudaimonia* as being 'made up out of many goods (*ek pollōn agathōn suntithemen*)' (*MM* 1184^{a}18–19) and of those goods as being parts of *eudaimonia*: 'In one way what we call just is whatever produces and maintains *eudaimonia* and its parts (*tōn moriōn*) for a political community' (*NE* 1129^{b}17–19; see *Rh.* 1360^{b}19–26). But these texts are entirely compatible with the idea of *eudaimonia* as a limit or measure of goodness. For they are entirely compatible with the idea that it is *eudaimonia* that determines what its parts are, not the antecedently identifiable parts that determine what it is. Moreover, 'part' covers a number of very different relations that Aristotle is at pains to distinguish in the *Ethics*. The relation of virtue or virtuous activity to *eudaimonia*, for example, is very different from the relation of the latter to external goods (see §29).

The nerve of Aristotle's argument about self-sufficiency is the idea of *eudaimonia* as a limit, then, rather than as an end composed of everything we choose because of itself. And it follows that (A) not (A*) is the premise the argument needs. *Eudaimonia* is not one good among many because it is the measure of the goodness of other goods. If it were one good among many, if it did not have this unique status as a measure or limit, it would be more choiceworthy when combined with any other good.

It scarcely needs saying, at this point, that choiceworthiness, like completeness and self-sufficiency, has emerged as a measure of intrinsic value or choiceworthiness. Hence our hypothesis about the meaning of *eudaimonia* has proved its worth. It explains why the many and the wise agree both that the best good is called *eudaimonia* and that it is unconditionally complete, self-sufficient, and most choiceworthy, even though they disagree completely about what *eudaimonia* actually is or about what concrete end really possesses these features.

22 THE FUNCTION ARGUMENT

This section—devoted to the argument proper—is the first of four dealing with various aspects of the function argument. §23 deals with the conclusion of the argument; §24 deals with the notion of a human being that the argument involves; §25 discusses the role of the argument in the *Ethics*.

The function argument opens as follows:

[A] Well, perhaps we shall find the best good if we first find the function (*ergon*) of a human being. For just as the good, that is [doing] well, for a flautist, a sculptor, and every craftsman, and, in general, for whatever has a function and action, seems to depend on its function, the same seems to be true for a human being, if a human being has some function. (1097ᵇ24–8; see *Pol.* 1326ᵃ13–14)

To understand (A), we must first understand what a function is. Aristotle identifies the function of a kind of thing, first of all, with its essence, with what defines it: 'What anything is is defined by its function: a thing really is what it is when it can perform its function, for example an eye when it can see. When something cannot perform its function, it is that thing in name only, like a dead eye or one made of stone' (*Mete.* 390ᵃ10–12).[31] But a thing's function is also identified with its end: 'everything that has a function is for the sake of its function' (*Cael.* 286ᵃ8–9; see *PA* 694ᵇ13–15); 'each thing's function is its end' (*EE* 1219ᵃ8).

The explanation of this double identification is that 'function' is act/result ambiguous: 'The function is said in two ways: of some the function is over and above (*para*) the employment, for example the house of house-building . . . with other things the function is the employment itself, for example sight in the case of seeing, study in the case of mathematical science' (*EE* 1219ᵃ13–17). The essence is the function as act; the end is the function as result:

We are insofar as we are activated (*d'energeia(i)*), insofar as we live and act (*tō(i) zēn gar kai prattein*). The function is in a way the producer activated (*energeia(i)*). Hence the producer is fond of the function because he loves his own being. And this is natural, since what he is potentially is what the function is actually (*energeia(i)*). (1168ᵃ6–9)

The function of a human being, then, is at once his essence and his

---

[31] See *PA* 640ᵇ33–641ᵃ6, 648ᵃ15–16, *GA* 731ᵃ25–6, *Metaph.* 1045ᵇ32–4, *NE* 1176ᵃ3–9, *Pol.* 1253ᵃ23–5.

end, at once an activity and its *allo* end. Since the unconditional human end is *eupraxia*, we can understand why function and action —*ergon* and *praxis*—are constantly conjoined in the function argument.[32]

The fact that a thing's function is its end explains why (A) says, without further argument, that if Øing is the function of an F, the good for an F is Øing well. For the end or goal of a flute-player (anyway, *qua* flute-player) does seem to be to play the flute well. Similarly, the end of any other craftsman (anyway, *qua* craftsman) seems to be to exercise his craft well.

The second component of the function argument is this:

[B] Then do the carpenter and the leatherworker have their functions and actions, while a human being has none and is by nature inactive (*argon*)[33] without any function? Or, just as eye, hand, foot, and, in general, every [bodily] part apparently has its functions, may we likewise ascribe to a human being some function over and above (*para*) all of theirs? (1097ᵇ28–33)

Now (B) is not so much a direct argument that human beings have a function as an indirect one, which relies on the implausibility of the view that they lack a function. For the alternative to having a function is being by nature inactive, and it is no more credible that human beings are by nature inactive than it is that they might be *eudaimōn* while asleep (1095ᵇ31–1096ᵃ2). When function is understood as essence and end, of course, the assumption that human beings have a function is somewhat more controversial, but it is also bolstered by a lot more of Aristotle's general philosophy.

(B) says that human beings have a function 'just as' bodily parts do. Does this mean that the human function is in every respect like the function of the eye? The fact that a function is both essence and end shows that there is no good reason to assume that it does. (B) also says, however, that the function of a human being will be over and above all of the functions of his bodily parts. Does this mean that it will be over and above each of them or of all of them taken together? It is difficult to be sure, but other texts show Aristotle committed to the stronger view:

Just as every instrument is for the sake of something, the parts of the body are also for the sake of something, that is for the sake of some action

---

[32] See 1097ᵇ26, 29, 1098ᵃ12–14.
[33] See 1167ᵃ11.

(*praxis*), so the whole body must evidently be for the sake of some complex action. Similarly, the body too must must be for the sake of the psyche, and the parts of the body for the sake of those functions for which they are naturally adapted. (*PA* 645^{b}14–20)[34]

This text claims not just that the parts of the body are for the sake of the complex action of the body as a whole, but that the body as a whole is for the sake of the psyche and psychic activity. Now this is compatible with the view that psychic activity consists in, and is, therefore, not over and above, the complex activity of the body (psychic activity would, in this case, be *allo* but not *para* bodily activity). Even within the psyche itself, however, practical activity is for the sake of study. Now study is matterless: 'bodily activity is in no way associated with the activity of *nous*' (*GA* 736^{b}28–9; see §§26–8). Hence study really is over and above all the bodily parts of a human being and their functions. If the human function is the function of *nous*, therefore, the human function, too, is over and above the functions of all the bodily parts (see §24). If it is not, we will have to find another explanation of why Aristotle seems to attribute this feature to it.

Human beings have a function, in any case, which is over and above the functions of their bodily parts. The next stage of the argument concerns the identification of that function:

[C] What, then, could this be? For living is apparently shared with plants, but what we are looking for is special (*idion*); hence we should set aside the life of nutrition and growth. The life next in order is some sort of life of sense-perception; but this too is apparently shared, with horse, ox, and every animal. The remaining possibility, then, is some sort of action of what has reason (*logon*). Now this [thing that has reason has two parts each of which has reason in a different way], one as obeying reason, the other as itself having it and exercising *nous* (*dianooumenon*). Moreover, life is also spoken of in two ways, and we must take life as activity, since this seems to be called life to a fuller extent. We have found, then, that the human function is the activity of the psyche that expresses reason or is not without reason. (1097^{b}33–1098^{a}8)

(C) assumes, without argument, that the human function must be 'special (*idion*)' to human beings. What does this mean? And why does Aristotle feel entitled to assume it? Aristotle sometimes uses *idion* in a technical sense, which he explains as follows:

---

[34] See *Mete.* 389^{b}23–390^{b}15, *DA* 415^{b}18, *PA* 642^{a}11, Kosman (1987).

A special property (*idion*) is something that does not reveal the essence of a thing yet belongs to that thing alone and is predicated convertibly of it. Thus it is a special property of man to be capable of learning grammar. For if he is a man, he is capable of learning grammar, and if he is capable of learning grammar, he is a man. (*Top.* 102ᵃ18–22)

But this technical sense cannot be intended in (C). For the function of a human being is his essence and, hence, cannot be one of the special properties that does not reveal the essence.³⁵ Aristotle must, then, be using 'special', as he often does, in the ordinary or non-technical sense of what is peculiar to a thing.³⁶ And, of course, it is not controversial that the human function is special to human beings in this sense. For the function of a human being is the human essence, and if human beings shared their essence with plants or beasts, they would belong to the same species as plants or beasts. For it is a thing's essence that determines its species (*Metaph.* 1030ᵃ11–14).³⁷

Notice that, on this account of (C), Aristotle is not assuming that whatever is special to a human being is his function. The specialness of the human function derives from the specialness of the human essence to which it is identical, but neither the function nor the essence is determined by what is special. Hence the function argument is not open to the criticism, often urged against it, that any property special to human beings is as good a candidate for the human function as rational activity. It is true, for example, that prostitution is special to humans, but it is false that it is part of our essence or function to prostitute ourselves.

The life-activity of growth and nutrition, which is the function of plants and vegetables, and the life-activity of perception, which is

---

³⁵ In the remainder of the discussion of *idion*, Aristotle distinguishes an unconditionally special property from 'a temporary (*pote*) or relative (*pros ti*) special property' (*Top.* 102ᵃ24–8). The former is special to its possessor at all times and in relation to all things, the latter is special to him only for a time or in comparison to some other things. Thus 'being on the right-hand side is a temporary property [of a man], while two-footed is a relative property; e.g. it is a property of man relatively to a horse and a dog' (102ᵃ26–28). Kraut (1979, 474–8; 1989, 312–9) argues that in (C) Aristotle is claiming only that the human function is special to humans in relation to the lower animals. But since even a relatively special property cannot reveal the essence, this must be mistaken. Whiting (1988, 37) claims that *idion* must refer to essence in the function argument. This is true, but it is not supported (as she suggests) by *Top.* 102ᵃ18–22.

³⁶ See Bonitz (1955) s.v. *idios* for references.

³⁷ Does this exclude study, which is shared with god, from being the human function? See §27.

the function of beasts, cannot be the human function.[38] 'The remaining possibility, then, is some sort of action of what has reason.' This is so because Aristotle is presupposing, what his biological researches have made evident, that there are just three life-activities: nutrition and growth, perception, and some sort of action of what has reason (*DA* 413^{a}20–415^{a}13). Since the human function is a life-activity (remember the act/result ambiguity of *ergon*), it must then be some sort of action of what has reason. Does this entail that the human function cannot be study? No. For Aristotle allows that study is itself a kind of action or *praxis* (*Pol.* 1325^{b}16–21) and is explicit that the human function may be some action or life-activity of the part of the psyche exercising *nous*.

Having identified the human function, Aristotle is now ready to bring out the connections between the human function and virtue (*aretē*):

[D] Now the function of a harpist is the same in kind, so we say, as the function of an excellent harpist. And the same is true unconditionally in every case, when we add to the function the superior achievement that expresses the virtue. For a harpist's function, for example, is to play the harp and a good harpist's is to do it well (*eu*). [E] Now we take the human function to be a certain kind of life and take this life to be the activity and actions of the psyche that accord with reason. [F] [Hence] the excellent man's function is to do these finely and well. [G] Each action or activity is completed well when its completion expresses the proper virtue. [H] Therefore, the human good turns out to be an activity of the psyche that expresses virtue. (1098^{a}9–17)

Part of (D) is reasonably uncontroversial given the identification of function with essence and end. For the essence of an F is clearly the same as the essence of an excellent F and an excellent F is clearly one that best achieves the end, which is that essence activated. But why is it virtue that ensures that an F will best achieve its end? Why is it that, as (G) puts it, 'each action or activity is completed well when its completion expresses the proper virtue'? The best answer is that this is just what a genuine virtue is. A genuine virtue is by definition something that completes an activity well or guarantees that it will achieve its end.[39]

---

[38] Life-activity is the relevant meaning of the ambiguous *zōē* (1098^{a}5–7). See §28.

[39] See *Ph.* 246^{a}10–15, *Metaph.* 1021^{b}20–3, *Rh.* 1366^{a}36–^{b}1; Plato, *R.* 352d8–354a4; §23. This makes (G) into a conceptual truth. But it means that we cannot

(D)–(G) establish that the goodness or excellence of a harpist consists in playing the harp well. But do they establish that the good for a harpist is playing the harp well?[40] They do not. But together with (A) they do. For (A) states that if F has a function, the good for F depends on the function. And, again, the fact that a thing's function is its end, or its essence activated, makes this an intelligible view. For to say that the good for an F is to best achieve its essential end is to say something that is at least a candidate for truth. We might balk, of course, at the idea that a human being has an essence or end. We might balk, too, at the idea that what is good for a human being is determined by his essence or end rather than by (say) what he happens to want. But we are now in the deep and disputed waters of natural teleology and ethical realism and have left far behind the idea that the function argument commits some easily diagnosed error.[41]

23 COMPLETE VIRTUES AND COMPLETE LIVES

The conclusion of the function argument is that the human good is an activity of the psyche expressing virtue. But to that conclusion Aristotle adds a difficult coda:

[I] And if there are more virtues than one, the good will express the best and most complete virtue. [J] Further, in a complete life (*biō(i)*). For one swallow does not make a spring, nor does one day; nor, similarly, does one day or a short time make us blessed and *eudaimōn*. (1098ª17–20)

How are (I) and (J) best understood?

In Book V of the *Ethics*, Aristotle refers to general justice as follows: 'This type of justice, then, is complete virtue, not unconditionally complete virtue, but complete virtue in relation to another . . . It is most of all complete virtue . . . the whole (*holē*) not a part of virtue' (1129ᵇ25–1130ª9). In vi. 12 he refers to virtue as a whole whose parts are *phronēsis*—and hence the virtues of character—and wisdom: 'Since it (wisdom) is a part of virtue as a

take it for granted that any of the things conventionally thought to be virtues—justice, moderation, courage, and the rest—are genuine virtues. No doubt the doctrine of the mean is in part intended to show that the conventional virtues are in fact genuine ones. The mean is discussed in Hursthouse (1980), Losin (1987), and Urmson (1973).

[40] See Glassen (1957) and Wilkes (1978).
[41] See Irwin (1988*b*, 363–5) and Whiting (1988).

whole (*tēs holēs aretēs*), it makes us *eudaimōn* because it is a state that we possess and activate' (1144ᵃ5–6). In the *Eudemian Ethics*, he identifies complete virtue with virtue as a whole and incomplete virtue with partial virtue:

> Now as *eudaimonia* was agreed to be something complete and life may be complete or incomplete—and this holds with virtue also (in one case it is whole (*holē*), in the other partial (*morion*))—and the activity of what is incomplete is itself incomplete, *eudaimonia* must be activity of a complete life (*zōēs*), which expresses complete virtue. (1219ᵃ35–9; see *Rh*. 1366ᵇ1–3)

This suggests that when Aristotle talks of the most complete virtue, he means virtue that is most *a-complete* or most inclusive.[42] But this is not so.

First, (I) invites us to choose from the set of virtues the best and most complete one. Hence the notion of completeness involved must allow us to compare virtues with respect to their completeness. Now a-completeness allows us to do this only when one of the virtues being compared is part of the other. Hence it does not allow us to compare *phronēsis* to wisdom since they are not parts of one another. But Aristotle does compare these two virtues and concludes that wisdom is more complete than *phronēsis* (1177ᵃ12–19, 1177ᵇ4–26). This is one reason to think that a-completeness is not what Aristotle has in mind in (I).

Second, is the whole of virtue even a member of the set from which (I) invites us to choose? If it is, the whole of virtue must be *a* virtue, just as the virtues of character are parts of the single virtue of *phronēsis*. But if the whole of virtue is a virtue and is, indeed, the most complete virtue referred to in (I), there must be an activity that expresses the whole of virtue, namely, complete *eudaimonia*. But there cannot be such an activity. For activity expressing wisdom is leisured while activity expressing *phronēsis* is unleisured or requires trouble (1177ᵇ4–26). Consequently, activity expressing the whole of virtue, which comprises both *phronēsis* and wisdom, would have to be both leisured and unleisured, which is impossible. Hence activity expressing the whole of virtue is impossible, and the whole of virtue is not a virtue.

Third, a similar argument can be mounted by appeal to pleasure. Studying is 'the pleasantest of the activities expressing virtue'

---

[42] See Ackrill (1974, 28).

($1177^a23–5$). Hence, study possesses one of the features character-
istic of *eudaimonia* ($1099^a7–21$, $1177^a22–3$). But activity expressing the whole of virtue, if there could be such a thing, would not be
pleasant since the pleasures of different activities or of different
psychic parts impede one another ($1154^b20–8$, $1175^a29–^b24$).[43]
Hence such activity, if it were possible, would not be *eudaimonia*
because it would not be pleasant. But activity expressing the most
complete virtue referred to in (I) is *eudaimonia*. Hence the most
complete virtue cannot be the most inclusive or a-complete one.

Two final points. Aristotle identifies primary *eudaimonia* not
with activity expressing the whole of virtue, but with activity
expressing wisdom ($1177^b19–26$). If the whole of virtue were the
most complete virtue referred to in (I), he could not consistently do
this. He also claims ($1178^b7–23$) that the gods are completely
eudaimōn and that the more like them we are the more *eudaimōn*
we are ($1178^b21–32$). It follows, given (I), that the gods' activity
must express the best and most complete virtue. But Aristotle
denies that the gods have *phronēsis* or the virtues of character. It
follows that the best and most complete virtue referred to in (I)
cannot be the most inclusive or most a-complete one.

What, then, are we to make of the texts about a-completeness
with which we began? Just this. *EE* $1219^a35–9$ tells us that
eudaimonia must be the expression of a whole or a-complete virtue;
it cannot be the expression of a partial or a-incomplete one. *NE*
$1129^b25–1130^a9$ and $1144^a5–6$ refer to two different things as a-
complete virtues, namely, the virtues of character as a whole and
those virtues together with wisdom. Hence, these texts are
irrelevant to the question of which (a–) complete virtue is, in the
relevant sense, most complete.

The kind of completeness relevant to (I) is not a-completeness,
then. But what kind of completeness is it? Surely, it is the kind—*b-
completeness*—which Aristotle discusses just before he launches
into the function argument. For he would hardly take the time to
discuss one kind of completeness at length only to introduce
another unexplicated at the eleventh hour. Now the relative b-
completeness of ends is determined by their relative choiceworthiness. Hence, since all virtues are choiceworthy because of
themselves and because of their *para* ends, we can compare the

---

[43] Carrie Swanson reminded me of the relevance of this.

relative b-completeness of two virtues in only one case, namely, where we choose one of them both because of itself and because of the other. But do any virtues have these features? Are virtues comparable with respect to their b-completeness? Indeed, they are. *Phronēsis* stands in the same relation to wisdom as medicine does to health. Therefore, it is for the sake of wisdom (1145^{a}6–9) and is inferior to it (1143^{b}34–5). Hence we choose *phronēsis* partly for its own sake and partly for the sake of wisdom. It follows that wisdom is a more b-complete virtue than *phronēsis*. Indeed, it is the most b-complete virtue. For activity expressing wisdom, being primary *eudaimonia*, is alone unconditionally complete. And activities inherit their completeness from the states of whose activations they are the *allo* ends (see *EE* 1219^{a}35–9).[44]

The completeness involved in (I) is b-completeness, then, and (I) is comparing virtues by reference to their choiceworthiness, by reference to how well they (or the activities that express them) satisfy desire.

(J), too, refers to completeness. Presumably, it refers to the same kind of completeness as (I); for it would be odd to switch from one kind of completeness to another without warning. Thus when (J) speaks of a complete life it means a b-complete life. But what is a b-complete life? The unconditionally b-complete good, *eudaimonia*, is self-sufficient because, when added to a life of a certain sort, it makes it choiceworthy and lacking in nothing. But a life of a few *eudaimōn* moments would not be choiceworthy and lacking in nothing. It would lack time. We would choose it, not by itself, but only together with something else, namely, more time spent being *eudaimōn*. How long would a life have to be, then, in order to be choiceworthy and lacking in nothing? Just long enough to be choiceworthy and lacking in nothing! There is no better general answer than that. A short life that is fulfilled may be choiceworthy and lacking nothing; a long life may lack much and not be choiceworthy at all (see §32).

24 Human Beings

The human function is the human essence or the human essence activated. It is the human end when its activation expresses the best

---

[44] Note that *EE* 1219^{a}35–39 refers to a complete *zōē* or life-activity not, like (J), to a complete *bios* or biographical life. See §28.

and most complete virtue. But what is the human essence? A natural thought is that this question is to be answered by metaphysics, biology, and psychology, and that the answer is already in when the function argument begins. The function argument would then provide the metaphysical, biological, and psychological foundations of the *Ethics*. But there is good reason to resist this natural thought. For, in the *Ethics*, as we are about to see, the notion of what a human being is undergoes progressive refinement. And the refining force is the *endoxa*-supported conclusion of the function argument. For the function argument establishes a conceptual connection between the human function, human virtue, and the human end that exerts conceptual pressure on what each of these three things can be.

Aristotle begins his discussion of ethical psychology in *NE* i. 13 with the notion of an *a-human being* or the hylomorphic compound of body and psyche inherited from the *De Anima* (412^a16-^b5). But he does not stay with this notion: 'It is clear that the virtue we must examine is human virtue, since we are seeking the human good and human *eudaimonia*. And by human virtue we mean virtue of the psyche, not the body, since we also say that *eudaimonia* is an activity of the psyche' (1102^a13-18). In this brief passage, the notion of an a-human being has been refined into that of a *b-human being* or complex human psyche. And within a few lines the notion of a b-human being undergoes further refinement: 'let us leave aside the nutritive part (*to threptikon*), since by nature it has no share in human virtue' (1102^b11-12). A human being is now a *c-human being* or a human psyche without its *threptikon*. For the human function determines that *eudaimonia* is a rational activity and, hence, that the ethically relevant conception of a human being must be that of the rationally active part of a b-human being.

The refinement in the notion of a human being that results in the notion of a c-human being proceeds by eliminating first the body and then the *threptikon* as having no share in rational activity. The next stage in the refinement is quite different. The parts of a c-human being are the desiring part (*orektikon*) and the rational part (*logon*). The rational part 'has reason to the full extent by having it within itself' (1103^a2). It is identical to *nous* (*Pol.* 1254^b8-9, 1334^b20). The desiring part, which is identical to the perceiving part (*DA* 431^a12-14), 'shares in reason' because it is able to listen to the rational part 'as to a father' (1103^{a}1–3, 1151^{a}15–28). Hence, a c-human being consists of a fully rational part and a quasi-rational part. But neither of these parts can be excluded by appeal to the function argument. For 'the human function is the activity of the psyche that expresses reason or is not without reason' (1098^{a}7–8), that is to say, it is either the function of the rational part or of the quasi-rational part or both.

But refinement does not stop with c-human beings, it simply takes a different form. For the conceptual pressure exerted by the function argument has not yet been completely relieved. The reason for this is clear. The human function is the human end when its activation expresses the best and most complete virtue. The best and most complete virtue is wisdom. The activity expressing wisdom is study. Study is primary *eudaimonia* and is, therefore, the human end. Study is the activity of *nous*. Consequently, the human function must be the function of *nous*, and a human being must—in some sense —actually be his *nous*. But in what sense? How can a c-human being be his *nous* when he is both his rational part and his quasi-rational part?

By the time we reach the end of *NE* x. 7 Aristotle is explicit that a c-human being is 'most of all (*malista*)' his *nous*:

Moreover, each person seems to be his *nous*, if indeed he is his controlling and better part . . . Hence for a human being the life expressing *nous* will be supremely best and pleasantest, if indeed this [i.e. *nous*] most of all is the human being. This life, then, will also be most *eudaimōn*. (1178^{a}2–8; see *Prt.* B62)

He is explicit—despite his use of conditionals—because we have already been told that the antecedent of those conditionals is true: 'And just as a polis and every other composite system seems to be most of all its most controlling part, the same is true of a human being' (1168^{b}31–3). The most controlling part of a c-human being is *nous*; therefore, a c-human being is most of all his *nous*. But what does it mean to say that a c-human being is most of all his *nous*?

One part of the key to this question lies in the following difficult text from *NE* ix. 8:

[A] At any rate, he [the person who always gains for himself what is fine] awards himself what is finest and best of all and gratifies the most controlling part of himself, obeying it in everything. [B] And just as a polis and every other system seems to be most of all its most controlling part, the same is true of a human being; hence someone loves himself most if he likes and gratifies this part. [C] Similarly, someone is called enkratic or akratic because his *nous* is or is not ruling, on the assumption that this is what each is. [D] Moreover, his [the one who gratifies his controlling part] own voluntary actions seem most of all to be those which accord with reason. [E] Clearly, then, this [the controlling part] or this most of all is what each is and the decent person likes this most of all. Hence he most of all is a self-lover. . . . [F] For the vicious person, then, the right actions conflict with those he does. The decent person, however, does the right actions, since every *nous* chooses what is best for itself and the decent person obeys his *nous*. (1168ᵇ29–1169ᵃ18; see 1166ᵃ10–23)⁴⁵

(A) and (C) entail that *nous* is the most controlling part. *NE* x. 7 (1178ᵃ2–8) also identifies the controlling part with *nous*. But how can *nous*, which engages only in study, actually control a c-human being and the practical activity in which he also engages?

Aristotle occasionally uses *nous* to refer to *phronēsis* or to both *phronēsis* and to *nous*. The following passage is a good example: 'Both of these are capable of causing local motion, both *nous* and desire: *nous*, that is to say, which calculates for the sake of an end and is practical (*praktikos*) and differs from theoretical *nous* in its end' (*DA* 433ᵃ13–16). If (C) and (F) are also examples of this usage, that would solve part of our problem. But it will not help with 1178ᵃ2–8. Hence, if we are to preserve consistency between Books IX and X, we must try another tack.

God is described as being the most controlling principle of the universe: 'If there is a substance of this nature (I mean one that is separable and immovable), as we shall try to prove there is,⁴⁶ if indeed there is such a kind of thing in the world, it must surely be the divine, and this is the first and most controlling (*kuriōtatē*) first principle' (*Metaph.* 1064ᵃ34–ᵇ1; see *EE* 1222ᵇ20–4). But God does not actually do anything to control the universe. He is immutably and eternally studying (1072ᵇ13–30, 1074ᵇ33–1075ᵃ5), more akin to the laws in a polis than to the judges who administer them (*Mu.* 400ᵇ5–401ᵃ10). He controls the world by being its *telos* or final cause, an object of desire and love, an unmoved mover (see §26). Now *nous* is 'something divine' (1177ᵇ27–8), studies only, is the most controlling part of a c-human being, and has a role in the

---

⁴⁵ This passage is discussed in Kraut (1989, 128–31) who argues that *nous* refers here to practical reason or *phronēsis*. Cf. Cooper (1975, 168–77).
⁴⁶ See *Metaph.* 1071ᵇ3–1073ᵃ13.

psyche that is explicitly likened to that of god in the universe (*EE* 1248^{a}25–9).[47] It seems reasonable to conclude that *nous* controls a c-human being in the way that god controls the universe, namely, by being its final cause, while *phronēsis*—which is for the sake of study or the activity of *nous* expressing wisdom—controls the psyche in the manner of an efficient cause. Hence, *nous* can be the most controlling part of a c-human being without compromising its status as something that studies only, but does not study 'any source of human *eudaimonia*' (1143^{b}19–20).

(F) attributes choice to *nous* and speaks of the c-human being as obeying its orders. This suggests that *nous* is more than the impassive final cause that we have represented it as being. What is going on? The most likely answer, but certainly not the only possible one, is this. In part, Aristotle is speaking somewhat metaphorically, representing the final cause as a kind of agent. He sometimes speaks of god in the same sort of active, agentive terms, as being like the general of an army or the ruler of the universe.[48] In part, he is speaking of *nous* synecdochically, as if it were the c-human being as a whole rather than the part that the c-human being is most of all: the c-human being chooses, the c-human being is most of all *nous*, so *nous* is said to choose. In part, he is representing as chosen by *nous* what it is, in fact, the nature of *nous* to do. Similarly, the c-human being is said to obey *nous* because it pursues the activation of *nous* as its end, and is guided in its actions by that end, but what effects those actions—their efficient cause— is *phronēsis* (1139^{a}31–3).

(A) also tells us that the person who gratifies his most controlling part 'awards himself what is finest and best of all'. Since study is 'supremely best' (1178^{a}5–6) and fine (1177^{a}15), this claim fits with the view that the most controlling part is *nous*. But the person under discussion in (A) is someone who gratifies his *nous* by engaging in practical activity, or activity expressing *phronēsis* (1169^{a}6–18). Since *phronēsis* is for the sake of *nous* this, too, is readily intelligible. Practical activity is at once for its own sake or for the secondary *eudaimonia* and for the sake of primary *eudaimonia*.[49]

---

[47] This passage is quoted and discussed in §27.

[48] See *Metaph.* 1075^{a}11–15, 1076^{a}3–4; §26.

[49] It is also possible—although not, I think, probable—that *NE* 1166^{a}10–23 represents a fourth stage of refinement in response to the function argument and that 1178^{a}2–8 represents the fifth and final stage of that refinement.

We can now understand (C) and (D). For *nous* to rule or control is for its activity to be the final cause of all the functions of the various parts that constitute a c-human being. Since both the enkratic and the akratic have true beliefs about *eudaimonia* and primary *eudaimonia* is study, both of them wish to study. In the enkratic, wish is stronger than appetite, so that study is the final cause of his actions. In the akratic, appetite is stronger than wish, so that study is not the final cause of his actions. Hence, in the former *nous* rules and in the latter it does not. (D) expresses essentially the same idea as (C). If *nous* controls a c-human being, he will act for its sake. Hence he will act in accord with reason. For reason is 'the part of the psyche that has reason, because it exhorts . . . correctly and towards what is best' (1102b14–16), and study is what is best.

(E) concludes from the fact that *nous* is the most controlling part of a c-human being that a c-human being is most of all *nous*. It follows that for a c-human being to be most of all *nous* is just for *nous* to be the element in him that is his final cause, the element for the sake of which all the other elements are (see *PA* 645^{b}14–20). And what is true of c-human beings is, (B) tells us, true of any other system: it is most of all that element in it that is its final cause. This is true of psyches, poleis, and households; it is equally true of the universe as a whole.[50]

A c-human being is most of all his *nous*. Is his function study, then, or is it just most of all study? In the *Ethics*, Aristotle does not tell us explicitly, but a fragment of the *Protrepticus* suggests that he once espoused the first alternative:

> If then man is a simple animal whose substance is ordered in a way that expresses reason (*logon*) and *nous*, his function will be nothing more than to attain the most exact truth and the truth about the beings. But if he is composed of several capacities and it is clear that he can by nature complete several [activities], the best of them is always his function (*aei toutōn to beltiston to ergon estin*), for example health is the function of the doctor and safety that of the ship's captain. Now we can name no better function of reasoning (*dianoias*) or of *nous* (*dianooumenou*) than the attainment of truth. Therefore, truth is the most controlling (*kuriōtaton*) function of this part of the psyche. (B65)

And this is, in fact, the answer that the theory he develops in the

---

[50] I agree with Keyt (1978, 379–80), therefore, that what one is most of all is precisely something to which one is *not* identical. Cf. Cooper (1975, 162–3), (1987*b*, 215 n. 15).

Ethics requires. For the human end is the human function activated, and the unconditional human end is primary *eudaimonia* or study. It follows that the human function must just be study (see §§27–8). The conceptual pressure exerted by the function argument has now been completely relieved. We see why it necessitates the refinement in the notion of an a-human being that, by eliminating the body and the *threptikon* as ethically irrelevant, results in the notion of a c-human being. We have seen why it necessitates yet further but quite different refinement in that notion, yielding the conclusion that a c-human being is most of all his *nous*. And we understand what it means to say that a c-human being is most of all his *nous*: it means simply that his *nous*, by contrast with his other parts, is his final cause.

25 The Role of the Function Argument in the Ethics

The *Ethics* does not take over the concept of what a human being is unrefined from the *De Anima*, then. Instead, it 'Nicomacheanizes' that concept, adapting it for ethical purposes by allowing it to respond to the conceptual pressures generated in the function argument. It would be misleading, therefore, to say without further ado that the function argument provides the biological and psychological foundations of the *Ethics*. For this suggests too crude an inheritance from biology and psychology, too crude a naturalism. It would be equally misleading to say without further ado that the function argument provides the metaphysical foundations of the *Ethics*. The function argument employs concepts, such as those of function, essence, and end, which—though perhaps biological in origin—belong to Aristotle's metaphysics. By using these concepts and by showing how they are related to the ethical notions of virtue and *eudaimonia*, the function argument establishes the close connections between metaphysics and ethics. But the ultimate test of the function argument is not the cogency of its metaphysical roots or of the connective tissue that relates them to the ethical foliage. This is established beyond reasonable doubt by the fact that Aristotle is repeatedly explicit that the test of the truth of theoretical arguments in ethics is their coherence with the *phainomena*, *legomena*, and *endoxa*. At the conclusion of the function argument, he reminds us of the latter fact. Let us hear that reminder a second time and allow it to resonate: 'We should examine the first principle not only from the conclusion and premises of a deductive argument, but from the *legomena* about it. For all the facts harmonize with a true account, whereas the truth soon clashes with a false one' (1098^b9–11). If the function argument is underwritten by the facts of ethical experience, it helps to underwrite them. If it is not, it fails altogether.

If we think of metaphysical foundations as enabling us to knit ethics into the web of naturalistic knowledge in general, lending support and insight by establishing coherence, the function argument is indeed the metaphysical foundation of the *Ethics*. But if metaphysical foundations must be somehow independent of experience or deeper than it, the *Ethics* has no metaphysical foundations.

4

EUDAIMONIA AND *EUDAIMŌN* LIVES

God is too perfect to think anything over and above himself.
And the reason for this is that while our well-being expresses
something different, god is himself his own well-being.

(*EE* 1245^b16–19)

Virtue is an instrument of *nous*, and because of it.

(*EE* 1248^a29)

A EUDAIMŌN life needs enough *eudaimonia*, enough time, and
enough external goods to be choiceworthy and lacking in nothing.
Study or theoretical activity expressing wisdom is primary
eudaimonia. Practical activity expressing *phronēsis* is secondary
eudaimonia and has primary *eudaimonia* as its *para* end. In this
chapter, we focus on these components of the *eudaimōn* life—
theoretical activity, practical activity, external goods—and their
significantly different roles in it. When it is complete, our account
of the foundations of the *Ethics* will also be complete.

26 STUDY

The discussion of wisdom in *NE* vi. 7 begins with two *phainomena*:
'we ascribe wisdom in the crafts to people who have the most exact
knowledge of them' (1141^a9–10); 'we also think that some people
are wise in general and not simply in some part of wisdom or in
some other such way' (1141^a12–14). On the strength of them,
Aristotle concludes:

Wisdom is the most exact (*akribestatē*) form of scientific-knowledge.
Hence the wise person must not only know what is derived from the first
principles of a science, but also grasp the truth about the first principles
themselves. Therefore wisdom is *nous* plus scientific-knowledge—scientific-
knowledge of the most valuable things with *nous* as its coping-stone.
(1141^a16–20; see 1141^b2–4).

But what licences the conclusion? What does it mean to say that wisdom is the most exact form of scientific-knowledge? And what are the most valuable things it studies? In *APo.* i. 27 Aristotle answers the first of these questions as follows:

One science is more exact than (*akribestera*) and prior to another [A] if it is at the same time knowledge that something is true and why it is true and not of the that separate from the why; [B] and if it is not said of an underlying subject (*hupokeimenou*) and the other is said of an underlying subject, for example arithmetic and harmonics; [C] and if it depends on fewer [posits], the other on an additional posit (*ek prostheseōs*), for example arithmetic and geometry. (I mean by on an additional posit, for example a unit is a positionless substance and a point is a substance having position—the latter depends on an additional posit.) (87ᵃ31–7)

(A) explains why wisdom involves *nous* of first principles. Without it, someone who possessed wisdom would not know why the derived principles are true. For to know why they are true—to know their causal explanations—one must demonstrate them from first principles of which one has *nous*.

(B) states in other terminology—matter is the underlying thing to which it refers—that exactness in a science is a function of its level of abstraction from matter. (C) is a variation on (B). For positing or *prosthesis* is the opposite of abstraction from enmattered particulars or *ahairesis*. Hence, the fewer posits the more abstract; the more abstract the more exact.[1] Theology is prior to and more exact than mathematics, therefore, and mathematics is prior to and more exact than physics or natural science (*Metaph.* 1026ᵃ10–13). For physics deals with beings that are essentially changing and cannot exist separate from matter (1025ᵃ18–1026ᵃ7); mathematics deals with beings that are unchanging but cannot exist separate from matter (1026ᵃ7–10); and theology deals with beings that are 'eternal and unchanging and separate' (1026ᵃ10–16). (B) and (C) together explain why wisdom is not the same as ethics or politics. Ethics and politics study enmattered particulars. Hence, they cannot be the most exact kind of scientific-knowledge (*NE* 1141ᵃ20–2).

It follows from this account of relative exactness that wisdom or the most exact form of scientific-knowledge has three features: it is

---

[1] See Barnes (1975, 181–2), Lesher (1973, 62–4), Ross (1949, 596–7).

the most abstract science, has the fewest posits, and is of the that and the why together. Hence study expressing wisdom must be of both the most abstract things and the most valuable ones.

To see what these things are and why they form a single class, we need to discuss some more of Aristotle's thoughts on god and *nous*.[2] God is eternally active *nous* that 'has itself as its object' (*Metaph*. 1075^{a}10): 'It must be itself that [divine] *nous* thinks, if indeed it is the most superior thing, hence [divine] *nous* is a *nous* of *nous* (*hē noēsis noēseōs noēsis*)' (*Metaph*. 1074^{b}33–5). What is the explanation of this strikingly opaque claim?

When *nous*, whether human or divine, studies matterless things, it becomes those things:

In some cases, the knowledge is the object. In productions, it is the essence without the matter; in theoretical sciences, it is the definition (*logos*), the thing defined (*pragma*), and the *nous* [of the definition or the thing defined]. Therefore, *nous* and the objects of *nous* (*tou nooumenou*) are not [always] different; in the case of things that have no matter, they—*nous* and the object of *nous*—are the same. (*Metaph*. 1074^{b}38–1075^{a}5)[3]

When *nous* studies a true and complete science consisting of essentially matterless universals, for example, it is identical to the science it studies and, hence, to the reality the theory reflects. To study *nous*, therefore, is just to study the matterless things that *nous* studies: '*Nous* is itself studiable in exactly the way that its objects are' (*DA* 430^{a}2–3).

Now 'the science that is most of all god's is divine science as is the science of god' (*Metaph*. 983^{a}6–7). And 'the most divine science is also the most valuable (*timiōtatē*)' (*Metaph*. 983^{a}5). For god is the best or most valuable thing (*Metaph*. 1074^{b}34;, 1075^{a}11–12). But god is not only the most valuable thing, he is also the most abstract one. For he alone is genuinely matterless (*Metaph*. 1026^{a}1–32). It follows that the most exact form of scientific-knowledge studies god, and so is the science of god or theology. Since *nous* is identical to the essentially matterless things it studies, it also follows that god, in a way, just is theology, a demonstrative structure of essentially matterless universals. But what is that structure? Looked

---

[2] Aristotle's god is discussed in Ackrill (1981*a*, 128–34), Norman (1969), and Ross (1923, 179–86). Wedin (1988, 160–254) is the most philosophically acute recent treatment of *nous*. God and *nous* are further discussed in §27.

[3] See *DA* 429^{a}18–29, 429^{b}10–22, 430^{a}3–5, 431^{a}1–2, 431^{b}17.

at epistemically it is theology; looked at ontologically, it is god himself.[4]

When god studies theology, then, he is, like all *nous* when it studies matterless universals, studying *nous*. But unlike human beings, for example, god is himself a matterless thing and the subject studied by theology. Hence in studying theology, he is studying himself. When a human being studies matterless universals, by contrast, he is not studying himself, only what is most of all himself. Thus god is *noēsis noēseōs*, the *nous* of *nous*, human beings are not.[5]

Now god is the final cause of everything else in the universe, which moves the world in the way that an immobile and impassive object of desire moves those things that desire it:

There is something that moves without being moved, being eternal, and substance and activity. And the object of desire and the object of *nous* move in this way; they move without being moved. The first principles of these are the same. (*Metaph.* 1072ᵃ25–7)

The most natural act for any living thing that has developed normally . . . is to produce another like itself (an animal producing an animal, a plant a plant), in order to partake as best it can in the eternal and divine. That is what all things strive for, and everything they do naturally is for the sake of that . . . Since it cannot share in the eternal and divine by going on continuously as one and the same living thing . . . it shares in it in the only way it can. What persists and goes on is not the animal or plant itself but something like itself—not the same individual but a member of the same species. (*DA* 415ᵃ26–ᵇ7)[6]

But god is also his own final cause. For the good or primary *eudaimonia* is eternal, continuous study, and that activity just is god: 'God is himself his own well-being' (*EE* 1245ᵇ19; see *MA* 700ᵇ32–701ᵃ1). Since well-being or *eudaimonia* is the best good (1094ᵃ22), this explains why Aristotle says that the good in the category of substance is god or *nous* (*NE* 1096ᵃ24–5). It follows that theology has the third feature required by the most exact science. It is at once of the that and the why, and not of the that

---

[4] *Metaph.* xii. 6–10 is an essay in the nascent stage of that science.
[5] See Norman (1969), Wedin (1988, 229–45), and §27.
[6] *Cael.* 279ᵃ22–30, 292ᵃ22–ᵇ25; *GC* 336ᵇ27–337ᵃ7; *Mete.* 339ᵃ19–32; *MA* 700ᵇ22–701ᵃ1; *GA* 731ᵇ20–732ᵃ9; *Metaph.* 1050ᵇ5–6, 1050ᵇ22–30, 1070ᵇ34–5, 1075ᵃ11–25. This account of the prime mover, which represents it as the teleological cause of everything and not just of the motions of the heavens, is convincingly defended in Kahn (1985).

separate from the why. For theology is the science of god, and god is his own why, his own final cause (see *Metaph.* 982ᵇ4–10).

Because god has the features we have been discussing, Aristotle claims that theology is identical to first philosophy or the science of being *qua* being (*Metaph.* 1026ᵃ13–32). The following is no more than a dogmatic sketch of the argument that leads him to this identification, but it could, I am confident, be defended in detail.

In the *Categories*, Aristotle divides the things that there are into ten very general classes or categories: substance, quantity, quality, relation, place, time, position, having, doing, and undergoing (1ᵇ25–2ᵃ10). And he argues that the category of substance is ontologically prior to all the others because, among other things, it is part of their definition in a way that they are not part of its definition. For the quality red to be, for example, is for some substance to be red, but of no substance is it true that for it to be is for it to be red (*Metaph.* 1019ᵃ1–4).

In the *Metaphysics*, however, Aristotle claims that substance must not only be ontologically prior to the other categories, it must also be epistemically prior to them (1028ᵃ31–ᵇ2). And this is, of course, a natural thing for him to claim. For if substance is ontologically prior, then, given Aristotle's realist conception of truth, it must be epistemically prior—more knowable in itself—as well. The problem is that ontological priority seems to belong to one kind of thing, namely, concrete particulars, such as this man or this bronze sphere, while epistemic priority seems to belong to another class altogether, namely, the essentially matterless universals that are the objects of unconditional scientific-knowledge.[7] To the resulting *aporia* Aristotle found a solution in the features of god we have been exploring. For god, being identical to theology, is as much an object of unconditional scientific-knowledge as is that science or the matterless universals it studies. Yet god is not a universal, but a substantial particular. For he is not just theology, he is theology activated in study: 'Life also belongs to god. For the activation of *nous* is life (*zōē*), and god is that activity; activity that by itself (*kath' hautēn*) is life both best and eternal' (*Metaph.* 1072ᵇ26–8). And theology activated is a particular not a universal:

---

[7] These two demands on substance are discussed in Lear (1988, 273–93) and Owen (1978).

Scientific-knowledge, like knowing, is of two kinds, one potential and one actual. Potentiality, being (as matter) universal and indefinite, is of what is universal and indefinite; but actuality, being definite is of something definite, and being a particular [*tode ti*], is of a particular. (*Metaph.* 1087ᵃ15–18)

God, therefore, seems to combine the ontological priority of concrete particulars with the epistemic priority of essentially matterless universals.[8]

God is certainly a substance, then, but to explain why theology is first philosophy, we need also to draw on the other feature of god we mentioned, namely, that he is the teleological cause of everything. Very roughly speaking, the picture is this. To say what qualities, quantities, relations, and so on are, we must make reference to a hylomorphic compound of matter and form, such as a particular man. But to say what a hylomorphic compound is, we have to make reference to its teleological cause: it is something that, in trying to realize its form, is trying to become as much like god as possible. Hence god enters into the definitions of all the beings, and is ontologically prior to all of them. Hence theology is first philosophy. For first philosophy is both the science that studies 'the first principles and causes of the things that are . . . *qua* being' (1025ᵇ1–2) and the science that studies essentially matterless things (*Ph.* 194ᵇ14–15; see *Metaph.* 1026ᵃ15–16). And god is at once the first principle and cause of all the beings and the only genuinely matterless thing.[9]

The activation of *nous* is study, but only the activation of *nous* that expresses wisdom—the 'supreme virtue' (1177ᵃ12–19)—is primary *eudaimonia*. And we now know what such study is. It is the activity of studying the structure of matterless universals that is both first philosophy and god or divine *nous*. For only it is the most

---

[8] Strictly speaking, then, it is not only essentially matterless universals, essences, and forms that are objects of scientific-knowledge; essentially matterless activities can also be objects of such knowledge.

[9] My account of first philosophy is indebted to Frede (1987, 81–95) and Patzig (1960), although it differs from theirs in various respects. Kosman (1984) is also largely congenial. The fact that god studies only essentially matterless universals seems to undermine the interesting suggestion canvassed by Lear (1988, 295) that 'god is actively thinking the primary substances to be found in the world'. The things in the world strive to be like god not by striving to be like the form of them that he contemplates (for he does not contemplate their forms), but by striving for the eternity that he possesses (*DA* 415ᵃ25–ᵇ7), a striving that is, admittedly, a striving of form against matter. See §2.

exact form of scientific-knowledge, only it is study of the most abstract and most valuable thing.

None the less Aristotle does sometimes speak of studying things other than theology in tones that suggest that it too should be counted as a very high kind of *eudaimonia*:

Of all beings naturally composed, some are ungenerated and imperishable for the whole of eternity, but others are subject to coming-to-be and perishing. The former possess value—indeed divinty—but we can study them less, because both the starting points of the inquiry and the things we want to know about present extremely few appearences to sense perception. We are better equipped to acquire knowledge about the perishable plants and animals because they grow beside us, and much can be learned about each existing kind if one is willing to take sufficient pains. Both studies have their attractions. For although we grasp only a little of the former, yet because of the value of what we grasp, we get more pleasure from it than from all the things around us; just as a small and random glimpse of those we love pleases us more than an exact view of other things, no matter how numerous or large they are. But because our information about the things around us is better and more plentiful, our knowledge of them has the advantage over the other. And because they are closer to us and more akin to our nature, they have their own compensations in comparison with the philosophy concerned with divine things . . . For even in the study of animals that are unattractive to the senses, the nature that fashioned them likewise offers immeasurable pleasures to those who are naturally philosophical and can learn their causal explanations. (*PA* 644^{b}22–645^{a}10)

It seems reasonable to conclude that a fuller sketch of the good might have to make room for kinds of *eudaimonia* that are higher than secondary but less high than primary. But, as this very text itself proclaims, only the study of theology, only study expressing wisdom, is of the very highest kind.[10]

27 HUMAN OR DIVINE?

God is *nous*; we are most of all *nous*. God's function, essence, or end is study; our function, essence, or end is study. It follows that 'our nature and essence is divine' (*PA* 686^{a}27–9). But does it follow that we are gods? Is human *nous* identical to divine *nous*? When we

[10] See *MM* 1197^{b}7–8, 1198^{b}9–20; *EE* 1249^{b}14–21; Defourny (1937); Hardie (1968, 336–57); Kraut (1989, 73–6).

study theology is our study one and the same thing as god? These are heady questions, but they admit of relatively sober answers.

We may begin our inquiry into them with the following controversial passage from the *De Anima*:

[A] Since, as in nature as a whole, to something that serves as matter for each kind (and is potentially each thing of that kind) there corresponds a cause that is productive in that it produces them, the two being related to one another as for example craft to its raw materials, of necessity these different factors must also be found in the psyche. And to the *nous*, so characterized, that becomes all things there corresponds the *nous* that makes all of them . . . [B] And it is the latter *nous* that is separate, impassive, and unmixed with matter, being in its substance an activity. . . . This *nous* is never not studying. [C] It is, however, only when separated (*chōristheis*) that it is just what it is (*hoper esti*) and is alone immortal and eternal. But we overlook the fact that while this is impassive [and immortal and eternal], the *nous* that is affected (*pathētikos nous*) is perishable and without the other cannot engage in study at all (*outhen noei*). (430ª10–25)[11]

(A) refers to two kinds of *nous*: passive matter-like *nous* and active form-like *nous*. How are we to understand them? Passive *nous* is perishable and so cannot be possessed by a god that is immortal and eternal (C). And because god lacks passive *nous*, because he is an essentially matterless activity, he cannot study enmattered universals such as those studied by physics.[12] If he could, he would not be the *nous* of *nous*. For *nous* is identical to its objects only when they are essentially matterless. But human beings, having passive *nous*, and having bodies and sense organs, can study enmattered universals. Through perception, memory, and induction enmattered universals get imprinted, so to speak, on our passive, matter-like *nous* enabling us to study them. But what enables us actually to engage in such study, what enables our passive *nous* to be activated, is a *nous* that makes all things (A), that is separate, impassive, unmixed with matter, and never not studying (B), and that is alone immortal and eternal (C). This *nous*

---

[11] Barnes (1971, 39–40), Hicks (1907, 498–510), and Hamlyn (1968, 140–2) convey some sense of the enormous controversy this passage has aroused. My translation of (C) is more than usually interpretative. We overlook the mortality of passive *nous*, and hence of ourselves, when we argue for the immortality of the human psyche. What we are really proving—if anything—is the immortality of divine *nous*.

[12] It follows that Aristotle's god is not omniscient.

is clearly divine *nous*. Since it is in our psyches along with our passive *nous*, there is 'something divine' in us (*NE* 1177^{b}28), something that Aristotle is willing to call ' the god' (*EE* 1249^{b}9– 21).

Because human *nous* is passive, because it can study enmattered universals, it is not the same as divine *nous*. But is it the same as divine *nous* when it studies theology or first philosophy? In *Metaph*. xii. 7, Aristotle contrasts human study with divine study as follows: 'If, then, god is always in that good condition [i.e. studying], in which we sometimes are, this compels our wonder; and if he is more (*mallon*) in that condition, this compels it yet more; and he is' (1072^{b}24–6). Part of the contrast—always/ sometimes—is clear enough: god is eternally and continuously doing what we are doing only occasionally. But what does *mallon* mean? Does it simply repeat the same contrast in other terms? The following text makes it unlikely that it does: 'the good itself will be no more (*mallon*) good by being eternal. For a white thing is no whiter if it lasts a long time than if it lasts a day' (1096^{b}3–5).[13] God is more in the condition of study than we are, then, but not simply because he is always in it. He would still be in it more even if (*per impossibile*) he were in it only for a short time. How can this be? A plausible answer is suggested by the following discussion of *mallon* in the *Protrepticus*:

We call something more (*mallon*) F than something, when the same word, 'F', applies to both, not only when it is F to a greater degree, but when it is prior and the other posterior, for example we say that health is more (*mallon*) a good, and similarly that which is by itself naturally worthy of choice in relation to that which produces it; yet we see that the same word ['good'] is predicated of both, though not unconditionally. For both useful things and virtues are said to be good. (B82)

God is more in the condition of study, then, because his study is prior to ours. But if his study is prior to ours, his *nous* is prior to ours. For god's *nous*—as (B) makes clear—just is his active study.

Of the many ways in which one thing can be prior to another for Aristotle, we may select one as clearly most relevant. The final cause of something is prior to it in being or substance (*GA* 742^{a}20– 2), and divine *nous* is the final cause of human *nous*:

---

[13] Cf. 'That which is white for many days is not more (*mallon*) white than what is white for one' (*EE* 1218^{a}13–14). I owe notice of the relevance of this text to Wedin (1988, 233–4).

It is clear that as god moves everything in the universe so he does in the psyche, for somehow the divine thing in us moves everything. The first principle of reason (*logou*) is not reason, but something superior. And what could be superior to scientific-knowledge and [human] *nous* but god? Not virtue. For virtue is an instrument (*organon*) of *nous*, and because of it. (*EE* 1248ª25–9)

But if divine *nous* is the final cause of human *nous* and superior to it, the two cannot be strictly identical.

None the less, when *nous* studies matterless things it becomes those things. Since a human being is most of all his *nous*, it follows that, during those moments in which he is studying theology, he is most of all god, most of all an immortal. That is why in advising us to do everything in order to study as much as possible, Aristotle really is advising us to 'immortalize (*athanatizein*)' ourselves (*NE* 1177ᵇ31–4). But what does it mean to be most of all god, most of all immortal, for a moment? It means no more than to be for a moment engaged in the activity that is both god and one's own final cause. We see this clearly in the following two passages:

Thus thought (*noein*) and study decay because something else within is destroyed, but *nous* itself is impassive (*apathes*). (*DA* 408ᵇ24–5)

Each person wishes for goods for himself. And no one chooses to become another person even if that other will have every good when he has come into being. For, as it is now, god has the good. Rather he chooses on the condition that he remains whatever he is. And each person would seem to be his *nous* or that most of all. (*NE* 1166ª20–3)

When a human being dies, his passive *nous* dies with him (only divine active *nous* is immortal). But the activity he engages in when he studies theology does not cease; it is always going on (god is eternal). We choose goods for the sake of engaging in that activity, but if we were identical to it, as god is, there would be no choices left; for, being god, we would already be eternally *eudaimōn*.

Nous itself is sometimes characterized in ways that suggest that it is an immaterial object planted in the psyche by god: '*Nous* seems to be an independent substance that comes in (*egginesthai*) to us and is not destructible' (*DA* 408ᵇ18–19); '[In foetal development] *nous* alone enters additionally from outside (*thurathen*) and alone is divine (*theion*). For bodily activity is in no way associated with its activity' (*GA* 736ᵇ27–9).[14] But it now seems clear that these texts

---

[14] See *NE* 1177ᵇ27–8, Balme (1972, 159–65).

are making a different sort of point altogether. Passive *nous* does not come in from the outside. It comes from the *katemēnia* and sperm just like all the other aspects of human matter and form (*GA* 736ᵇ5–737ᵃ34). What comes in from the outside is something that, as (B) puts it, is 'in its substance an activity'. And to say that that activity comes in from the outside is simply to say that its final cause is not the sperm or *katamēnia*, but something outside them: god.[15]

We are most of all god when we study theology, then, but we are never actually gods. How, then, can we share our function and essence with god? The answer is, in fact, reasonably straight-forward. A function can be possessed in different ways and to different degrees. A good knife and a mediocre one have the same function, but the former's is completed by the appropriate virtue, the latter's is not (see *Metaph.* 1021ᵇ12–25). In the same way, god's function is completed in a way that ours is not. Unlike us, god is eternally engaged in study. Unlike us, he engages in study by himself (*Metaph.* 1072ᵇ26–8), but we cannot engage in study without him. For his activity is the final cause of ours. We share god's function, to be sure, but that just makes us god-like, it does not make us god.

It is because we are not god, indeed, that 'a *eudaimōn* person is a human being and so will need external prosperity also. For his nature is not self-sufficient for study, but he needs a healthy body and to have food and other services provided' (1178ᵇ33–5). For, if our *nous* was god, the easiest way to immortalize ourselves would be to shuffle off these mortal coils and join god, so to speak, in endless *eudaimonia*.[16] We cannot do that because our study depends on our body and will cease to be when it does.

28 *Eudaimonia* and *Eudaimōn* Lives

In *NE* x. 6–8, Aristotle discusses two separate questions. The first concerns *eudaimonia*. It is this. Which of the following three activities is *eudaimonia*? Is it pleasure, practical activity, or study? The second concerns not activities but types of *lives*. It is this. Which life is most *eudaimōn*?

---

[15] This is strongly suggested by *GA* 744ᵇ11–28.

[16] Other gods, less impassive and more vengeful than Aristotle's, prevent us from taking this easy way out by forbidding suicide.

Now Aristotle uses two words corresponding to 'life', namely, *zoē* and *bios*. The first, which refers to the sort of life biologists and zoologists (among others) study, is ambiguous: 'Life is also spoken of in two ways and we must take life expressing activity (*kat'* *energeian*), for this seems to be so called more legitimately (*kuriōteron*)' (1098ᵃ5–7). Here the contrast is between life as a second potential and life as an activity that is the activation of that potential. When we are asleep, we are alive in the first sense; when we are awake and actually engaged in activity, we are alive in the the second sense (1095ᵇ32–3, 1098ᵇ30–1099ᵃ6). The latter—*life-activity*—is more legitimately called 'life' because, in Aristotle's view, the term 'life' is transferred from the activation of the potential to the potential itself (*Metaph.* 1050ᵃ21–3).

Bios, which refers to the sort of life in which a biographer might be interested, is also ambiguous, but not in the same way as *zoē*. *Bios* refers, first of all, to a *biographical life*, to a span of time throughout which someone possesses the second potential whose activation is life-activity. In the following passage, *bios* is clearly used in this sense: '[In sleep] the good and the bad person are least distinct, which is why *eudaimōn* people are said to be no worse off than wretched ones for half their life (*tou biou*)' (1102ᵇ5–7).[17] *Bios* also has a second sense, however, which is exemplified in the following passage from *NE* i. 5:

It would seem that people not unreasonably reach their conception of the good, that is of *eudaimonia*, from the lives they lead (*ek tōn biōn*). For there are most of all three that are most favoured: the life of gratification, the political life, and, third, the life of study. The many, the most vulgar, would seem to conceive of *eudaimonia* as pleasure, therefore they like the life of gratification. Hence they appear completely slavish. For the life they decide on is a life (*bion*) for cattle. And yet they have some argument on their side, since many in positions of power feel the same way as Sardanapallus. The cultivated people, those who are active (*praktikoi*), conceive of *eudaimonia* as honour, since this is more or less the end of the political life (*biou*). . . . [But] it would seem, they pursue honour to convince themselves that they are good; at any rate, they seek to be honoured by people with *phronēsis*, among people who know them, and for virtue. It is clear, then, that in the view of active people at least, virtue is superior. Perhaps, then, one might conceive virtue more than honour to be

---

17 See 1098ᵃ17–20, 1101ᵃ14–16.

the end of the political life (*biou*). . . . The third life is the life of study: we will examine it in what follows. $(1095^b14-1096^a5)^{18}$

Here *bios* refers to a *mode* of biographical life.[19]

Now a *bios* in this second sense is identified—the passage makes clear—by the conception of *eudaimonia* operative within it. The many, because of the lives they live, take pleasure to be *eudaimonia* and hence pursue everything else for the sake of pleasure. For in taking pleasure to be *eudaimonia* they are taking it to be the best good, the good for whose sake everything else is pursued (1095^a14-28). In the same way, the cultivated take virtue to be *eudaimonia*, and so pursue everything for the sake of virtue, while the wise, we may infer, take study to be *eudaimonia* and pursue everything for its sake.

Eudaimonia is a kind of life (*zōē*). For it is a life-activity, the activation of a certain potential. Thus 'the activation of *nous* is life (*zōē*)' (*Metaph.* 1072^b26-7). But *eudaimonia* is neither a biographical life (*bios*) nor a mode of one. A biographical life is something within which *eudaimonia* may occur. And a mode of biographical life is identified by the conception of *eudaimonia* operative within it —a conception which may or may not be correct.

Given these facts, we would expect the question of whether a biographical life is *eudaimōn* to be settled in large part by the answer to the question of what mode of life it exemplifies, and we would expect that answer to be settled by which life-activity is really *eudaimonia*. It seems reasonable, therefore, to begin with the question of which of the three competing life-activities—pleasure, practical activity, and study—is *eudaimonia*. Having answered it, we should be better equipped to answer the question of which mode of biographical life is most *eudaimōn*.

In *NE* x. 6 (1176^a33-^b9), Aristotle reviews the findings of i. 7–8, which we discussed in §21–4, and concludes that *eudaimonia* must have the following four features:

1. It must be an activity, the activation of a state, not a state.
2. It must be self-sufficient.
3. It must be choiceworthy by itself not for any *para* end.

---

[18] I have adopted the rearrangement of the text proposed by Irwin (1985*b*, 7). The final sentence clearly states, what in my view is true, that the remainder of the *Ethics*, and not just x. 6–8, is about the life of study (see below).

[19] I have benefited in this paragraph and the next from two interesting studies of *bios*, Cooper (1975, 157–60; 1987*b*, 213–15 n. 14).

4. It must (because of the function argument) be an activity expressing virtue.

And these are the features he uses to determine which of the three candidate activities is really *eudaimonia*. Pleasant amusements are activities (1153^a12-15),[20] hence they possess (1). They are choiceworthy because of themselves not solely for a *para* end, hence they also possess (3), at least to some extent. People congratulated for their *eudaimonia* —such as tyrants and others in supreme power—spend their leisure engaged in such amusements (1176^b9-17). Hence those amusements seem to possess (2) as well. There are *phainomena*, therefore, to support the claim of pleasant amusements to be *eudaimonia* (see 1095^b21-2). But Aristotle dismisses their claim just as he dismissed it in *NE* i. 6 (1095^b19-22). 'These powerful people have had no taste (*ageustoi*) of pure and civilized pleasure and so resort to bodily pleasures' $(1176^b19-21$; see $1139^b13-16)$. Hence they are not reliable sources of ethical *endoxa*. Moreover, those who are such sources— namely, excellent or virtuous people—tell against the claim of amusements not for it. Amusements cannot be the unconditional end because virtuous people seek them in order to relax, so that they can be more active in the future $(1176^b30-1177^a1)$;[21] the *endoxa*-underwritten function argument shows that *eudaimonia* is not amusement, but activity expressing virtue; serious activity of the better part of a person is 'more excellent' and so has 'more the character of *eudaimonia*'; even a slave can enjoy pleasant amusements but 'no one would allow that a slave shares in *eudaimonia*' $(1176^b24-1177^a11)$.

The next contender is activity expressing *phronēsis* or the virtues of character. Clearly, it is an activity expressing virtue. It is also self-sufficient to a degree and is choiceworthy because of itself. It thus has a claim on each of (1)–(4). But it is not *eudaimonia* all the

---

[20] Pleasures are also the *allo* ends of activities. For 'pleasure', like 'function' and '*eudaimonia*', is act/result ambiguous. In vii. 1–14, Aristotle focuses on pleasure as act; in x. 1–5, he focuses on pleasure as result. This has caused confusion and controversy and it is still not clear just why he changes his focus in this way. But there need be no inconsistency involved in doing so. See Gosling and Taylor (1982, 193–344).

[21] Aristotle is not denying here that simple amusements are chosen because of themselves not *di' hetera*. What he is claiming is that, unlike *eudaimonia*, amusements have a *para* end, namely, relaxation for the sake of future activity. See Kraut (1989, 164).

same or, at any rate, not primary *eudaimonia*. For, first of all, it is not as self-sufficient as study:

> The self-sufficiency we spoke of [at 1097^{b}6–16] will be found in study most of all. For admittedly the wise person, the just person, and the other virtuous people all need the good things necessary for life. Still, when these are adequately supplied, the just person needs other people as partners and recipients of his just actions, and the same is true of the temperate person, the brave person, and each of the others. But the wise person is able, and more able the wiser he is, to study even by himself; and though he presumably does it better with co-workers, still he is most self-sufficient. (1177^{a}27–^{b}1)^{22}

Thus study possesses (2) to a higher degree than practical activity does. Second, we pursue practical activity both because of itself and because of a *para* end:

> From the virtues concerned with action we try to a greater or lesser extent to gain something over and above the action itself (*para tēn praxin*). . . . But the actions of the politicians require trouble also. Over and above (*par'*) political activities themselves these actions seek positions of power and honours; or at least they seek *eudaimonia* for the politician himself and his fellow citizens, which is something different (*heteran*) from politics itself, and clearly is sought on the assumption that it is different. Hence among actions expressing the virtues those in politics and war are pre-eminently fine and great; but they require trouble, aim at some [further] end, and are not chosen [solely] because of themselves (*di' hautas*). (1177^{b}2–18)

It follows that activity expressing *phronēsis* lacks (3) and cannot be primary *eudaimonia*. For *eudaimonia*, being unconditionally complete, cannot be pursued for either an *allo* or a *para* end.

A little later, however, practical activity is at least awarded a second prize:

> For a human being the life expressing *nous* will be supremely best and pleasantest, if indeed this most of all is a human being. This life, then, will also be most *eudaimōn*. The life expressing the other kind of virtue [i.e. *phronēsis* and the virtues of character] is so in a secondary way (*deuterōs*) because the activities expressing this virtue are [merely] human. (1178^{a}6–10)

^{22} At *EE* 1245^{b}4–9, Aristotle says that friends 'should study together (*suntheōrein*) . . . [for] each really wishes to share the end that is most of all choiceworthy with his friend'. Thus even though someone may not need friends in order to study, he seems to have a reason, stemming from friendship, to want to study with them.

But there is a problem about the precise identity of the prizewinner. Is it activity expressing *phronēsis–1*, which is pursued solely because of itself, not because of any *para* end?[23] Or is it activity expressing *phronēsis–2*, which is pursued in part for its own sake and in part for the sake of study, its *para* end?

Let us suppose that the virtuous act that best promotes study in a given situation is X. X will, therefore, express *phronēsis–2* and the virtues of character. But is there any guarantee that X will express *phronēsis–1*? Clearly, there is not. Different ends are usually best promoted by different acts. If I want to act moderately at a dinner party, for example, simply for its own sake or to express *phronēsis–1*, I may decide to have just two glasses of wine. But if I want to act moderately both for its own sake and for the sake of study, if I want my act to express *phronēsis–2*, I may—thinking of the especially clear head I will need to do first philosophy next morning—decide to set the limit at one glass. But what this means is that an act expressing *phronēsis–1* need not express *phronēsis–2*. Hence the two contenders are not equivalent, and we must choose between them.[24]

If secondary *eudaimonia* must, then, be either activity expressing *phronēsis–1* or activity expressing *phronēsis–2*, which is it? The only plausible answer is that it is activity expressing *phronēsis–2*. For all three Aristotelian ethical treatises are explicit that *phronēsis* must be for the sake of study. We discussed *NE* 1145ᵃ6–11 in §17, but the pronouncements of the *Eudemian Ethics* and the *Magna Moralia* merit brief notice:

> Since a human being, also, is by nature composed of a thing that governs and a thing that is governed, each should live by reference to its own ruling first principle. But that is of two sorts. For medicine is a governing principle in one way and health in another, since the first is for the sake of the second. Thus it is in the case of the part of the psyche that studies. For the god (*ho theos*) is a governor not in a prescriptive fashion but is that for the sake of which *phronēsis* prescribes . . . Hence if some choice and possession

[23] Cooper (1987*b*, 208) argues that activity expressing *phronēsis–1* is secondary *eudaimonia*. Kraut (1989, 1–7) argues that activity expressing either *phronēsis–1* or *phronēsis–2* is secondary *eudaimonia*. Both answers face severe difficulties.

[24] This is even clearer if we turn from *phronēsis* to politics. Politics–1 would control a polis so as to produce practical activity. Politics–2 would control it so as to produce study. It is obvious, that politics–1 will result in very different actions from politics–2. Perhaps politics–1 would exclude study from the polis altogether except insofar as it contributes to activity expressing *phronēsis–1*.

of natural goods—either goods of the body or money or of friends or the other goods—will most of all produce the study of the god (*tēn tou theou malista theōrian*), that is the best and finest limit (*horos*). But whatever, through deficiency or excess, hinders the serving and studying of the god (*ton theon therapeuein kai theōrein*) is bad. (*EE* 1249ᵇ9–21)[25]

Phronēsis is, as it were, a kind of steward of wisdom, procuring leisure for it and its function (i.e. study], by subduing and moderating the passions. (*MM* 1198ᵇ17–20)[26]

It follows that the activity expressing *phronēsis–1* is not activity expressing *phronēsis* at all. For no activity expresses *phronēsis* unless it has study as its limit or end.

We would expect, therefore, that Aristotle would restrict *eudaimonia* to beings who, possessing *nous*, are capable of study. And in both of his major ethical treatises that is precisely what he does:

The other animals have no share in *eudaimonia*, being completely deprived of the activity of study. The whole life of the gods is blessed, and human life is blessed to the extent that it has something resembling this sort of activity. But none of the other animals is *eudaimōn*, because none of them shares in study at all. Hence *eudaimonia* extends just as far as study extends, and the more someone studies the more *eudaimōn* he is, not coincidentally but insofar as he studies, since study is valuable by itself. And so *eudaimonia* will be some sort of study. (1178ᵇ24–32)[27]

None of the other animals that are naturally inferior to human beings have any share in *eudaimonia*: no horse or bird or fish is *eudaimōn*, nor anything else that does not, as the proverb says, by its nature have a share in something divine; it is by sharing in good things in some other way that these things live either well or badly. (*EE* 1217ª24–9)

It is because *eudaimonia* is an activity of *nous*, indeed, that human *eudaimonia* 'expresses something different (*kath' heteron*)', while 'god is himself his own well-being' (*EE* 1245ᵇ16–19). For human

---

[25] It is a matter of dispute, since the phrases are ambiguous, whether *ho theos*, *tou theou theōrian*, and *ton theon therapeuein kai theōrein* refer to god and his study or to *nous* and its study of god. See Woods (1982, 193–8). If we must choose between these, then the latter is clearly to be preferred. For, first, *phronēsis*, while it prescribes for the sake of our active *nous*, cannot prescribe for the sake of god himself, and, second, while things can hinder our *nous* from studying, nothing can hinder god from doing so. In fact, however, Aristotle is surely referring to the active *nous* in us, which is divine, as the god (see §27).

[26] See *MM* 1208ª5–20, *Pol.* 1255b35–7. The bona fides of the *Magna Moralia* as a source of Aristotelian ethical doctrine are defended in Cooper (1973).

[27] This passage is carefully discussed in Kraut (1989, 54–67).

primary *eudaimonia* is the expression of something divine, something superior to and so different from the merely human (*NE* 1177ᵇ26–31), but god's *eudaimonia* just is god himself.[28] The activity commended as secondary *eudaimonia*, then, must be activity expressing *phronēsis–2*, activity that is choiceworthy because of the secondary *eudaimonia* to which it is identical and because of the primary *eudaimonia* that is its *para* end. When our activity expresses *phronēsis* and is for the sake of study it is secondary *eudaimonia*, but if we made activity expressing *phronēsis* our absolute end, such activity would not be *eudaimonia* of any kind.

Secondary *eudaimonia* is activity expressing *phronēsis*. But why is such activity *eudaimonia* at all? The function argument establishes that *eudaimonia* is an activity of the psyche in accord with reason that is completed by its proper virtue. *Phronēsis* is the virtue proper to practical activity and so completes it (1144ᵃ6–7). Hence the claim of activity expressing *phronēsis* to be some kind of *eudaimonia* is underwritten. But when it emerges that *sophia* is a more complete virtue than *phronēsis*, activity expressing the latter is demoted to secondary status.

The remaining contender for being primary *eudaimonia* is study. And it, Aristotle argues, possesses all of (1)–(4). It is an activity, not a state; it is the most self-sufficient activity (1177ᵃ27–ᵇ1); it and it alone is choiceworthy solely because of itself not because of any *allo* or *para* ends (1177ᵇ1–2); it is activity expressing the best and most complete virtue (1177ᵃ12–17). It is also the most continuous activity and the most pleasant (1177ᵃ21–7).

Study has emerged as primary *eudaimonia*, then; activity expressing *phronēsis–2* as secondary *eudaimonia*; and pleasure as no kind of *eudaimonia* at all. We now turn to the question of which mode of life is most *eudaimōn*.

The mode of life identified by having pleasure as its operative conception of *eudaimonia* is quickly dismissed as a contender (1177ᵃ1–3). It contains neither activity expressing *phronēsis–2* nor

---

[28] *EE* 1245ᵇ16–19 is often interpreted to mean that human *eudaimonia* requires friends, while god's depends only on himself, since this is the topic of much of the preceeding discussion. But this makes it difficult to understand why Aristotle introduces the text by saying: 'Yet according to this argument [that since god does not need friends, god-like people should not need them either] the excellent person will not even study (*noēsei*) anything [over and above himself]'.

study. Hence it is not *eudaimōn* to any degree (see §29). It is a life for cattle (1095^{b}20); and cattle, lacking *nous*, are not in any way *eudaimōn*.

In *NE* i. 6, the end of the political life is identified not with virtuous activity, but with virtue itself. And virtue is also quickly ruled out as a candidate for being *eudaimonia*. For it is possible to possess virtue while being asleep, inactive, or suffering the worst evils or misfortunes 'and if that's the sort of life (*zōnta*) he has no one would count him *eudaimōn*' (1095^{b}31–1096^{a}2). In x. 7, virtue is again ruled out as being *eudaimonia* because activities expressing the virtues of character have *para* ends (1177^{b}12–15). The politician may pursue virtue—or politics itself whose end is virtue—for its own sake, but in fact his actions have a *para* end, namely, leisure. And this is clear from his actions themselves even if his conception of *eudaimonia* is at odds with it. We may infer, though Aristotle does not explicitly do so, that the political life, like the life of pleasure, is not the *eudaimōn* life.[29]

There follows a brief passage in which study is compared to political activity and shown to be *eudaimonia* (1177^{b}19–24). Then, for the first time in x. 7, lives rather than activities are explicitly compared. But the comparison is difficult and requires careful analysis

[A] The complete *eudaimonia* of a human being will be this activity [study], if it has received a complete length of life (*biou*). For nothing incomplete is proper to *eudaimonia*. [B] Such a life would be higher than the [merely] human level. For someone will live it (*biōsetai*) not insofar as he is a human being, but insofar as he has something divine in him. And the activity of this divine thing is as much superior to the activity expressing the other virtue as the thing itself is superior to the compound. Hence if *nous* is something divine in comparison with a human being, so also will the life (*bios*) that expresses it be divine in comparison with human life (*bios*). [C] We should not listen to the proverb-writers and 'think human, since you are human', or 'think mortal, since you are mortal'. Rather, as far as we can, we ought to immortalize ourselves, and do everything to live (*zēn*) expressing the most supreme thing in us.[30] For however small this may be,

---

[29] Unlike Plato, Aristotle does not explicitly rank the three major modes of life he recognizes in terms of how *eudaimōn* they are. But it seems reasonable to believe that he would accept Plato's ranking. Those who lead the political life are closer to being *eudaimōn* than those who live the life of pleasure. See Reeve (1988, 144–59).

[30] The shift from *bios* to *zōē* here shows that the focus of the life (*bios*) expressing *nous* is the life-activity (*zōē*) of study.

it surpasses everything in power and value. [D] Moreover, each person seems to be his *nous*, if indeed he is his controlling and better part. It would be absurd, then, if he were to choose not his own life (*bion*) but something else's. And what we have said previously will apply now: what is proper to each thing's nature is supremely best and pleasantest for it. Hence for a human being the life (*bios*) expressing *nous* will be supremely best and pleasantest, if indeed this most of all is the human being. This life, then, will also be most *eudaimōn*. [E] The life expressing the other kind of virtue is so in a secondary way because the activities expressing this virtue are [merely] human. . . . Besides, *phronēsis* is yoked together with the virtues of character and they with it. For the first principles of *phronēsis* express the virtues of character and correctness in the virtues of character expresses *phronēsis*. And since these virtues are also connected to feelings, they are concerned with the compound. Since the virtues of the compound are human virtues, the life (*bios*) and *eudaimonia* expressing them is also human. That of *nous*, however, is separated. (1177^b24–1178^a22)

The life expressing *nous* is more *eudaimōn* than the life expressing *phronēsis*, (B) tells us, because the activity of *nous* is superior to the activity of the 'compound'. (E) establishes that the latter activity is activity expressing *phronēsis*, and that the compound—since *phronēsis* requires *nous* and cannot exist without it (§§11–18)—is the c-human being discussed in §24.

(A) suggests that the life expressing *nous* is a life that has had enough study or primary *eudaimonia* in it to be choiceworthy and lacking in nothing. (B) claims that a life of that sort is not possible for us insofar as we are merely human, but only insofar as there is something divine in us, namely, *nous*. It thus draws on doctrines discussed in §§26–7. (C) advises us to do everything to lead such a life, since it is by far the best kind. (D) adds that, since we are most of all our *nous*, it would be absurd for us to live a life other that the one expressing *nous*, which, being supremely best and pleasantest, is in fact the most *eudaimōn*.

But what exactly is the life expressing *nous*? Is it the biographical life in which *nous* alone is expressed? Or is it that part of a biographical life expressing *phronēsis*-2 that expresses *nous*. It must be, and can only be, the latter. For no human being can live a life in which *nous* alone is expressed and none could be *eudaimōn* doing so. For our appetites and emotions need to be satisfied if we are to be *eudaimōn* and will interfere with our study if they are not (see §§29–32).

What, then, is the life expressing *phronēsis*? Is it the life expressing *phronēsis–1* or the life expressing *phronēsis–2?* It is, and can only be, the latter. For activity expressing *phronēsis–1* is not *eudaimonia* of any kind. And a life without *eudaimonia* of any kind in it could hardly be *eudaimōn* even in a secondary way.

(A)–(E) is not, then, a comparison of the life expressing *nous* alone with the political life.[31] For the life expressing *nous* is not the life expressing only it; and the life expressing *phronēsis*, since it has virtuous activity and not the virtues themselves as its end, is not the political life. What are being compared in (A)–(E) is the part of (what we would call) a person's life that expresses the merely human thing in him and the part that expresses the divine thing in him. But it would be an error, though a forgivable one, to think that a single thing leads both of these lives. It is rather the case that one thing—a human being—leads the former and that another—*nous* —leads the latter. The life and *eudaimonia* of *nous*, as (E) reminds us, is separated from the life and *eudaimonia* of the compound (see *DA* 413b24–6). Yet these two lives, though separated, are—like those of a steward and the head of a household —linked; for the first is for the sake of the second.[32]

Study is primary *eudaimonia*, then, and a *eudaimōn* life is one in which enough study is appropriately distributed (see §32). But study, even though it is primary *eudaimonia*, is not enough by itself to make a life *eudaimōn*. The life must also be sufficiently long (1177b24–6) and equipped with sufficient external goods (1178b33–5). But added in the appropriate way to a life provided with these things, study makes that life *eudaimōn* or choiceworthy and least lacking in anything.

29 External Goods

Aristotle's advice on how to achieve the *eudaimōn* life is twofold. First: 'As far as we can, we ought to immortalize ourselves and do everything to live expressing the most supreme thing in us' (1177b33–4). Second: 'In so far as he [someone who is studying] is

---

[31] Cf. Cooper (1987b) and Kraut (1989, 39–77).

[32] '*Bios*,' Cooper (1975, 160) writes, 'means always "(mode of) life", and in any one period of time one can only have one mode of life.' Perhaps. But two things can presumably have two modes of life in one period of time. Hence, what we think of as a person can have two modes of life simultaneously, one led by the *nous* and the other by the c-human being that collectively (as we would say) he is.

a human being, however, and lives together with a number of other human beings, he chooses to do the actions expressing virtue. Hence he will need the sorts of external goods required for living a human life' (1178^{b}5–7). The first piece of advice is clear enough: 'Do everything possible to immortalize yourself.' Taken in isolation it sounds pretty ruthless. The second piece of advice—or normative description—is less ruthless and less clear. Why should someone whose unconditional end is study choose to do actions expressing the virtues of character? Why should someone who wants to study bother being ethical? Aristotle's answer is necessarily complex and will take four sections to develop. This section is concerned with external goods and their role in the *eudaimōn* life; §30 discusses the relationship between the virtues of character and external goods; §31 focuses on friends, 'the greatest external good' (1169^{b}9–10); §32 discusses the question of how primary *eudaimonia*, secondary *eudaimonia*, and external goods are combined by practical activity— and also with it—in a *eudaimōn* life.

Aristotle recognizes three types of goods: 'some called external (*ektos*), some goods of the psyche, others goods of the body; and the goods of the psyche are said to be goods to the fullest extent and most of all, and the actions and activities of the psyche are ascribed to the psyche' (*NE* 1098^{b}12–16; see *MM* 1184^{b}1–6). Goods of the psyche are states—the virtues—and the activities that are their *para* ends, namely, primary and secondary *eudaimonia*. External goods and goods of the body, on the other hand, are capacities:

Other goods [than the virtues] are capacities (*dunameis*), for instance, office, wealth, strength, beauty. For these are things that the good man can use well and the bad man ill. Hence such goods are called capacities. Goods indeed they are (for everything is judged by the use made of it by the good man, not by that of the bad); and it is incidental to these same goods that luck (*tuchēn*) is the cause of their production. For from luck comes wealth, and also office, and generally all the things that rank as capacities. (*MM* 1183^{b}27–35)

Now a capacity is 'a source of change in another things or in the same thing considered as other' (*Metaph.* 1020^{a}4–6; see *Cael.* 301^{b}18–19). And the changes in question can be opposites—either good or bad:

What is true of sciences and capacities (*tōn epistēmōn kai dunameōn*) is not true of states. For while one and the same capacity or science seems to have results that are opposites [either good or bad], but a state that is an opposite cannot have results that are opposites. From health, for example, we do not get opposite results but only healthy ones. (*NE* 1129ᵃ11–16)

Hence, external goods and goods of the body are things that the virtuous person uses to change the world or himself for the better, and that the vicious one uses to change himself or the world for the worse. *MM* 1183ᵇ27–35 claims that external goods and goods of the body are the result of luck. This point is also stressed in other texts: 'No activity is complete if it is impeded, and *eudaimonia* is something complete. Hence the *eudaimōn* person needs to have goods of the body and external goods added, and needs luck also, so that he will not be impeded in these ways' (*NE* 1153ᵇ16–19); 'It is not possible to be *eudaimōn* without external goods, which luck controls' (*MM* 1206ᵇ33–4). But the goods of the psyche are not controlled by luck: 'The goods external to the psyche come of themselves and by luck, whereas no one is just or temperate on account of luck' (*Pol.* 1323ᵇ27–9). There is a fundamental contrast, therefore, between external goods and goods of the body, on the one hand, and goods of the psyche, on the other. For, first, the goods of the psyche are states and their activations while goods of the body are external goods. And second, the goods of the psyche are—for a reason we shall explore in a moment—not controlled by luck, while at least some of the goods of the body and external goods are.

But there is also an important division to be drawn within the class of goods that luck controls. We can see this by following up on the significance of a remark Aristotle makes in *NE* vi. 4 while discussing the difference between action and production. The remark is this: 'In a way craft and luck are concerned with the same things, and as Agathon says: "Craft is fond of luck, and luck of craft"' (1140ᵃ17–20). Craft and luck are concerned with the same *endechomena*, with the same things that admit of being otherwise, namely, those not studied by *phronēsis* that hold neither with unconditional necessity nor for the most part. But when craft enters the picture it does away with the need for luck or radically reduces its control. This idea is already in Hippocrates and Plato: 'They [the sick] did not want to look on barefaced luck, so they entrusted themselves to craft instead' (*de Arte* 4, 5–6; see *VM* 1, 12); when the craft of wisdom is present in someone, 'the one in whom it is present is not still in need of good luck' (*Euthd.* 280b2–3; see *Grg.* 448c5–7). But it is also explicit in Aristotle's own writings: 'Where there is most *nous* and reason, there is least luck; and where there is most luck there is least *nous*' (*MM* 1207ª4–6; see *Metaph.* 981ª1–5). It is this fact, indeed, to which Agathon is attesting. His point is the one that we might make by saying 'I am a great believer in luck and I find that the more I know the more luck I have'. Luck likes craft because craft ensures—what is then no longer—good luck. And craft likes luck because craft is seldom able to reduce the control of luck to zero.[33]

But not all of the goods controlled by luck are studied by craft to the same degree. Good birth and good looks, for example, especially the former, are not something that craft can do much about once we are already on the scene. These goods seem to be more controlled by luck than, for example, good health, which is itself more controlled by luck than, for example, good shoes. Still, it is not clear just what the limits of craft are: new knowledge opens up all sorts of possibilities for reducing the role that luck plays in our lives (see §32). But neither is it clear what things must remain forever in the lap of the gods (see *EE* 1247ª3–7). Hence luck and craft are concerned with the same things only 'in a way'.

It is for these reasons, no doubt, and because our bodies are parts of us, that Aristotle sometimes seems to waver on whether to class goods of the body as internal goods or as external ones: 'Goods of the body and of the psyche are internal; good birth, friends, money, and honour are external' (*Rh.* 1360ᵇ26–9); 'a *eudaimōn* person is a human being and so will need external prosperity also [in order to be *eudaimōn*]. For his nature is not self-sufficient for study, but he needs a healthy body and to have food and other services provided' (1178ᵇ33–5). For the fact is that some goods of the body are, like goods of the psyche, less controlled by luck, while others, like some external goods, are more controlled by it.

External goods are also subject to two other kinds of subdivision. The first divides them according to their choiceworthiness:

Some sources of pleasure are necessary; others are choiceworthy by themselves, but can be taken to excess. The necessary ones are the bodily ones, that is those that concern food, sexual intercourse, and the sorts we took to be the concern of licentiousness (*akolasian*) and moderation. Other

---

[33] Craft and luck are further discussed in Reeve (1989, 37–45).

sources of pleasure are not necessary, but are choiceworthy by themselves, for example victory, honour, wealth, and similar good and pleasant things. ($1147^{b}23-31$)

We choose food, drink, and sex because we have to, urged on by somatic discomfort. Hence we do not choose them because of themselves, but we do choose other external goods, such as honour and friends, because of themselves (see §31).

The second subdvision is between external goods that are goods of competition (*perimachēta agatha*) and those that are not: 'Those who make self-love a matter of reproach ascribe it to those who award the biggest share in money, honours, and bodily pleasure to themselves. For these are the goods desired and eagerly pursued by the many on the assumption that they are the best; and hence they are also the goods that are competed for' ($1168^{b}15-19$; see $1169^{a}20-1$). The many compete for money, honours, and bodily pleasures, but not, it seems, for friends, beauty, or good birth.

What is the role of external goods of the sorts we have been discussing in the *eudaimōn* life? In the following three texts Aristotle addresses this issue:

[A] For, first of all, in many actions we use friends, wealth, and political power just as we use instruments (*organōn*). [B] Further deprivation of certain [externals]—for example good birth, good children, beauty—mar our blessedness (*hrupainousi to makarion*). For we do not altogether have the character of *eudaimonia* if we look utterly repulsive or are ill-born, solitary or childless, and have it even less, presumably, if our children or friends are totally bad, or were good but have died. ($1099^{a}33-^{b}6$).

[C] Some of the other external goods are necessary conditions (*huparchein anagkaion*), [D] others are naturally useful and cooperative as instruments (*organikōs*). ($1099^{b}27-8$)

[E] The wise person, the just person and the other virtuous people all need the good things necessary for life (*pros to zēn anagkaion*). [F] Still, when these are adequately supplied, the just person needs other people as partners and recipients of his just actions; and the same is true of the moderate person and the brave person and each of the others. ($1177^{a}28-32$)

Are the roles discerned for external goods in (A)–(B) the same as those discerned in the other texts? The use of *organōn* in (A) and *organikōs* in (D) is good evidence that the roles mentioned in (A) and (D) are identical. And this is good evidence that those mentioned in (B) and (C) are also identical. The occurrence of *anagkaion* and the use of friends as examples in both (A)–(B) and (E)–(F) is likewise good evidence that in both texts the same contrast is again in view. Presumably, then, there are just two roles being distinguished in all these texts, namely, the A-role and the B-role, as we may call them. But what precisely are these roles?[34]

The difference between the A-role and B-role suggested by (E)–(F) seems to be this: B-role goods are required by the agent in order to engage in an activity, and so can vary from one type of agent to another. A-role goods are required by the activity regardless of who the agent is. The A-role and B-role, understood in precisely this way, are discernible in the following texts: 'someone who is studying needs none of these [external] goods for the activity at least; indeed, for study itself at least they are even impeding factors (*empodia*)' (1178^b3–5); 'a *eudaimōn* person is a human being and so will need external prosperity also [in order to be *eudaimōn*]. For his nature is not self-sufficient for study but he needs a healthy body and to have food and other services provided' (1178^b33–5). The first text tells us that A-role external goods are not needed for study, that too many of them impede study, presumably because of the extra time needed to manage them appropriately. The second text tells us that B-role external goods are needed by us—although not, for example, by god—in order to study.

Given these two roles for them in the *eudaimōn* life, we would expect the deprivation of external goods to have a variety of effects on virtuous activity and, hence, on *eudaimonia*, all the way from making it impossible to making it a bit more difficult. And this is precisely what we find.

---

[34] Cooper (1985, 183–4), in one of the best discussions of external goods, suggests that the contrast is 'between those external goods that provide the normal and expected contexts for the exercise of the virtues [B-role], and external goods that are used instrumentally as means to the ends aimed at in virtuous activities [A-role]'. But B-role goods are necessary for the life-activity of the agent, they are not just normal and expected contexts for the exercise of the virtues. And A-role goods are more like parts or components of virtuous activities than they are like external means to some further end. Irwin (1985a, 95–7) argues that the contrast is between instrumental goods (A-role) that are not choiceworthy because of themselves and intrinsic goods (B-role) that are choiceworthy because of themselves being parts of *eudaimonia*. But friends, for example, who are intrinsic goods (see §31), can play either the A-role or the B-role.

Aristotle allows, for example, that deprivation of some external goods makes it impossible for a person even to acquire the virtues: 'Moreover [if *eudaimonia* results from virtue and some sort of learning or cultivation] it will be common to many. For anyone who is not deformed with regard to virtue will be able to achieve *eudaimonia* through some sort of learning and attention' (1099^{b}18–20). The relevant goods are presumably of the sorts referred to in the following passage:

There are three things that make someone good and excellent. The three are nature, habit, and reason (*logos*). First, he must be born a human being and not some other animal; so, too, he must have a certain quality of body and of psyche. But there is no benefit in having some qualities from birth, for they are altered by habit; and some qualities are by nature made to be turned by habit to good or bad. (*Pol.* 1332^{a}38–^{b}3)

It is possible to lack some of these things, but it is a rare occurrence. For nature 'leaves nothing to luck' (*Cael.* 290^{a}31) and 'always makes the best things possible' (*Cael.* 288^{a}2–3). Hence for the most part human beings can become virtuous through habituation and socialization.[35] It is for this reason, and because nature 'is more exact and better than any craft' (1106^{b}14–16), that Aristotle exempts goods of the psyche from the control of luck and contrasts them with the external goods controlled by luck or craft.

Aristotle's richest account of the impact of external goods on *eudaimonia* and on the *eudaimōn* life, however, and of the difference between it and that of virtuous activity, is the following one in *NE* i. 11:

[A] Many events are matters of luck and some are smaller, some greater. Hence, while small strokes of good or ill luck will not influence his [a virtuous person's] life, many great strokes of good luck will make it more blessed, since in themselves they naturally add adornment to it and his use of them is fine and excellent. Conversely, if the opposite [i.e. many and great strokes of ill luck], they oppress and spoil (*thlibei kai lumainetai*) his blessedness, since they involve pain and impede (*empodizei*) many activities. And yet, even here what is fine shines through, when he bears many severe strokes of bad luck with good temper, not because he feels no distress but because he is noble and magnanimous. [B] And since it is activities that control life (*hai energeiai kuriai tēs zōēs*), as we said, no blessed person could ever become wretched (*athlios*), since he will never do

---

[35] For further discussion see §30, especially n. 46.

hateful and base actions. For a truly good person possessed of *phronēsis*, we suppose, will bear strokes of luck suitably, and from his resources at any time will do the finest actions that he can . . . If this is so, then the *eudaimōn* person could never become wretched. [C] Still, he will not be blessed (*makarios*) either, if he falls into luck as bad as Priam's. Nor, however, will he be inconstant and prone to fluctuate, since he will neither be easily shaken from his *eudaimonia* nor shaken by just any sort of bad luck. He will be shaken from it, though, by many serious misfortunes, [D] and from these a return to being *eudaimōn* will take no short time; at best it will take a long and complete length of time that includes great and fine successes. (1100^{b}22–1101^{a}13)

What does 'control' mean in (B)? Simply this. If activity expressing virtue is present in a life, some *eudaimonia* is present in it, although not necessarily enough to make the life itself *eudaimōn*. For activity expressing virtue just is *eudaimonia*. If activity expressing vice is present, some wretchedness is present. For activity expressing vice just is wretchedness. If no activity of either sort is present, then—no matter what the story is about external goods, whether they are present in abundance or almost entirely absent—the life is neither *eudaimōn* nor wretched.[36] Hence virtuous activity does control *eudaimonia* in a way that external goods do not. The former has an all or nothing impact on *eudaimonia*; the latter has a variable impact that extends from slightly marring *eudaimonia* to preventing it altogether.[37]

The person described in (A)–(D) needs to be contrasted, therefore, with the one described in the following passage: 'Life includes many reversals of fortune, good and bad, and the most prosperous person may fall into a terrible disaster in old age, as the

[36] Irwin (1985*a*, 102) offers a different account of these passages: 'In saying that virtuous actions control or cause happiness, he does not mean that they are sufficient for it, or that happiness consists only of them and their necessary consequences. He means that in the right circumstances virtuous actions make the decisive contribution to happiness; we are to assume a reasonable level of external goods and then notice the role of virtue and virtuous action.' This account confuses *eudaimonia*, which is an activity, with a *eudaimōn* biographical life, which is not. Virtuous activity is sufficient for *eudaimonia* since it just is *eudaimonia*. But it is not sufficient to make a biographical life *eudaimōn*.

[37] The verbs Aristotle uses to express the impact of external goods on *eudiamonia* —each of which covers a lot of territory—make this clear: *hrupainō* (1099^{b}2) means to defile, disfigure, contaminate, infect; *thlibō* (1100^{b}28) means to reduce, compress, oppress, afflict, distress; *lumainomai* (1100^{b}28) means to outrage, maltreat, harm, injure, spoil, ruin; *empodizō* (1100^{b}29; see 1153^{b}9–25) means to put in bonds, fetter, hinder, thwart, interfere with, present an obstacle to, impede. See Liddell, Scott, and Jones (1966) s. vv.

Trojan stories tell us about Priam. But if someone has suffered these sorts of misfortunes and comes to a wretched end no one counts him *eudaimōn*' (1100ª5–9). The person envisaged here performs vicious actions and so becomes wretched in the end. That is why no one counts him as *eudaimōn*. Was this person ever virtuous? There is no reason to think so. If he had been virtuous, he would never— (B) is explicit on the matter—have fallen into vice and wretchedness. Thus while *eudaimonia* is to some extent at the mercy of luck, wretchedness, like virtue, is not.[38]

According to (C), it takes many serious misfortunes to shake a good man from his *eudaimonia*, and (D) is explicit that a return to being *eudaimōn* after such misfortune 'will take a long and complete length of time that includes great and fine successes'. (D) is often taken to be a psychological remark about recovery time,[39] but it is probably not such a remark. *Eudaimonia* is an activity; it can return in an instant, especially to a virtuous person who 'has, so to speak, no regrets' (1165ᵇ29). What cannot return quickly is what would make a life in which serious misfortunes had occurred a *eudaimōn* life, one choiceworthy and lacking in nothing, but that is as much a logical or conceptual point as a psychological one. A life containing serious misfortunes could only count as choiceworthy and lacking in nothing if it contained a lot of compensating good things appropriately distributed in it. Imagine what would have to be added on to Priam's life before anyone would consider it choiceworthy and lacking in nothing.

30 External Goods and the Virtues of Character

The virtues of character are states and states are defined as follows: 'By states (*hexeis*) I mean what we have when we are well or badly off with respect to the feelings (*pathē*). If, for example, our feeling is too intense or too weak, we are badly off in relation to anger, but if it is intermediate, we are well off; and the same is true in other

---

[38] There is no reason to think, either, that the description of the typical effects of age on character at *Rh*. 1389ᵇ13–1390ª24 are intended to apply to a virtuous person who 'will bear strokes of luck suitably, and from his resources at any time will do the finest actions that he can'. The text does not, therefore, justify the claim, made by Nussbaum (1986a, 338–9), that virtue contains 'the seeds of its own disaster'.

[39] See Nussbaum (1986a, 336–40).

cases' (1105^{b}25–8; see *Ph*. 247^{a}3–4). Hence, the virtues are what we have when we arc well off with respect to the feelings, that is, the appetites and emotions (1105^{b}21–3).

We are well off with respect to our feelings when they 'listen to reason' (1102^{b}28–1103^{a}1), but not just any old kind of listening will do. Our feelings must listen to reason in the same way as the moderate or courageous person's not just in the same way as the enkratic's. The enkratic's wish or reason simply overpowers his feelings; the virtuous person's feelings and reason aim at the same thing: 'the moderate person's appetitive part must agree with reason; for both aim at what is fine' (1119^{b}15–18). That is why the desiring part of the psyche is said to listen 'still better' to reason in the virtuous person than it does in the enkratic (1102^{b}26–8).

When the feelings have the same aim as wish, they are said to be 'in a mean' between excess and deficiency, but this mean is not determined abstractly; it is not, for example, an arithmetic mean, nor is *moderato in omnibus* an Aristotelian principle. Rather, the mean is defined in relation to 'the reason by reference to which the *phronimos* would define it' (1107^{a}1–2). But what is that reason? And how does the *phronimos* work out the mean in relation to it?

Aristotle's answer to the first question is this: 'In all the states of character we have mentioned [the virtues of character] and, indeed, in all other matters, there is a target (*skopos*) that the person who has reason (*logon*) focuses on and, as a result, tightens or loosens accordingly, and this is the limit of the various mean states (*kai tis estin horos tōn mesōteron*)' (1138^{b}21–3). The limit or target is primary *eudaimonia*, since *phronēsis* is for its sake. And the metaphor of loosening and tightening suggests a responsiveness of feeling to wish, which ensures their harmony. Some of Aristotle's advice about how we might achieve this harmony helps explain its nature:

If we aim to hit the mean we must first of all steer clear of the more contrary extreme . . . For since one extreme is more in error, the other less, and since it is hard to hit the mean with accuracy, the second-best tack is, as they say, to take the lesser of two evils. We shall succeed best in this by the method we describe. We must also examine what we ourselves drift into easily. For different people have different natural tendencies towards different ends, and we come to know our own tendencies by the pleasure and pain that arises in us. We must drag ourselves off in the contrary direction. For if we pull far away from error, as they do in straightening bent wood, we shall reach the mean. And in everything we must beware above all of pleasure and its sources. For we are already biased in its favour when we come to judge it. Hence we must react to it as the elders reacted to Helen, and on each occasion repeat what they said, for if we do this, and send pleasure packing, we shall be less in error. ($1109^a30-{}^b12$)

By noticing our natural proclivities, we can correct for them. Over time, with habit and practice, our feelings typically change becoming more responsive or less resistant to wish, more in harmony with it.

Now feelings are concerned with external goods, especially goods of competition: 'those who are greedy for these goods gratify their appetites and in general their feelings and the non-rational part of the psyche' (1168^b19-21). For 'appetite's concern is what is pleasant and what is painful' (1111^b16-18); the emotions all 'involve pleasure or pain' (1105^b21-3); and the goods competed for are all 'sources of pleasure' (1147^b23-31). Hence, we would expect the virtues of character to be particularly concerned with external goods. And, indeed, they are. Courage is concerned with painful feelings of fear and pleasant feelings of confidence; moderation is concerned with the pleasures of taste and touch ($1118^a23-{}^b8$);[40] generosity and magnificence are concerned with wealth; magnanimity is concerned with honour; mildness is concerned with anger, which is itself a painful condition caused by 'what is believed to be an insult' (*Rh.* 1378^a32); the virtue that is a mean between being ingratiating and being quarrelsome, is concerned with pleasures and pains generated in social exchanges; the virtue that is a mean between boastfulness and self-deprecation is concerned with such feelings as confidence, envy, and jealousy, which cause us to have too high or too low an opinion of ourselves; wit is concerned with what is socially amusing; friendliness with social pleasures other than amusements ($1107^a33-1108^b7$). Special justice is concerned with *pleonexia*, with wanting more and more without limit of the external goods of competition (1129^b1-4). General justice is 'complete virtue, not unconditionally complete virtue, but complete virtue in relation to another' (1129^b25-7), so it is concerned with external goods just as the other virtues of character are.

---

[40] Young (1988) is a good recent discussion of moderation and its apparently odd restriction to the pleasures of taste and touch.

It is because the virtues of character are connected with external goods in this way that Aristotle can be confident to some degree that the virtues he lists are all the virtues that there are (1115^a5). Moreover, this connection also explains, I think, why he believes that the full virtues, unlike the natural ones, are reciprocal and must be possessed as a unified whole ($1144^b30-1145^a2$). For any feeling, not in a mean, not responsive to wish, has the potential to overthrow wish and result in vicious action. But no feeling is restricted to causing just one vice; a single feeling, not in a mean, can cause actions expressing the whole range of vices. Suppose, for example, that someone suffers from uncontrollable anger, but that his other feelings are—at least when his anger is not aroused—responsive to wish. If he is angry at the enemy, his anger may overstrengthen his confidence making him rash rather than courageous; if he is angry with a sexual partner, his anger may overexcite his sexual desire making him licentious; if he is angry with a beneficiary, his anger may cause him to give less money than he should; if he is angry with someone whom he should honour, he may give less honour—or, overcompensating, more honour—than he should; if he is angry with his guests, his anger may cause him to be quarrelsome or hurtfully boastful or cruelly witty; if he is angry with his comrades in arms when it comes time to divide the spoils, his anger may overstimulate his appetite for external goods, so that he exhibits special injustice.[41] Hence someone who possesses *phronēsis* and who reliably does what best promotes *eudaimonia* must have all the virtues if he is to have any of them.[42]

The virtues of character are concerned with external goods, then.

---

[41] The *Iliad*, which is among other things a study in anger, provides many illustrations of the capacity of that emotion to generate vices other than irascibility. Thus Agamemnon's anger at Achilles' suggestion that he return Chryseis to her father results in his unjustly forcing Achilles to give up Briseis. Achilles' anger at Hektor for killing Patroklos results in his licentious or immoderate treatment of Hektor's body.

[42] 'The magnificent man is generous', Aristotle says, 'but the generous one is not necessarily (*outhen mallon*) magnificent' (1122^a8-9). Does this raise a problem for the doctrine of the reciprocity of the virtues? It does, but it seems to be a soluble one. The reciprocity of the virtues is clearly to be understood as the claim that the virtues are one and the same state as one another, while possibly differing in their being (see 1130^a10-13, 1141^b23-4). Suppose that generosity and magnificence are the same state, S, and that X has S, but isn't wealthy enough to give away more than moderate amounts, while Y has S, but is sufficiently wealthy to be lavish. Then, while X's actions can express S, X can only be generous not magnificent, since his expenditures can never be of sufficient size to be magnificent. Y's actions can also express S, and some of them will involve moderate, some very large, expenditures. Since the latter

And the clue to the nature of their concern is their relation to justice. This is spelled out with special clarity in the following passages:

> The actions producing the whole of virtue [and therefore expressive of it[43]] are the lawful actions that the laws prescribe for education promoting the common good. (1130[b]25–6)

> What is just is found among those who have law in their relations. Where there is law, there is injustice, since the judicial process is judgement that distinguishes what is just from what is unjust. Where there is injustice there is doing injustice . . . And doing injustice is awarding to oneself too many of the things that are good unconditionally and too few of the things that are bad unconditionally. That is why we allow only reason, not a human being, to be ruler. For a human being awards himself too many goods and becomes a tyrant, but a ruler is a guardian of what is just and hence of what is equal. (1134[a]30–[b]2)[44]

The things that are referred to here as good unconditionally—that is to say, that are good for the virtuous person—are external goods (1129[b]4–10). Hence what *phronēsis* or reason does when it rules in a polis is to ensure that people acquire at least habituated virtue, so that external goods, normally competed for, will be distributed equally or in proportion to worth (1131[a]20–9, below;). The result will be that the needs 'that hold everything together' (1133[a]26–31) will be satisfied in a way that ensures the long-term stability of the polis, the long-term stability of what is alone self-sufficient to supply those needs. For politics 'aims not at some advantage close at hand, but at advantage for the whole of life' (1160[a]21–3).

This account of the involvement of the virtues of character with external goods, allows us to understand why someone who needs such goods would want to live in a just polis exchanging them with others in a just way, but it also enables us to see why, even if external goods were simply there for the taking, and competition for them was not a problem, someone whose end is primary *eudaimonia*, would still want (some of) the virtues of character:

> Those who seem to be the best off and to be in the possession of every

actions will be magnificent, Y is both generous and magnificent. It follows that the generous man is not necessarily magnificent, but that generosity and magnificence are none the less one and the same state. Cf. Irwin (1988*a*) and Kraut (1988).

[43] See 1103[b]9–25.
[44] See 1094[b]9–10, 1102[a]7–10, 1137[a]26–30.

good, have special need of [special] justice and moderation, for example those—if, as the poets say, there are such—who dwell in the Isles of the Blessed. They above all will need philosophy, moderation, and [special] justice, and all the more the more leisure they have, living in the midst of abundance. (*Pol.* 1334ᵃ28–34)

Without philosophy (or wisdom) no one can study, but without special justice and moderation his unruly appetites and emotions will deprive him of the peace of mind needed for study (see *MM* 1198b9–20).⁴⁵

Someone whose end is primary *eudaimonia*, then, has good reason to choose the virtues of character as instrumental means to the stable, long-term acquisition of his end, but that means that he has an incentive to try to come to value them for their own sakes. For if he succeeds, he will find exercising them less arduous than if he simply sees them as intrinsically undesirable means to what he does value. But, of course, he cannot do the impossible. He can come to value the virtues for their own sakes, everything else being equal, only if there is something intrinsically valuable in them for him to discover (*Metaph.* 1072ᵃ29). But, on Aristotle's view, there is something intrinsically valuable in the virtues: activity expressing them is secondary *eudaimonia*, as the function argument shows and those who have had the relevant experiences attest. But to have those experiences one must have *phronēsis*; for without *phronēsis* one cannot have full virtue.

Now *phronēsis* is the same state as politics. And one only has to glance at the account of politics in §20 to see that most people are unlikely to have the ability to acquire *phronēsis*. In the *Politics*, Aristotle is explicit about this:

Phronēsis is the only virtue peculiar to the ruler. All other virtues it seems are necessarily common to ruler and subject. The virtue of the subject is certainly not *phronēsis* but true belief; he is like the maker of the flute while his ruler is like the fluteplayer or flute user. (1277ᵇ25–30)⁴⁶

---

⁴⁵ Given the reciprocity of the virtues this implies that a solitary studier will have all the virtues though his actions will express only some of them.

⁴⁶ See *Pol.* 1277ᵃ5–1277ᵇ7, 1278ᵃ40–ᵇ5, 1288ᵃ32–ᵇ2. This view about *phronēsis* may seem to conflict with *NE* 1099ᵇ18–20 where Aristotle says that *eudaimonia* is 'common to many (*polukoinon*)', indeed to all those who are not deformed in their capacity for virtue. The conflict is more real than apparent, however. For, first, the context makes it clear that Aristotle is making a comparative judgement: if *eudaimonia* is the result of 'some sort of virtue and learning', then it will be a more common possession than it would be if it were a gift from the gods or

The rulers have *phronēsis* or full virtue; the subjects have habituated virtue and so true practical beliefs. Hence the subjects in a polis are virtuous only as an instrumental means to the external goods they desire; they do not see the intrinsic value of ethical activity because they have never tasted it.[47] Their virtue is thus like the diminished type of courage exemplified by citizens who 'stand firm against dangers with the aim of avoiding reproaches and legal penalties and of winning honours' (1116^{a}17–29).[48]

Those with *phronēsis* have both the incentive, then, and the ability to find the virtues intrinsically valuable or desirable because of themselves.

3 1 VIRTUOUS FRIENDS

The core features of friendship (*philia*), on Aristotle's view, are (1) mutual wishing of good or beneficial things, (2) mutual awareness of that mutual wishing, resulting in (3) equal exchanges of those things: '[friends] must wish good things for each other and be aware of it' (1156^{a}4–5); 'in every way each friend gets the same things and similar things from each, and that is what must be true of friends' (1157^{a}34–5; see *Rh.* 1380^{b}35–1382^{a}19). The require-ment that friends exchange good things equally explains why 'friendship is said to be an equality (*isotēs*)' (1157^{b}36); why 'friendship and justice would seem to be concerned with the same things' (1159^{a}25–6; see 1161^{a}10–11); and why 'friendship would seem to hold a polis together' preventing civil war from breaking it apart (1155^{a}22–3) It also explains why so much of Aristotle's discussion of friendship is given over to the topic of what consitutes equal exchange between unequal partners who want different things from each other (see *NE* viii. 7–ix. 3).[49]

the product of luck or chance (1099^{b}9–20). The comparative nature of the claim is explicit in the parallel section of *EE* (1215^{a}12–19). Second, Aristotle seems to be allowing here that those who acquire habituated virtue also acquire some measure of (secondary) *eudaimonia* (see 1099^{b}29–32). Hence even if we took his claim that *eudaimonia* is widely shared to be absolute rather than comparative, it would still not conflict with the view that full-blown *phronēsis* is possessed by only a comparative few.

[47] See Plato, *R.* 358a4–6, where Glaucon attributes this view of virtue to the many.

[48] See Plato, *R.* 429a8–d1, 601d1–602a1; Reeve (1988, 81–95, 236–45).

[49] These facts about *philia* show that 'friendship' is at the very least a controversial translation.

Now there are three kinds of lovable or choiceworthy things: the good, the pleasant, and the useful (1155^{b}19–20, *Top.* 118^{b}27–8). And it is because of these that people love or befriend each other:

[A] Friendship has three forms corresponding to the three objects of love. For each object of love has a corresponding type of mutual loving, combined with awareness of it, and those who love each other wish good things to each other insofar as they love each other. (1156^{a}7–10)

People who love each other because of the good are virtue friends or character friends (1164^{a}12, 1165^{b}8–9); people who love each other because of pleasure are pleasure friends; people who love each other because of utility are utility friends.

Virtue friends, who wish good things to one another and exchange it, exhibit complete friendship:

[B] Complete friendship is the friendship of good people similar in virtue. For they wish good things to one another in the same way, that is insofar as they are good, and they are good by themselves. And those who wish good things to their friend for the friend's own sake are most of all friends. For they have this attitude because of the friend himself, not coincidentally. Hence these people's friendship lasts as long as they are good—and virtue is something that endures. (1156^{b}7–12).

Pleasure or utility friends, by contrast, are not friends for their friend's own sake:

[C] Those who love for utility or pleasure are fond of a friend because of what is good or pleasant for themselves, not insofar as the beloved is who he is, but insofar as he is useful or pleasant. (1156^{a}14–16)[50]

The contrast drawn in (B) and (C) is puzzling. For the three types of friendship are structural analogues of one another. How is it, then, that virtue friends wish good things to their friend 'for the friend's own sake' while the two other types of friends fail to do so?

(A), (B), and (C) refer to wishing good things to someone 'in so far as' he is good, pleasant, or useful. What does it mean? A natural thought is this. If X loves Y because of his goodness (pleasure, utility), he wishes good things to Y insofar as Y is something good (pleasant, useful). Thus utility friendships break up when the partners are no longer useful; pleasure friendships break up when the partners no longer please each other; and virtue friendships

---

[50] See 1164^{a}20–2, 1167^{a}14–18.

break up if either partner becomes vicious (1157ª3–16, 1165ª36–ᵇ36). Is this Aristotle's thought?

The following passage claims that friends want themselves and their friends to remain human beings capable of giving and receiving good things: 'If, then, we have been right to say that one friend wishes good things to the other for the sake of the other himself, the other [and the friend himself⁵¹] must remain whatever sort of being he is. Hence it is to the other as a human being that a friend will wish the greatest of goods' (1159ª8–11). But utility friends, pleasure friends, and virtue friends have different conceptions of what a human being is: 'Whatever someone regards as his being, or the end for which he chooses to live, that is what he wishes to pursue with his friend' (1172ª1–3; see *Rh.* 1381ª9–10). Thus utility friends conceive of themselves and their friends as profit seekers; pleasure friends conceive of themselves and their friends as pleasure seekers; virtue friends conceive of themselves and their friends as seekers of virtuous activity (1164ª20–2). But utility friends and pleasure friends are wrong about what the human essence, end, or function is. Hence they do not love someone 'for who he is' or 'for the friend's own sake'. For they are wrong about what their friends are and wrong about their ends or sakes. Virtue friends, on the other hand, are right about these things. For the human essence, end, or function is virtuous activity. Hence virtue friends do love someone for what he is and for his own sake. For to love someone for his own sake is to love him for the sake of what he really is or is most of all; and that is his function, essence, or end.

The failure of pleasure and utility friends to love for the sake of their friends leads Aristotle to claim that such friends 'were never friends to each but to what was expedient for themselves' (1157ª15–16). He concludes that pleasure and utility friends are 'friends coincidentally and by being similar to virtue friends' (1157ᵇ4–5).

Pleasure and utility friends are out for their own pleasure or for what is useful to themselves, then, and only coincidentally pursue the pleasure or utility of their partners as a means to their own pleasure or utility. It follows that pleasure and utility friends are selfish. But what about virtue friends? Are they selfish?

---

⁵¹ See 1166ª20–3, 1168ᵇ5–6, and below.

'All the features of friendship', Aristotle claims, 'extend from oneself to others' (1168^{b}5–6), since they are exemplified most of all in one's relations to oneself:

It is said that we must love most of all the friend who is most of all a friend. One person is most of all a friend to another if he wishes good things to the other for the other's sake, even if no one will know about it. But these are features most of all of one's relations to oneself. And so are all the other features that define what a friend is. (1168^{b}1–5)

It follows—and that it does is important for many of Aristotle's subsequent arguments—that the virtuous person is not an *egoist about value*. What he values is virtuous activity not (or not primarily) that the virtuous activity is his own. If this were not so, our friendship for others could not be an extension of our friendship for ourselves. But the virtuous person is an *egoist about desire*.[52] For he 'awards himself what is finest and best of all' (1168^{b}30–1) and 'wishes good things most of all to himself' (1159^{a}12).[53] Moreover, this is what he ought to do—the virtuous person 'should love himself most of all' (1168^{b}10). For he does everything for the sake of his *nous* (1166^{a}16–17), and *nous* (or primary *eudaimonia*) is the most valuable and lovable thing. It seems to follow that, far from being less selfish than pleasure or utility friends, virtue friends are more, or more successfully selfish, than either of them.

However, this is not the whole story. For Aristotle also contrasts virtuous people and vicious ones with respect to their selfishness in a way that suggests that the former are not selfish at all:

vicious person does seem to go to every length for his own sake, and all the more the more vicious he is—hence, he is accused of doing nothing away from himself (*aph' heautou*).[54] The decent person, on the contrary, acts for

---

[52] Egoism about value says: 'What makes X valuable is that I want it'. Egoism about desire says: 'Get valuable things most of all for yourself'. Egoism about value is always threatened with undercutting itself since it cannot explain what is valuable about wanting or having what is not itself valuable by any standard other than simply being wanted. See Nozick (1989, 151–61). The somewhat stark statement that Aristotle is not an egoist about value will be qualified, though not retracted, below.

[53] See 1168^{b}28–9, 1169^{a}17.

[54] Irwin (1985*b*, 253), following Burnet (1900, 421), translates: 'he is accused e.g. of doing nothing of his own accord'. The pre-Burnet translation, which I have adopted, is more readily intelligible. See Engberg-Pedersen (1983, 38).

what is fine, all the more the better he is, and for the sake of his friend, disregarding his own interests (*to d' autou pariēsin*). (1168ᵃ30–5)

This results in a manifest *aporia*, but it is one that Aristotle is fully aware of, and that he attempts to solve—as he attempts to solve all *aporiai*—by refining the notion that causes the problem. There are, he argues, two kinds of selfishness: *bad-selfishness* and *good-selfishness*, as we may call them. If someone is bad-selfish, he awards himself the biggest share of the goods of competition— money, honours, and bodily pleasures—and gratifies his feelings or the non-rational part of his psyche (1168ᵇ15–22). If someone is good-selfish, he 'gratifies the most controlling part of himself, obeying it in everything' (1168ᵇ30–1).

Because the non-virtuous (incorrectly) identify themselves with their non-rational part, while the virtuous (correctly) identify themselves with their rational part, most of all with their *nous*, both good- and bad-selfishness are forms of selfishness. But good-selfishness is yet good and bad-selfishness bad. For bad-selfish people will fight with each other for external goods, thereby destroying the polis and harming everyone. Good-selfishness, on the other hand, actually benefits everyone: 'when everyone strives (*hamillōmenon*)⁵⁵ to achieve what is fine and strains to do the finest actions, everything will be as it should in the community and each person individually will receive the greatest goods, if indeed virtue is such' (1169ᵃ8–11; see 1162ᵇ6–13). Part of the reason for Aristotle's confidence on this front is clear from §30. If everyone does exhibit the virtues of character (or if the rulers exhibit them and their subjects the natural virtues), external goods will be distributed justly and fairly and the desires for them will be stably satisfied in the long-term. But his confidence that the virtuous competitors will themselves receive the greatest goods seems itself to give rise to an *aporia*.

If X and Y are both good-selfish, they will not compete over external goods, but they will strive—and strive good-selfishly—to do fine actions. X will allow Y to have a larger share of external goods because in doing so he gets a larger share of what is fine (1169ᵃ25–9). Sometimes he will even allow Y to do the fine action

---

⁵⁵ *Hamillaomai* should be contrasted with *perimachomai*, which Aristotle uses to characterize the goods of competition. The latter, which literally means 'to fight all around one', suggests very intense rivalry. The former can mean 'to strive without the idea of rivalry'. See Liddell, Scott, and Jones (1966) s. vv.

since this is even finer than doing the action himself (1169ª32–ᵇ1). It seems to follow that if both X and Y are good-selfish, they cannot both receive the finest goods as Aristotle claims they must.⁵⁶

This *aporia* has some charm, but its charm is superficial. If X and Y are unequal in virtue, the less virtuous person must love the more virtuous person more than he is loved, so that the more virtuous person gets the finer of the available goods (1158ᵇ23–8). For virtuous people, not being egoists about value, love really valuable things in proportion to their value. If X and Y are equal in virtue, however, they should each benefit equally (1158ᵇ29–1159ª3). And they do. If X allows Y to do the fine action, he too does something fine, but both X and Y know that Y's action is possible only because X allows, and both know that X's allowing is possible only because Y, by acting, allows Y to allow, and so on.⁵⁷ The reiteration of allowing that has appeared on the scene is the mark of 'reciprocal choice (*antiprohairesis*)' (*EE* 1236ᵇ3) or co-operation, which is itself the mark of the very best kind of friendship. Thus the *aporia* is revealed as empty. For equally virtuous friends both achieve the finest things by striving for them.

A second *aporia* concerning virtue friendship is more difficult:

There is also a dispute about whether a *eudaimōn* person needs friends or not. For it is said that the blessed and self-sufficient have no need of friends since they already have the (external) goods, and, hence, being self-sufficient, need nothing added. But a friend, being another yourself, cannot supply anything you yourself cannot.⁵⁸ Hence, it is said, 'when the god gives well, what need is there of friends'. However, in awarding the *eudaimōn* person all the goods it would seem absurd not to give him friends. For having friends seems to be the greatest external good. (1169ᵇ3–10)

On the one hand, we have as a Socratic *endoxon* that *eudaimōn* people cannot be friends, because they already have all the good things they need or want.⁵⁹ On the other, we have as an *endoxon* backed by experience that friends are the greatest external good.

⁵⁶ See Price (1989, 112–3) who infers, unjustifiedly, that good-selfishness is 'radically faulty'.
⁵⁷ Someone who refuses ever to be benefited, who always wants to be allowed to be the benefactor, is *aēdēs*, disagreeable or unpleasant (1171ᵇ25–7).
⁵⁸ *ton de philon, heteron auton onta, porizein ha di' hautou adunatei.* Irwin (1985b, 257) and Ross (1980, 238) suggest that what Aristotle is saying is that a friend, being another self, supplies what you cannot. But this derails his train of thought.
⁵⁹ 'Socratic' because raised by Socrates in the *Lysis* (214b5–215a1): 'Is there

Aristotle first deals with the latter *endoxon* providing two reasons to accept it. The *eudaimōn* person will need friends to be virtuous towards (1169^{b}10–16) and, being naturally political, he has desires that only friends can satisfy (1169^{b}16–22). Aristotle concludes that 'the *eudaimōn* person must have friends' (1169^{b}21; see 1155^{a}4–5). But before this conclusion can be taken as established the truth in the opposing *phainomena* must—as in all good dialectical clarifications—be shown to be compatible with it. Hence Aristotle asks: 'what are the other side saying and in what way is it true?' (1169^{b}22–3).

The *eudaimōn* person does not need utility friends and has little need for pleasure friends. This supports the Socratic *endoxon* (1169^{b}23–8). Yet he still does need virtue friends. But why does he need them? What good can they possibly do him? Aristotle gives three different arguments by way of explanation. The first is this:

[A] We said at the beginning that *eudaimonia* is a kind of activity, and clearly activity comes into being and does not belong in the way that a possession does. Being *eudaimōn* is found, then, in living and being active. The activity of a good person is excellent and pleasant in itself, as we said at the beginning. Moreover, what is our own is pleasant. [B] We are able to study (*theōrein*) our neighbours more than ourselves and their actions more than our own. [C] Hence a good person finds pleasure in the actions of excellent people who are his friends, since these actions have both the things that make them naturally pleasant. [D] Therefore, the blessed person will need good friends, since (*eiper*) he decides to study virtuous actions that are his own, for the actions of a virtuous friend are such. (1169^{b}30–1170^{a}4)[60]

(B) is controversial, but we might simply accept it as having a fair

anything that two things that are alike can do for one another that each cannot do for himself?' But since it is found in Euripides (*Orestes*, 667), which Aristotle cites, and is later supported by appeal to the views of the many (1169^{b}23–4), we need not suppose that its provenance is exclusively Socratic.

[60] Both this argument and its longer partner at 1170^{a}13–^{b}19 assume that the *eudaimōn* person has friends. But neither is open, I believe, to the criticism levelled against the latter by Cooper (1980, 318–19) of failing to explain 'the value to a person of *having* friends'. Aristotle assumes that the *eudaimōn* person will have friends in order to prove that he *needs* them. Since having is not the same as needing, no circularity is involved. But even the assumption that the *eudaimōn* person will have friends is surely shorthand for a counterfactual assumption that we might express as follows: if the *eudaimōn* person were to have friends, he would find pleasure in their company. If this counterfactual is true of the *eudaimōn* person, the remainder of Aristotle's argument will show—if it is sound—that he needs friends whether or not he has them.

amount of intuitive plausibility.[61] For if it is even slightly easier to study a friend's actions than one's own, say because 'most people are bad judges of their own' (*Pol.* 1280^a15–16), that should be sufficient for Aristotle's purposes, since a virtuous person will then be slightly benefited by having virtue friends.

But this supposes, as (D) asserts, that the *eudaimōn* person does decide to study virtuous actions that are his own, and one might wonder why he decides to do that. Perhaps the most obvious answer is the most plausible. He chooses to study virtuous actions so as to understand better how to produce them: 'Those such as Pericles are the ones we regard as having *phronēsis*, because they are able to study (*theōrein*) what's good for themselves and for people in general' (1140^b8–10). He chooses, more particularly, to study those virtuous actions that are his own because, as (C) tells us, they have in addition both of the features that make them naturally pleasant to study.

(C) is clearly the crux of the argument, yet it is difficult even to understand. How can the virtuous actions of *another* have both of the features that make actions naturally pleasant to study, if one of those features is—as (A) and (D) both tell us—that the actions are *one's own*? A few distinctions will help us to explore Aristotle's answer. Let us say that an action Ø is *weakly* X's own if it is a token of a type of action that X himself would do or would have done. Ø is *strongly* X's own if he is partly or wholly responsible for Ø. Is (A)–(D) about weak ownership or strong ownership?

If it is about weak ownership, we might try to reconstruct it as follows. A virtuous person loves his own virtuous actions for their own sake. Since he is not an egoist about value, it follows that he must love the virtuous actions of his virtue friends for their own sake. Since his friends are virtuous, their actions are of the sort that he himself would do. Therefore, his friends' actions are naturally pleasant for him to study. For they have the features that make his own activities naturally pleasant, namely, they are valuable and they are weakly his own.

The problem with this argument is patent. The notion of weak ownership adds absolutely nothing to it. For it is simply another way of saying that the actions of a virtuous friend are of a certain sort, namely, the virtuous sort. This conflicts with the strong impression the argument gives that someone loves the actions of his virtue friend because they are his own and not simply because they are virtuous (see 1166ª30–2 and below). Weak ownership seems too weak, then, for Aristotle's purposes. So let us turn to strong ownership. Strong ownership seems paradoxical, but we have already seen a way to lessen the paradox in the case of at least some actions, namely, those which exhibit reciprocity or reciprocal choice. For the friend who acts and the friend who allows him to act might each reasonably claim to be partly responsible for such actions. Since many of the actions of friends who are striving with one another to be virtuous are going to be reciprocal in this way, friends can legitimately claim strong ownership of many of the actions of their friends.

It seems clear, however, that Aristotle is not restricting himself to such actions when he says that a virtuous person owns the actions of his virtue friends. He seems rather to be saying that he owns *any* of their actions. Can this more general sort of ownership be strong ownership? To answer this question we need to try to make sense of Aristotle's puzzling claim that 'the decent person . . . is related to his friend as he is to himself, since the friend is another self' (1166ª30–2).[62]

Aristotle claims that 'loving is like production' (1168ª19), and that the things a person helps produce are his second, but separate, selves: 'A parent loves his children as himself. For what has come from him is a sort of other himself—a separate one (*kechōristhai*)' (1161b27–9); 'a friend wishes to be a sort of separate (*diairetos*) self' (*EE* 1245ª34–5).[63] Moreover, he clearly thinks that a virtuous person produces his virtue friends by sustaining and increasing their virtue:

> The friendship of decent people is decent, and increases the more often they meet. And they seem to become still better from their activities and their mutual correction. For each moulds the other in what they approve of. Hence the saying 'noble deeds from noble people'. (1172ª10–14)[64]

This strongly suggests that a virtue friend is someone's second self simply because the latter has helped make him the virtuous person that he is.[65] On the assumption that production is transitive, we can

---

[62] See *NE* 1168b7, 1170b6–7; *EE* 1245ª30–5, 1240b3.
[63] See *DA* 415ª26–b7; *NE* 1120b13, 1168ª6–9; §§22, 26.
[64] See 1170ª4–13, 1180ª31–2.
[65] This idea is discussed in Millgram (1987), to which I am indebted here.

now explain how *all* the actions of X's virtue friends are actions that he is partly responsible for and so strongly owns.

The notions of a friend being a second self, and of his actions being those of his friend, do have some genuine content, then, content that helps explain, at least to some extent, why a virtuous person enjoys studying the actions of his virtue friends, and why he is therefore benefited by having such friends. But this explanation works only because virtuous people are not strict egoists about value. For a person's second selves are not identical to him and their actions are not his in exactly the way that his own actions are. None the less, one might say that Aristotle is sailing as close as possible to value egoism. For he does seem to suppose that the reason someone values his virtue friends and finds their actions pleasant to study is, at least in part, that he sees them both as to some degree his own products.

Aristotle's second argument on the benefits to the *eudaimōn* person of having virtue friends is briefer and more straightforward. It runs as follows:

It is thought that the *eudaimōn* person must live pleasantly. But the solitary person's life is hard, since it is not easy for him to be continuously active by himself. With others and in relation to them, however, it is easier and hence his activity will be more continuous . . . Further, good people's life together allows a sort of cultivation of virtue, as Theognis says. (1170ª4–13).

Alone, one will constantly have to interrupt virtuous activity in order to acquire necessary external goods. Moreover, the vast majority of the virtues of character can be activated only together with other people (1177ª28–32), and even study, the most self-sufficient activity, is done 'better with co-workers' (1177ª34). The virtues are brought about and maintained by virtuous activity (1104ª18–27), so that striving with other virtuous people—whose 'thought is well supplied with topics for study, (1166ª26–7)— whether in philosophical argument (1172ª5) or in practical activities, encourages the kind of ethical creativity and imagination that is difficult for the solitary to match. Hence virtue friends confer genuine benefits even on someone who is already virtuous and *eudaimōn*.

Aristotle's final argument (1170ª13–ᵇ19) relies essentially on the same ideas as the first. He begins by arguing that 'living is choiceworthy to a good person most of all, since being is good and pleasant for him' (1170^{b}3–4). Then he draws on the view that a friend is a second self to establish that 'the excellent person is related to his friend in the same way as he is related to himself' (1170^{b}5–7). He concludes that 'his friend's being is choiceworthy for him in the same or a similar way' to his own (1170^{b}7–8). But because of the conceptual connection between *eudaimonia* and the choiceworthiness of lives, it follows that 'whatever is choiceworthy for a *eudaimōn* person he must possess, since otherwise he will to that extent lack something' (1170^{b}17–18). Aristotle concludes that a completely *eudaimōn* person 'must have excellent friends' (1170^{b}18–19).

These three arguments do help us to see, I think, how completely *eudaimōn* people can still benefit one another; they help explain why such people need one another in order to be completely *eudaimōn*. But it is important not to be lulled by them into ignoring either their two predecessors (1169^{b}10–21) or the role that virtue friendships with less than completely virtuous people play in getting a person into the condition in which he is completely *eudaimōn*, and in sustaining him in that condition from then on. To satisfy his needs for external goods, a man who is going to be completely *eudaimōn*—and I use the term 'man' advisedly—needs to be virtue friends with the naturally virtuous craftsmen who manufacture many of those goods. To satisfy his natural human need for family life, sexual love, and children, he must find a virtuous woman with whom to be friends—though her virtue, too, since she is incapable of full-blown *phronēsis*, will be inferior to his (1161^{b}11–1162^{a}33, *Pol.* 1260^{a}13).[66] When he becomes fully *eudaimōn* he no longer needs to get these things because he already has them and has arranged for them to be reliably supplied, but even when fully *eudaimōn*, he still needs fully virtuous friends to appreciate more easily how *eudaimōn* he himself is, to enable him to be more continuously active, to maintain and increase his virtue, and to enjoy for themselves.

32 PRACTICAL ACTIVITY

To have a *eudaimōn* life we need *eudaimonia* (primary and secondary) and external goods, the latter consisting of external

---

[66] For fuller discussion see Price (1989, 162–78) and Sherman (1989, 144–56).

goods of competition and virtuous friends of various kinds. And the reason we need all these things is that our nature is complex. We have wishes, emotions, and appetites, all of which need to be satisfied. The problem facing *phronēsis*, then, since it is good-selfish, is to arrange for some sort of distribution of *eudaimonia* and external goods in our lives. But what sort of distribution? Aristotle seems to impose just three conditions on it. (1) The distribution of external goods and secondary *eudaimonia* must be for the sake of primary *eudaimonia* (§28). (2) That distribution must be a more efficient means to primary *eudaimonia* than any of the available alternatives (§§11–18). (3) Primary *eudaimonia* must be possessed or engaged in 'not for just any chance period of time but for a complete life' ($1101^a15–16$). And if the resulting distribution of external goods and *eudaimonia* satisfy these three conditions, then, on Aristotle's view, they make the entire life *eudaimōn*, or choiceworthy and lacking in nothing. Now none of these conditions is a maximizing or optimizing condition; none tells us that the distribution of secondary *eudaimonia* and external goods arranged by *phronēsis* must serve to maximize the amount of primary *eudaimonia* (or time spent studying) in a life. And indeed there is no clear evidence that Aristotle ever entertained such a condition. He does indeed say that 'the more someone studies, the more *eudaimōn* he is' (1178b29–30), but he nowhere suggests that *phronēsis* will have failed in its own terms if it fails to provide a life with the most study possible. It follows that lives with unequal amounts of primary *eudaimonia* in them can all be choiceworthy and lacking in nothing, and that *phronēsis* will have done its work adequately if it provides enough primary *eudaimonia* to make a whole life possess this feature, even if by making other decisions it could have made it more *eudaimōn*. It seems, then, that unlike most thinkers about practical reason, Aristotle is not a maximizer or an optimizer. In his view, enough is as lacking in nothing as a feast.[67]

We cannot determine the success or failure of *phronēsis* in a life, then, by looking at the sheer amount of primary *eudaimonia* it contains. But it is also seems true that concealed in the notion of 'enough' there is a reference to distribution as well as to quantity. For it seems that two lives could contain the same amount of primary *eudaimonia* without both containing enough of it, in the

[67] Slote (1989) is an interesting recent defence of a similar view.

relevant sense. After all, a life in which all the primary *eudaimonia* occurred early and that ended like Priam's would hardly be as choiceworthy and lacking in nothing, it seems, as one in which the same amount of primary *eudaimonia* was distributed throughout the adult years. It follows that *phronēsis* must pay attention to distribution as well as quantity, if it is to succeed. But distribution, like quantity, is fixed by nothing more precise than the requirement that the overall life should be choiceworthy and lacking in nothing.

Because *phronēsis* looks to make a whole life choiceworthy, it aims, like politics, 'not at some advantage close at hand, but at advantage for the whole of life' (1160ª21–3). Hence it seems to be a kind of rational prudence. But if it is, how are we to explain the fact, dramatically illustrated by the following passage, that the *phronimos* is willing to act in ways that seem to amount to abandoning long-term advantage altogether?

The excellent person labours for his friends and for his native country and will die for them if he must; he will sacrifice money, honours, and goods of competition in general, to achieve what is fine for himself. For he will choose intense pleasure for a short time over mild pleasure for a long time; a year of living finely over many years of undistinguished life; and a single fine and great action over many small actions. (1169ª18–25)

To answer this question, we need to reflect on the role of character and virtue in life. Whatever one does, one ends up with a character of some sort. *Phronēsis* (initially in the person of one's elders and betters) tries to ensure that it will be of the best sort, the sort that will, for the most part, result in actions that promote its own aims. On the strength of the argument outlined in §§26–31, Aristotle is persuaded that the best character to have, the one that will best promote the aims of *phronēsis*, is a virtuous one. But the virtues of character, once possessed, exert their influence on action, influence that is not open to renegotiation in a particular case. Hence if, in the particular circumstances with which luck presents him, virtue requires a *phronimos* to sacrifice his life for his friend or country, he will. If it requires him to choose between a short fine life and a long mediocre one, he will choose the former. Since luck can be controlled by craft but cannot be eliminated, the result is that the character that it is for the most part best to have may send one to an early grave. But that proves only that 'a good man's fortune may grow out at heels',[68] it does not prove that there is anything wrong with his character or that *phronēsis* is not rational prudence. For rational prudence can do no better than non-negotiable luck allows. To demand that it always achieve its goal is simply to forget that we are enmattered human beings not gods (see 1100^b14-21).

That is one problem solved, but there is another more insistent variant of it to which, as we shall see, the solution is more or less the same. This problem emerges from a very natural line of thought. If a life must have enough study in it to be choiceworthy and lacking in nothing, and you see that yours will not have enough in it unless you do this vicious action, should you not do it? Now, if you are a *phronimos*, you will not do it; that is certain. For a *phronimos* has the virtues of character and it is out of these he will act. Hence the question really comes down to this: If your aim in life is as Aristotle describes it, should you be a *phronimos*? If you are persuaded by the argument of §§26–31, you will answer, yes. If you are not, then at least you will know where your attack on Aristotle is to be appropriately directed.

We now know what the goal is at which *phronēsis* aims. But what does it actually do to achieve its goal? How does it arrange for external goods and primary *eudaimonia* to be so distributed in a life that the whole life is choiceworthy and lacking in nothing? *Phronēsis* is practical not directly productive, but since it is the same state as politics, it is an architectonic virtue, able to control the capacities, crafts, and sciences so that they optimally contribute to primary *eudaimonia*. The nature of that control is clear in the case of politics, since it is interpersonal, but interpersonal control does have an obvious intrapersonal analogue.

A person who possesses *phronēsis* also possesses other capacities, and typically other skills and sciences as well. He may, for example, be a doctor whose medical knowledge enables him to cure people including, in many instances, himself or his friends. What his medical knowledge does not tell him, however, is how best to use itself in order to ensure his own *eudaimonia*, but *phronēsis* tells him precisely that. Now, it says, is the time to use your medical skill to cure, now is the time to use it to ensure a painless and dignified death. In the same way, *phronēsis* controls a capacity, however humdrum, ensuring that it is exercised in a way that optimally

---

[68] Shakespeare, *King Lear*, II. ii. 160.

promotes *eudaimonia*. In the same way, it controls study itself, albeit for study's own sake, saying, for example, that study must now be curtailed to ensure a better distribution of more of it throughout life as a whole.[69] Because *phronēsis* is an architectonic virtue of this sort, human actions typically have a complex structure. A doctor's medical skill is expressed in productions, but if that skill is also controlled by *phronēsis*, those productions—whether or not they are successful —involve an activation of *phronēsis* that is a *praxis* or canonical action. And that *praxis* is valuable or desirable independent of the value that attaches to the product of the underlying craft. If the craft is both successful and expresses *phronēsis*, *phronēsis* will achieve one of its *para* ends, namely, the leisured activity of study. But if it fails, or if *phronēsis* fails in its control through bad luck or through the inexactness that plagues perception of enmattered particulars, *phronēsis* will still achieve its other *para* end, namely, activity expressing the virtues of character, or secondary *eudaimonia*. Thus someone who possesses *phronēsis* will be to some degree *eudaimōn* even if he fails to achieve primary *eudaimonia*.[70]

But surely *phronēsis* will often fail to achieve its *para* end of primary *eudaimonia* unless it actually becomes politics, unless those who possess *phronēsis* come to rule a polis. We can see this by looking for a moment at what politics would typically have to accomplish in order best to achieve its goals.

It would have to arrange for a sufficient supply of external goods of competition by controlling the productive crafts. But it is not enough to ensure that external goods are supplied today, politics must also ensure that they will continue to be supplied tomorrow. Hence it will have to ensure, for example, that there are craft schools to educate craftsmen of the future.

And it will not do to ensure the production of such goods, if they are literally competed for. Hence politics must ensure that people do not compete. And there is only one reasonably stable way to do

---

[69] The idea that virtue is an *epistēmē epistēmōn*, 'a science of [how to use] sciences', is already being explored in the *Charmides*. In the *Euthydemus*, this superordinate science is identified with politics. See Reeve (1989, 124–44).
[70] This paragraph addresses the problem raised by Charles (1986, 140–4) of whether Aristotle's claim that a *praxis* is present in every moral action is a substantial thesis or a trivial one. It should be clear now that it is a substantial thesis based on a view about the crafts and capacities and on an analysis of *phronēsis* as an architectonic virtue that controls them so as to optimally promote *eudaimonia*.

this. It must ensure that people acquire either the natural virtues of character or the full virtues if they are able, and that the laws, courts, and judges are just. But it will not do to ensure that the present generation will be virtuous if the next generation will not, so politics must provide for the ethical education, through habituation, of future generations just as it provided for the production of future producers.

These virtuous citizens are not needed simply as a means to political tranquillity and lack of open warfare over external goods, however, they are also needed as friends and marriage partners. For the best and most stable kinds of friendships are those between virtuous people who desire the good for each other for the other's own sake. Hence the most stable polis will be one whose citizens are as far as possible bound together by such friendships.

Moreover, the productive crafts are not the only ones that politics will need to achieve its goals. It will also need the military sciences, to guarantee peace and stability in an uncertain world, and the theoretical sciences, both for their own sake as objects of study, and because of their beneficial spin-offs. And to ensure their continued existence it will need to organize military academies and universities. Moreover, it will have to regulate and oversee all of these lest they drift away from their end or purpose of benefiting everyone throughout life.

If politics does all that, it will have best satisfied the needs of all the members of the polis including those of the rulers themselves. And, so far as knowledge can, it will have made human *eudaimonia* minimally dependent on luck. For it will have organized the crafts and sciences that together reduce as far as possible the control of luck.[71]

Could *phronēsis* that fails to become politics do all that? Obviously, it could not. No individual could possibly master all the crafts and sciences. Even to appear on the scene, indeed, *phronēsis* needs what only a polis can provide, namely, habituation in virtue. *Phronēsis* is thus a political not an individual achievement.[72] That

---

[71] The attitude to luck manifest in this account of politics contrasts sharply with the one attributed to Aristotle in Nussbaum (1986a, 235–394).

[72] It is this fact that enables Aristotle to avoid the 'encyclopaedic conception of virtue and wisdom [*phronēsis*]' raised as a problem by Irwin (1988a, 75–7). *Phronēsis* is not itself encylopaedic. But it needs the other crafts and sciences in the encyclopaedia if it is to accomplish its aim with maximum success. Hence it will optimally achieve its aim only by becoming politics.

is why the *Ethics*, whose focus is on individual *eudaimonia*, none the less begins and ends with a discussion of politics.

33 THE ROLE OF THE *ETHICS* IN THE *EUDAIMŌN* LIFE

The *Ethics*, Aristotle tells us repeatedly, is a practical work, one that contributes to practical knowledge.[73] We can now see what that claim means and why it is true.

The audience to whom the *Ethics* is addressed consists of people who, having habituated virtue, also have reliable *endoxa* about *eudaimonia*. But their *endoxa* conflict with others and so give rise to *aporiai*. The *Ethics* aims to solve those *aporiai* by means of dialectic, bringing to light the truth that the *endoxa* contain, and thereby converting a vague and conflict-ridden grasp of *eudaimonia* into clear-sighted *nous* of what it is. The *Ethics* thus provides to those with habituated virtue precisely what they need in order to be fully virtuous and to possess *phronēsis*. It gives them a clear target to aim at and so makes them 'more likely to hit the right mark' (1094ᵃ24).

But the credibility of the *Ethics* on the identity of the right mark ultimately depends at least to some degree on experience. Hence the *Ethics* is unlikely to convince those who have had no taste of study or who, having tasted it, find it unpleasant or boring or empty. It is of no small significance, therefore, that Aristotle refers to himself and his audience as 'philosophers' (1096ᵃ15–16). For philosophers have both tasted study and found it to their liking. What gives their taste authority, what simultaneously privileges and legitimates it, however, is the fact that it is underwritten by science and dialectic in a way that the conflicting tastes of the many and the politicians are not.

---

[73] See 1095ᵃ5–6, 1099ᵇ29–32, 1103ᵇ27–9, 1179ᵃ34–ᵇ31; §3.

CONCLUSION

THE previous chapters have been largely silent on the philosophical merits of Aristotle's arguments, in the belief that analysis should precede criticism. But in these concluding remarks, I want to say something about how, possessed now of a unified account of the foundations of the *Ethics*, we ought to assess them and the work that Aristotle has built on them. Has the *Ethics* anything to teach us? And if so, what are its most important lessons?

Aristotle argues, as we have seen, that *nous* is related to *phronēsis* in two ways. First, it provides *phronēsis* with knowledge of universals of the sort that he believes it must have if is to achieve *eudaimonia* as reliably as possible. Second, the activity of *nous* is itself primary *eudaimonia* or the ultimate end at which *phronēsis* aims. Both of these conclusions are clearly controversial, albeit to quite different degrees.

It might be thought, for example, that *phronēsis*, as a kind of practical knowledge, is radically independent of theoretical scientific-knowledge. For it might be thought that many people possess the former without possessing the latter. The great moral teachers—Socrates, Christ, and Buddha—have hardly been men of science; Tolstoy's peasants, for all their apparent practical wisdom, scarcely knew what science was.

There is clearly some merit in this thought—but it takes some refining. Let us first distinguish, as we have often had cause to do in other cases before, between nascent *phronēsis* and *phronēsis* proper. *Phronēsis* proper, being the same state as politics, sits astride all of the completed crafts and sciences, and makes its judgements about what to do armed, in the ideal case at least, with the human equivalent of omniscience. Nascent *phronēsis* makes the best use of available crafts and sciences where these are pertinent to the practical problem it is trying to solve.

Now, in a given historical situation, it may well be that no crafts or sciences are pertinent in this way. And if that is so, someone obviously can exhibit nascent *phronēsis* in that situation without possessing any craft-knowledge or scientific-knowledge.[1] That's an obvious point, I suppose, but it is worth making, because it reveals the contextual, historical nature of nascent *phronēsis*, something that focus on *phronēsis* proper tends to occlude. Consequently, we might agree that *phronēsis* draws on crafts and sciences without having to accept that anyone who lacks scientific-knowledge (or lacks access to it) cannot be practically wise.

It may be, too, though this is itself a controversial matter, that there are some practical questions to which no craft or science is ever relevant. Here are some putative examples: How does god want us to live? What does morality require of us? What is right and what wrong? Since these seem like fundamental moral questions, we might plausibly claim, that *phronēsis*, insofar as it is a *moral* virtue, really is entirely independent of science. Morality, as we might suppose, has to be available to all rational beings however limited their intellectual abilities.

No simple answer is available to this criticism of Aristotle's views. For, just as when we were considering the function argument, we are once again embroiled in the dispute about realism and naturalism in ethics. Since no resolution of this dispute is in sight, we can only conclude that Aristotle's conception of *phronēsis* is indeed a controversial one.

But if we back away from this dispute for a moment and suppose it resolved along naturalistic lines, and if we distinguish between the nascent and proper varieties of *phronēsis*, then it seems to me that Aristotle's conception of the first kind of relation between *phronēsis* and *nous* is a compelling one. Practical knowledge needs theoretical knowledge if it is reliably to achieve its goal of making life go as well as possible. This does not mean, as we saw in §32, that in order to possess *phronēsis* someone must himself have mastered all of the crafts and sciences, it means only that he must have reliable access to their findings. This is one reason that makes Aristotle represent *phronēsis*—rightly in my view—as an ineliminably political achievement. (Another is that *phronēsis* is itself the result of acculturation and the preservation and transmission of experience.)

---

[1] It is also true, of course, that some scientific-knowledge might be relevant in the situation, but it would take too long to discover whether or not that this is so. Or it might be that the relevant knowledge is available to the *phronimos*, but it would take too long for him to apply it.

Let us turn now to the second of the two relationships that, on Aristotle's view, holds between *phronēsis* and *nous*, namely, that—to be precise about it—the activation of *phronēsis* is for the sake of study or the activation of *nous* expressing wisdom. Since this relationship is mediated by the claim that study is primary *eudaimonia*, we may begin there.

One criticism can be got out of the way at once. It is this. Aristotle's conception of *eudaimonia* is too exclusive to be credible. And the reason it can be dismissed is that it confuses *eudaimonia*, which consists both of primary and secondary *eudaimonia*, with primary *eudaimonia* alone. The latter is an exclusive end, but *eudaimonia* itself is not. And what is true of *eudaimonia* is even more true of the *eudaimōn* life. For it consists of primary *eudaimonia*, secondary *eudaimonia*, and external goods, so arranged that the latter two are for the sake of the former. Thus the *eudaimōn* life, if not *eudaimonia* itself, is a structured inclusive end, consisting of primary *eudaimonia* and all the intrinsically valuable or desirable things—all the things that are desirable by or because of themselves—that promote it. It is therefore in many ways the sort of end that a lot of contemporary philosophers take happiness to be. For they, too, believe that happiness is some kind of inclusive end composed of intrinsic goods.

But despite its superficial similarity to these sorts of accounts of happiness, Aristotle's conception of the *eudaimōn* life has three features that make it problematically different from them. (1) Primary *eudaimonia* is not an end that we choose, but one that is fixed by our nature, by what we are. (2) Intrinsic goods, other than primary *eudaimonia*, are choiceworthy in part because of their relation to it and not just because they are intrinsically valuable. (3) Primary *eudaimonia* is study.

Currently dominant economic models of rational choice conceive of rationality as applicable only to means, not to ends. We are rational, on these models, if we take the best or most efficient means to our ends, whatever those ends happen to be, but our ends themselves are beyond rational appraisal. ''Tis not contrary to reason', as Hume famously put it, 'to prefer the destruction of the whole world to the scratching of my little finger.'[2] On the interpretation that I have defended, *phronēsis* has something in

---

[2] Hume (1739, 416).

common with these models of practical rationality. It, too, fails to apply to our ultimate end. This is bound to disappoint the growing number of philosophers who look to Aristotle for a conception of practical reason that might be used to correct these economic models precisely by giving us an account of rational deliberation about ends.[3] This is one reason that (1) is problematical. Such philosophers might, however, be heartened by the fact that dialectic seems to offer us a way of assessing even ultimate ends and getting clearer about them. Aristotle refuses to consider such dialectical clarification as a form of deliberation or as relevant to choice, at least where *eudaimonia* is concerned. But we might wonder whether, if (2) were out of the picture, this would amount to any more than a terminological decision that we might abandon with impunity (see *Top.* 104^{b}1–2).

(1) is also problematical, however, because it seems to presuppose some kind of natural teleology. In §§22–5, I tried to argue that this presupposition is less crude than it is sometimes presented as being by critics because it is the result of a negotiation between our intuitions about *eudaimonia* and our naturalist theory of ourselves. None the less, philosophers who believe that it is a person's desires that determine his ends, so that different people are likely to have very different ends, will not take much comfort from that fact.

(2) is problematical because it gives one good, primary *eudaimonia*, so much power over choice, and this would be a problem regardless of what primary *eudaimonia* turned out to be. For a contemporary philosopher will want to know how it is that one intrinsic good comes to dominate all the others in this way. He will want to know how intrinsic goods are to be ranked. Certainly, Aristotle is not left mute in the face of such a challenge. He can appeal to such formal criteria as completeness and self-sufficiency. He can even appeal to his account of pleasure, which we have not explored in detail, to argue that some intrinsic goods are objectively more pleasant than others. These appeals may help cut some ice against the opposition, but much of their success is likely to depend on the strength of the case that can be made out that something other than the *eudaimōn* life itself, conceived of as an inclusive end, really best satisfies them.

---

[3] See e.g. Wiggins (1975; 1978).

This, obviously enough brings us to (3). It will be illuminating, I think, to approach it somewhat asymptotically, by looking for a moment at the role it plays in Aristotle's politics.

Phronēsis proper is an ideal, one that we are unlikely ever to realize completely. And it is an ideal that, as it were, projects an associated political ideal, namely, a polis in which *phronēsis* rules. Like Plato before him, Aristotle argues that a polis of this sort could not be a participatory democracy, and we can imagine a number of different argumentative routes he might take to that conclusion. The first appeals to the complexity of what the ruler needs to be able to understand in order to rule. The thought here is that the ruler must at least be able to comprehend what scientists and other experts tell him, and that the uneven distribution of raw intelligence makes it impossible for everyone to do this. The second appeals to the uneven distribution of ethical virtue in a society. The thought here is that even with proper upbringing, socialization, and schooling not everyone will have the kind of will and desires that guarantee that they will use available knowledge to promote the *eudaimonia* of the polis as a whole. The third appeals to the nature of primary *eudaimonia*, its connection to *phronēsis*, and to the unequal capacities of people to experience it and to appreciate its true nature.

Of these routes to the conclusion that a polis ruled by *phronēsis* cannot be a participatory democracy, let us focus on the third as most relevant to our present discussion of *eudaimonia*, and because, to some extent at least, it seems to incorporate the other two. Aristotle argues that study is primary *eudaimonia* and that *phronēsis* is what best achieves it. He assumes that even in an ideal society only a few will have the ethical and intellectual virtues necessary either to achieve *phronēsis* or to engage in study. It is probable that he makes this assumption on biological and ultimately on metaphysical grounds: the forms that we see exhibited in the world, which include the forms of people with very different abilities, characters, and interests (moneymakers, politicians, philosophers), are eternal; they always have been present in the world and they always will be.[4] No doubt it is a controversial assumption, the grounds of which are no less so. But its controversiality simply serves to throw (3) into stark relief. For if

---

[4] See *GA* 731^b24–732^a3, 742b17–743^a1; *DA* 415^a25–^b7; Cooper (1987*a*, 246–7).

primary *eudaimonia* were not study, if it were not something so *outré* and exclusive, both it and *phronēsis* might well be accessible to people of very different types, even if those types were somehow eternal and immutable. So at the bottom of Aristotle's conception of the ideal polis lies (3), his conception of primary *eudaimonia* itself.

Now I raise this argument not to argue backwards from the attractiveness of democracy to the unattractiveness of Aristotle's conception of primary *eudaimonia*, although that is not an entirely unappealing stratagem, but in order to raise as vividly as possible the problem of ideology.

Aristotle's argument that study is primary *eudaimonia* has, as we saw, an ineliminable experiential foundation. Only those who have tasted study are likely to be able to determine whether the argument is a success. But the people who have experienced study, and found it to their liking, are philosophers. Hence, as we saw in §33, the *Ethics* is directed primarily to them. But surely, as Aristotle himself admits, people form their conceptions of *eudaimonia* from the lives they lead. And if that is so, then we might see in the philosophers' attestation to the superiority of study to all other intrinsic goods not objective evidence of its superiority, but rather evidence of the power of upbringing and ideology to influence experience.

By returning to politics we can further strengthen this criticism. Imagine for a moment a marginalized intellectual, who has been engaged in philosophy and the intellectual life since his teens, and is almost entirely lacking in political power or influence, sitting down to determine what the best kind of life and the best kind of polis are. Imagine that and you have to a large degree imagined Aristotle in his ethics and politics class in the Lyceum. For Aristotle entered Plato's Academy at the age of 17, stayed there for twenty years, and spent almost his entire adult life either there or in the Lyceum. Moreover, he was a metic—a resident alien—in Athens and was barred from playing an active role in Athenian political life. Since people often recoup in fantasy what they lack in reality, is it any wonder that he and his fellow philosophers 'discovered' that *their* values are the true ones and that an ideal polis would recognize this and make philosophers its rulers?[5]

---

[5] Whitehead (1975) is important in this regard as are Aristotle's own remarks about metics at *EE* 1233^{a}28–30 and *Pol.* 1275^{a}35–38, 1326^{a}18.

This is a crude objection, as I have formulated it, but it is one that surely occurs at some time or other to any reader of the *Ethics* and *Politics*. It is also one to which Aristotle has an answer. For, on his view, it is only if science and dialectic underwrite the philosopher's experience that his experience has any probative force. Of course, this will not satisfy a critic who believes that not even science, let alone dialectic, can escape the stranglehold of ideology. But to the less extreme, it will surely offer some comfort. The net effect of it, however, is that Aristotle's conclusions about primary *eudaimonia* become hostage to history and to advances in science and dialectic. It is a fate shared with all the findings of nascent science and nascent dialectic.

In my view, and it is surely one that will meet with little opposition, science and dialectic have not just taken these Aristotelian conclusions hostage, they have decisively killed them off. No one now believes that everything in the world is trying to become as much like Aristotle's god as possible, or, indeed, that there is such a god for them all to try to become like. No one believes, therefore, that study or the contemplation of that god can possibly be primary *eudaimonia* or what, so to speak, human life is all about. A major doctrine of the *Ethics*—if I am right *the* major doctrine—has therefore been falsified by science and dialectic and become incredible.

But this fact does nothing to detract from the enormous elegance and power of Aristotle's argument; it does nothing to diminish—at least in my experience—the pleasure that the *Ethics* affords a reader. But we do not have to turn from the true to the beautiful in order to defend Aristotle's achievement. We can see this by looking not at the further relations between *phronēsis* and *nous*, but to *phronēsis* itself, to what it accomplishes with what *nous* gives it, and to how it accomplishes it.

There are various ways in which one might go about constructing an account of practical reason. One might, for example, try to come up with a logic of practical reason, like deontic logic or the logic of decision. But this is not what Aristotle does. Instead, he spends his time talking about the psychology of the *phronimos*. What would someone have to be like in order to register things as they are and to care about them and be moved by them proportionately to their true value and importance? Aristotle's answer, spelled out in considerable psychological detail, is that he must have the virtues of character. We ought, I think, to be sympathetic to this sort of answer. A logic of practical reason ought to be a model of a practically wise person, not a formal system. Here, and perhaps elsewhere, the *phronimos* is 'the standard and measure' (1113ᵃ33). So that is one important contribution to live philosophy that the *Ethics* makes, but it is not the only one. Another, and the one on which I shall end, is philosophical method. Dialectic looks like, and has sometimes been compared to, so-called conceptual analysis, but it is really quite different. For dialectic must be sensitive to science and to other empirical disciplines in a way that conceptual analysis often is or was not. And this sensitivity is, I think, a major strength and one that should be taken as canonical. Dialectic is not a directly empirical discipline, but it draws on such disciplines, and so succeeds, where so much other philosophy fails, in remaining in touch with reality, in touch with the world.

APPENDIX
Form and Matter in Aristotle's Embryology

Socrates and Xanthippe have a child, call it Z. Both Socrates and Xanthippe contribute something to Z, but they do not both contribute the same thing. Socrates contributes form but no matter; Xanthippe contributes matter but no form. So much is canonical doctrine throughout the *Generation of Animals*. Here are some representative texts:

The male provides both the form and the source of movement while the female provides the body, i.e. the matter. (729^a9)[1]

The body comes from the female and the soul from the male; and the soul is the substance (*ousia*) of some particular body. (738^b25–7)

The residue [i.e. the seed] of the male provides no matter at all for the foetus that gets formed. (764^b12–13. See 729^b35 ff.)

This doctrine is PRINCIPLE 1 of Aristotle's embryology. PRINCIPLE 2 tells us how the male seed (*sperma*, *gonē*) and the female menses (*katamēnia*) combine to produce Z. It receives its most extensive and helpful statement in the following text:

One may also grasp from these examples how the male contributes to generation. For not every male emits seed, and in those that do emit it the seed is no part of the foetus that is produced, just as nothing comes away from the carpenter to the matter of the timber, nor is there any part of carpentry in the product, but the shape and the form are produced from the carpenter throught the movement in the matter. His soul (in which the form is) and his knowledge [of building] move his hands or some other part in a movement of a particular kind —different when the product is different, the same when it is the same —the hands move the tools and the tools move the matter. Similarly the male's nature, in those that emit seed, uses the seed as a tool containing actual movements, just as in craft productions the tools are in movement; for the movement of the craft is in a way in them. (730^b8–23)

Thus what Socrates' seed does to Xanthippe's menses in order to produce Z is to introduce a certain movement into it; a movement that is transmitted from Socrates' form (essence, soul) into his seed and from his seed into Xanthippe's menses. So the movement in Xanthippe's menses is caused by the movement in Socrates' seed and—initially at least— is qualitatively identical to it. Here is a second text that makes this point unequivocally and explicitly:

---

[1] See 716^a4 ff., 727^a27–8, 727^b11–15, $^b31$–3, 729^a9–32, 730^a14–15, 730^a28–$^b2$, 732^a1 ff., 765^b8 ff., 766^b12–15.

When it [the seed] comes into the uterus it constitutes and moves the female's residue [the menses] in the same movement in which it itself is actually moving. (737^a20–2)

Thus we may express PRINCIPLE 2 as follows: The male seed introduces the male form into the female menses simply and solely by causing a movement in it that is qualititatively identical to the actual movement generated in the seed by the form or soul of the male whose seed it is.

The initial effect of this movement is to begin the formation of the foetal heart. Once the heart is formed, the foetus grows of its own accord, drawing its nourishment from its mother through the umbilicus (735^a12–26). Thus when Socrates' seed has communicated its own movement to Xanthippe's menses, its work is done:

As the parts of the animal to be formed are present potentially in the matter [the menses], once the principle of movement has been supplied, one thing follows on after another without interruption, just as it does in the puppets in the 'marvels'. (741^b7–9)

The remainder of foetal development is due to the foetus itself, to the operations of its own heart.

The third principle of Aristotle's embryology is by no means peculiar to it but belongs to his general metaphysics. It is this:

[PRINCIPLE 3] So far as things formed by nature or by human craft are concerned, the formation of that which is potentially is brought about by that which is in actuality. (734^a28–31; see 734^b19 ff.)

Xanthippe's menses have the potential to be moved in such a way as to become Z and all its parts, but they cannot become the actual matter of Z or any other foetus until they are moved or concocted by the actual motions in Socrates' seed.[2]

Once the movement from Socrates' seed has been transmitted into Xanthippe's menses, however, a number of different things can happen to it that determine Z's gender and various other of its inheritable characteristics. The three principles that govern these happenings are summed up as follows:

But it is necessary to take hold of the general principles. [PRINCIPLE 4] The one just stated, that some of the movements are present potentially and others actually. But in addition two more; [PRINCIPLE 5] that what gets mastered departs from type, into the opposite; [PRINCIPLE 6] that what slackens passes into the movement that is next to it: slackening a little, into a near movement; more, into one that is farther away; finally, [the movements] so run together that it [the foetus or child] doesn't resemble any of its own or kindred, rather all that's left is what is common [to all], and it is [simply] man. (768^b5–12)

To figure out what exactly these three principles amount to, however, we

[2] See 737^a18 ff., 740^b18 ff., 743^a26–9.

will need to probe more deeply into the movements involved in reproduction.

The movement in Socrates' seed is a structure of *dunameis* (capacities, powers) that corresponds to the structure of the form that originates it (see 767^b35 ff.). One of these *dunameis* (<Socrates>) corresponds to the components in his form that are peculiar to him. Another (<male>) corresponds to the components of his form shared only with other males. A third (<human being>) corresponds to components shared only with other human beings. A fourth (<animal>) corresponds to components shared only with other animals. And so on. These *dynameis* are actual sub-movements of the actual (complex) movement in Socrates' seed. In addition to these actual sub-movements, however, the movement in Socrates' seed also contains a heirarchy of *dunameis* that are merely potential. One of these is —notice the different brackets—{Socrates' father}, which is the analogue of <Socrates>. Another is {Socrates' grandfather}. A third is {Socrates' great-grandfather}. And so on. these actual and potential movements are among those to which PRINCIPLE 4 refers.

Turning now to Xanthippe's menses we find a similar yet significantly different structure. For the movements in her menses that correspond to those in Socrates' seed are not actual movements but only potential ones:

Some of the movements are present actually others potentially: actually—those of the male progenitor and of the universals such as *man* and *animal*, potentially—those of the female and those of the ancestors. (768^a11–14)

Thus, corresponding to <Socrates>, <male>, <human being>, and <animal>, we have {Xanthippe}, {female}, {human being}, and {animal}. And corresponding to {Socrates' father}, {Socrates' grandfather}, and so on, we have {Xanthippe's mother}, {Xanthippe's grandmother}, and so on.

Let us focus, for simplicity's sake, on one sub-movement of the overall movement in Socrates' seed, namely, <Socrates>, and watch what happens to it during reproduction. If <Socrates> is transmitted to the menses and 'stands fast (*meinē(i)*)' (768^a32), Z will resemble Socrates. But <Socrates> may fail to stand fast. And if it does, then one of the things that happens to it is that it can 'slacken' or degrade—in a way that is governed by PRINCIPLE 6—into one of the potential movements that constitute the complex movement in Socrates' seed:

The movements that are working up [the menses] slacken (*luontai*) into ones that are near them, for example, should the movement of the male slacken, it shifts-over first by the minimal difference into that [i.e. the movement] of his father; second, into that of the grandfather; and in fact in this way also among the females, the [movement] of the female progenitor [shifts-over first] into that of her mother, or if not into that, into that of her grandmother; and so on up the line. (768^a14–21)

Thus if <Socrates> fails to master Xanthippe's menses, it may (as one possiblity) slacken or degrade into <Socrates' father>, that is to say , into the actual motion that corresponds to <Socrates' father> or that is the latter activated or actualized.

What causes <Socrates> to slacken or degrade in this way? The obvious answer is something about Xanthippe's menses; and this is indeed the answer Aristotle endorses:

> The cause of the movements' slackening is that what acts also gets acted upon by what is being acted upon, as what cuts get blunted by what is being cut and what heats gets cooled by what is being heated, and generally what moves (except the first mover) gets moved by some movement in return, for example, what pushes is pushed back in some way, and what squeezes is squeezed back. Sometimes, it is even acted on altogether more than it acts, what heats may get cooled, or what cools get heated, sometimes not having acted at all, sometimes [having acted but] less than being acted upon. (768^{b}15–24)

To understand this answer fully, however, we need to know more about what {Xanthippe} actually is.

If we think of Xanthippe's menses as a sort of prime matter or natureless material, it is difficult to see how, having no nature of its own, it could offer any resistance to the imposition of <Socrates>. It is clear, however, that we are not to think of it that way. Xanthippe's menses are in fact very much like Socrates' seed; they are 'seed that is not pure but needs working on' (728^{a}26–7). But because Xanthippe's vital heat is lower than Socrates' she cannot complete the final stage of working them up or concocting them into pure seed by herself:

> The woman is as it were an infertile male; for the female exists in virtue of a particular incapacity, in being unable to concoct (*pettein*) seed out of the nutriment in its last stage (which is either blood or the analogous part in the bloodless animals) owing to the coldness of her nature. (728^{a}17–21)

None the less, she can work up the menses (or the seminal residue in them) to within that single step of being pure seed. Thus the potentialities her menses contain are much closer to actualization than those, let us say, of prime matter (if Aristotle believed in it) or of earth, water, fire, and air.[3]

At this point, it is useful to engage in a little counterfactual speculation. Suppose that Xanthippe could take the final step, that she could concoct her menses the whole way. The result would be a female child that resembled Xanthippe herself. Consequently, we might think of her menses as having a natural tendency to form such a child, a tendency that Aristotle expresses by referring to the *dunameis* present as potential movements

---

[3] See 735^{a}9–11: 'It is possible to be relatively nearer and farther in potentiality, as the geometer asleep is farther than the one awake, and the latter is farther than the one studying [geometry].'

within it. It is these natural tendencies that offer opposition to <Socrates> and that, in the situation we are exploring, cause it to slacken or degrade into <Socrates' father> or worse <Socrates' grandfather>, and so on. Whether Xanthippe's menses will cause <Socrates> to slacken or not depends, as we saw, on the tendencies in it, but it also depends on Socrates' seed and on the relationship between its *dunameis* and those of the menses:

> The male and the female . . . must also stand in a certain proportional relationship (*summetrias*) to one another;[4] for all things that come into being as products of craft or nature exist in virtue of a certain ratio (*logon*). Now if the hot [in the seed] preponderates too much it dries up the wet things [i.e. the menses]; if it is very deficient it fails to make them become constituted [as a foetus]; what it must have is a proportional relationship that is in a mean relative to the thing being worked up. Otherwise it will be as in cooking; too much fire burns the meat, too little doesn't cook it, and in either case what you are trying to produce fails to reach completion. (767^{a}13–23)

What is required, then, for the motions in Socrates' seed to stand fast once they have been transmitted to Xanthippe's menses is that the right sort of proportionality exists between the vital heat in the seed and the wetness in the menses.

The items involved in slackening are the movements in the seed and the tendencies or potential movements in the menses, and the locations of these movements and potential movements during slackening is very clearly the menses itself, not the seed. Moreover, the effect of slackening is one of degree: <Socrates> can slacken into <Socrates' father> or further into <Socrates' grandfather> or further still into the movements of one of his yet more distant ancestors. But these features do not seem to be shared by another phenomenon that can occur during reproduction, namely, *mastering*. First, the items involved in mastering seem not to be movements but the seed and the menses themselves:

> But the male seed differs [from the female menses] in that it contains a first principle within itself of such a kind as to set up movements and to concoct thoroughly the ultimate nourishment, whereas the female's seed contains matter only. So when it [the male seed] has the mastery, it takes it [the female seed] over to itself (*eis hauto agei*), but when it is mastered it [the male seed] changes to the opposite or else to extinction (*eis tounantion metaballei hē eis phthoran*). But the female is opposite to the male. (766^{b}12–16)

Second, what happens to something that is mastered is, as PRINCIPLE 5 tells us, that it 'departs from type into the opposite', and this seems to be an all or nothing affair rather than a matter of degree. Third, it seems to follow that when A masters B, it is B that departs from type into the opposite, so that if the male seed gets mastered, for example, as sometimes happens,

---

[4] See 723^{a}26–31, 727^{b}11–12.

then it and not the menses or the foetus being formed changes into its opposite.

Let us elaborate on the story of mastery that has now emerged. It is something like this. Socrates' seed tries to transmit <Socrates> and its other component sub-motions into Xanthippe's menses. If it succeeds, the story is as before, and Z is a male child that resembles Socrates. If it fails, and is instead mastered by, for example, [Xanthippe], then its own motion is changed into one that has <Xanthippe> as a sub-movement in place of <Socrates>. This changed seed now makes a second assault, as it were, on Xanthippes' menses and succeeds in transmitting its altered motions to them. If the only change in Socrates' seed is the one just recorded, then Z will be a male child that resembles Xanthippe. But if, in addition, <male> were mastered by {female}, then Z would be a female child resembling Xanthippe. And so on for all the other sub-motions, potential or actual, that make up the seed and the menses.[5]

The problems with this picture are essentially threefold. First, since it entails that the male seed does not always transmit its own motion—the one it inherits from the form or soul of the male whose seed it is—to the menses, it conflicts with PRINCIPLE 2. Second, it renders Aristotle's account of slackening incoherent. Before a male movement can slacken, it must be transmitted to the seed. Suppose, therefore, that <Socrates> masters {Xanthippe} in round one, so that it is transmitted to the menses, but that once there it slackens into <Socrates' father>. What causes it to slacken is, as we know, {Xanthippe}, but how can that be so when {Xanthippe} has already been decisively mastered in round one? Third, the picture entails that after its intitial encounter with Xanthippe's menses Socrates' seed stays around, although possibly in an altered condition, to make what we have been calling a second assault. But this cannot be right. PRINCIPLE 1 tells us that the seed transmits its form (in the shape of a complex movement) to the menses, but contributes no matter whatsoever to the generative process. The following text tells us that once the seed has made this contribution, what is left of it, namely, the body of the seed now bereft of the motion it has transmitted to the menses, simply evaporates:

But the body of the seed . . . dissolves and evaporates, having a fluid and watery nature. That is why one should not look for it always to come out again, nor to be any part of the constitued shape (*tēs sustasēs morphēs*), any more than the curdling-juice which sets (*sunistanta*) the milk: it too changes and is no part of the mass that is being constituted. (737ª7–16)

It follows that there is no room in Aristotle's account of reproduction either for a modified seed or for more than a single round of interaction between the seed and the menses.

---

[5] This is the picture that seems to be presupposed in Cooper (1988*c*).

If this is so, however, what are we to make of the texts that suggest that the seed changes over to its opposite as a result of being mastered by the menses? I suggest that 'seed' is being used in them as a shorthand for 'the movement that the seed transmits to the menses'. For Aristotle is clear that these two expressions are more or less equivalent and interchangeable:

It makes no difference whether we say that it is the seed or this movement [the movement the seed transmits to the menses] that makes each of the parts grow. (767^b18-20)

Thus what really happens in mastery is that <Socrates> or some of the other actual or potential motions in that seed master {Xanthippe} or some of the other corresponding potential motions in the menses, or vice versa.

Slackening and mastery are now much more of a piece: both involve movements; both take place in the menses. This allows us to see mastery as the inverse of *complete* slackening. Here is what I have in mind. Suppose (*a*) that {Xanthippe} causes <Socrates> to slacken first into <Socrates' father>, then into <Socrates' grandfather>, then into <Socrates' great-grandfather>, and so on, so that none of the movements in this sequence stand fast, and (*b*) that <Socrates> does not cause {Xanthippe} to slacken to any degree. In this case, {Xanthippe} masters <Socrates>, and their offspring Z will resemble Xanthippe. If things go the other way, so that <Socrates> stands fast and {Xanthippe} completely slackens, then <Socrates> masters {Xanthippe} and Z will resemble Socrates. And so on.

Armed with this theory, Aristotle is able to explain many of the facts of genetic inheritance. He can explain why some children are males, others female—<male> sometimes masters {female} and is sometimes mastered by it; why some children (whether male or female) resemble their mothers while others resemble their fathers—{Xanthippe} sometimes masters <Socrates> and is sometimes mastered by it; and why some children resemble their more distant ancestors on either their father's or their mother's side—<Socrates> and {Xanthippe} sometimes slacken. Finally, he can explain why some children resemble no one in their family or are simply monsters—<Socrates> slackens into <animal>. Such explanatory richness is obviously a major intellectual achievement. But is it sufficient to explain all of the facts of genetic inheritance? And has it been purchased at the price of consistency?

The problem of explanatory adequacy I want to discuss concerns inheritance from a male (female) relative on the mother's (father's) side. Can the theory explain, for example, how Z can resemble his mother's father. More specifically, can it explain why he has his maternal grandfather's nose rather than his mother's or his father's? It can. <Socrates> has as one of it sub-movements, the movement that corresponds to Socrates' nose. This movement tries to master the corresponding sub-movements in {Xanthippe} but instead causes it to slacken into the corresponding movement in |Xanthippe's mother| and is then mastered (and deformed or altered) by it.[6] Let us call this deformed sub-movement of <Socrates>, <NOSE>. Now <NOSE> got into Xanthippe's mother's form from Xanthippe's mother's father; for everything gets into someone's form excusively from his or her father. All we have to do, then, is to suppose that <NOSE> was undeformed by the corresponding sub-movement of the movements in Xanthippe's mother's mother, and we have the explanation we need. For when the sub-movement in |Xanthippe| corresponding to Xanthippe's nose slackened into the corresponding sub-movement of |Xanthippe's mother|, and this deformed the corresponding sub-movement of <Socrates> into <NOSE>, and this operated to form Z's nose, the outcome was that Z got his maternal grandfather's nose.

Now for the problems of consistency. The first of these stems from Aristotle's views on intellect or *nous*. PRINCIPLE 1 suggests, if it does not flatly state, that the male is the sole formal cause of the foetus and resulting child. The line of inheritance is from the male form to the seed and from the seed to the menses and the foetus. But the following difficult text suggests that the most important component of the child's form, his *nous*, comes from somewhere else altogether:

All principles whose actuality is bodily are clearly unable to be present without body (for example, walking without feet). Hence too they cannot enter [the foetus] from outside [the seed and the menses]. For they can neither enter by themselves, since they have no existence separate [from matter], nor enter in as the principles of an already formed body; for the seed is a residue produced by a change in the nutriment. It remains then that *nous* alone enters additionally from outside [the seed and the menses?] and alone is divine; for [the] bodily actuality is in no way associated with its actuality. (736[b]22–9)

Now in the *Parts of Animals*, Aristotle is explicit that natural science (*physikē*)—and therefore embryology—treats only of those parts of soul and form that do not include *nous* and the intelligible entities studied by it (*PA*641[a]32–[b]10). It is these parts, and these parts only, he says, that constitute an animal's nature or *phusis*. This suggests that PRINCIPLE 1 is intended to apply not to the human form as a whole but only to the natural part. We need to explain, of course, just where Aristotle thinks *nous* does come from, but that is a discussion that properly belongs elsewhere (see §27).

The second problem of consistency is by far the most pressing. Suppose

---

[6] Sub-movements of this sort are countenanced at 772[b]31–5: 'If the thing doing the working up (*dēmiourgountos*) gains the mastery, both [sets of sexual organs of the sort that are sometimes present in deformed offspring] are similar [to the male's]: if it is completely mastered (*kratēthentos holōs*), both are similar [to the female's]; but if it masters here and is mastered there, the one [set] is male and the other female. (For whether we consider the reason why the whole animal is male or female, or why the parts are so makes no difference.)'

that Z is a male who resembles Xanthippe. If we look at his form, it surely contains components, such as <male> that it inherits from Socrates' form. But it also seems to contain elements, such as <Xanthippe>, that it inherits from Xanthippe's form. The trouble is that this is inconsistent with PRINCIPLE 1, the most fundamental principle of Aristotle's entire embryology. For we now seem to have the female contributing form rather than just matter to the foetus.[7]

To see our way through this problem, we need to absorb the full impact of Aristotle's infamous doctrine that a female is 'as it were a deformed male' (737[a]27–8) and that being female is 'a sort of natural deformity' (775[a]15–16). When the <male> component of the movements in Socrates' seed is overcome by the [female] component of the movements in Xanthippe's menses, it is changed. And it is this changed movement that then works up the menses into a foetus. Hence what is doing the working up is not an acutal movement contributed by Xanthippe (or Xanthippe's form)—all the movements in her menses are potential only —but an actual movement that ultimately derives from Socrates' form. Of course, this movement has been altered or 'deformed' by the menses, but it is still Socrates' movement. And it is precisely for this reason that a female is a deformed male: she is the result of a deformation of a movement deriving from the male form. Generalizing, we can say that whenever a movement deriving from a male form is altered or deformed by the natural tendencies in the female menses, the resulting foetus will itself be deformed (see 767[b]5–6). But it will be deformed, as opposed to having an undeformed form contributed by its mother, precisely because it is always the father who contributes the actual movements that shape the menses. All the menses can do is either be mastered by those movements or deform them, it cannot generate any actual movements of its own. Thus PRINCIPLE 1 is safe: the male contributes the form only; the female the matter only.

PRINCIPLE 1 is safe. But why did Aristotle ever bother to accept it? Why did he not simply allow that both the male and the female contribute formal elements to the foetus? The answer, I think, lies at the very basis of the hylomorphic explanations that Aristotle favours above all others both in his embryology and elsewhere. For hylomorphic analysis cannot easily admit of partial or incomplete forms. It cannot allow, for example, that part of Z's form comes from Xanthippe and part from Socrates. And the reason it cannot is that to explain how it is that such partial forms unite into a single form capable of enforming or animating a unified animal like Z, it would have to presuppose the existence of a background unified form to ensure that they unite in the right way.[8]

Hylomorphic analysis requires unified forms then. It follows that

[7] Furth (1988, 133–41) argues that this objection is fatal to Aristotle's theory.

[8] This problem becomes even more vivid when we retire into the craft analogy that underwrites hylomorphic analysis and that Aristotle so frequently draws on as

Aristotle really does need to attribute complex tendencies to matter if he is to be able to explain the manifest facts of reproduction. Without the tendencies in Xanthippe's' menses, as should now be clear, Aristotle's embryology simply collapses. The same is true, indeed, of his hylomorphic explanations of natural phenomena in general. For unless matter has complex tendencies, unless it refuses to be as malleable as undifferentiated prime matter, Aristotle simply has no way to explain why relations between the forms exemplified in nature fail to hold universally. In other words, he has no explanation of *hōs epi to polu*.

By the same token, Aristotle has to attribute a certain complexity to forms themselves if his embryology is to work. We have seen, for example, that Socrates' form must contain items like <Socrates>, items that distinguish it from the form of any other member of the same species, with the possible exception of an identical twin. This has obvious repercussions for our understanding of what a form is and puts in question some common views on this topic. First, Xanthippe and Socrates belong to the same species, for example, but their forms cannot be identical. It follows that forms are not the same as species. Second, Socrates' form and Xanthippe's form differ intrinsically and not merely because they are the forms of individuals whose contingent or accidental properties differ.[9] Moreover, Socrates' form can be passed on to his offspring unchanged, and it will be so passed on if every sub-motion in it masters the corresponding sub-motion in Xanthippe's form. It seems to follow that Socrates cannot be literally identical to his form.

---

an aid to the imagination. For suppose that Socrates is making half a house and that Xanthippe is making half a house. What could possibly explain the fact that for the most part the halves they make can be combined to form a single house? The only plausible answer seems to be that they both make their halves by following the appropriate parts of one and the same unified plan.

[9] These two consequences are discussed by Cooper (1988*c*, 15, 33–8).

REFERENCES

ACKRILL, J. L. (1965). 'Aristotle's Distinction between *Energeia* and *Kinesis*.' Bambrough (1965, 121–41).
—— (1974). 'Aristotle on *Eudaimonia*.' Repr. in Rorty (1980, 15–33).
—— (1980). 'Aristotle on Action.' Rorty (1980, 93–101).
—— (1981*a*). *Aristotle the Philosopher*. Oxford: Oxford University Press.
—— (1981*b*). 'Aristotle's Theory of Definition: Some Questions on *Posterior Analytics* II 8–10.' Berti (1981, 361–84).
ALLAN, D. J. (1961) (ed.). *Aristotelis: De Caelo*. Oxford: Clarendon Press.
—— (1970). *The Philosophy of Aristotle*. 2nd edn. Oxford: Oxford University Press.
ANSCOMBE, G. E. M. (1965). 'Thought and Action in Aristotle.' Bambrough (1965, 143–58).
ARMSTRONG, D. M. (1983). *What is a Law of Nature?* Cambridge: Cambridge University Press.
ARMSTRONG, G. C. (1935) (ed.). *Aristotle's Magna Moralia*. Cambridge, Mass.: Loeb Classical Library.
BALME, D. M. (1972) (tr.). *Aristotle's De Partibus Animalium I and De Generatione Animalium I*. Oxford: Clarendon Press.
—— (1984). 'The Snub.' Repr. in Gotthelf and Lennox (1987, 306–12).
—— (1987). 'Teleology and Necessity.' Gotthelf and Lennox (1987, 275–85).
BAMBROUGH, R. (1965) (ed.). *New Essays on Plato and Aristotle*. London: Routledge and Kegan Paul.
BARNES, J. (1969). 'Aristotle's Theory of Demonstration.' Repr. in Barnes, Schofield, and Sorabji (1975, 65–87).
—— (1971). 'Aristotle's Conception of Mind.' Repr. in Barnes, Schofield, and Sorabji (1975, 32–41).
—— (1975) (tr.). *Aristotle's Posterior Analytics*. Oxford: Clarendon Press.
—— (1980). 'Aristotle and the Methods of Ethics.' *Revue internationale de philosophie* 34: 490–511.
—— (1982). *Aristotle*. Oxford: Oxford University Press.
—— (1984) (ed.). *The Complete Works of Aristotle*. Princeton, NJ: Princeton University Press.
—— (1987). 'An Aristotelian Way with Skepticism'. Matthen (1987, 51–76).
—— SCHOFIELD, M., and SORABJI, R. (1975) (eds.). *Articles on Aristotle*. Vols. 1–4. London: Duckworth, 1975–9.
BERTI, E. (1981) (ed.). *Aristotle on Science: The Posterior Analytics*. Padua: Editrice Antenore.

BOLTON, R. (1987). 'Definition and Scientific Method in *Posterior Analytics* and *Parts of Animals*.' Gotthelf and Lennox (1987, 120–66).

BONITZ, H. (1955). *Index Aristotelicus*. 2nd edn. Graz: Akademische Druck- und Verlagsanstalt.

BRATMAN, M. (1987). *Intention, Plans, and Practical Reason*. Cambridge, Mass.: Harvard University Press.

BRINK, D. O. (1989). *Moral Realism and the Foundations of Ethics*. Cambridge: Cambridge University Press.

BURNET, J. (1900) (ed.). *The Ethics of Aristotle*. London: Methuen.

BURNYEAT, M. (1980). 'Aristotle on Learning to Be Good.' Rorty (1980, 69–92).

——— (1981). 'Aristotle on Understanding Knowlege.' Berti (1981, 97–139).

BYWATER, I. (1894) (ed.). *Aristotelis: Ethica Nicomachea*. Oxford: Clarendon Press.

CHARLES, D. (1984). *Aristotle's Philosophy of Action*. Ithaca, NY: Cornell University Press.

———(1985). 'Aristotle's Distinction between Energeia and Kinesis: Inference, Explanation, and Ontology.' *Language and Reality in Greek Philosophy*, 173–81. Athens: *Instituto toy Biblioy*.

——— (1986). 'Aristotle: Ontology and Moral Reasoning.' *Oxford Studies in Ancient Philosophy* 4: 119–44.

CHARLTON, W. (1970). *Aristotle's Physics: Books I and II*. Oxford: Clarendon Press.

——— (1988). *Weakness of Will: A Philosophical Introduction*. Oxford: Basil Blackwell.

CLARK, S. R. L. (1975). *Aristotle's Man*. Oxford: Clarendon Press.

CODE, A. (1986). 'Aristotle's Investigation of a Basic Logical Principle.' *Canadian Journal of Philosophy* 16: 341–57.

COOPER, J. M. (1973). 'The *Magna Moralia* and Aristotle's Moral Philosophy.' *American Journal of Philology* 94: 327–49.

——— (1975). *Reason and Human Good in Aristotle*. Cambridge, Mass.: Harvard University Press.

——— (1980). 'Aristotle on Friendship.' Rorty (1980, 301–40).

——— (1985). 'Aristotle on the Goods of Fortune.' *Philosophical Review* 94: 173–96.

——— (1987a). 'Hypothetical Necessity and Natural Teleology.' Gotthelf and Lennox (1987, 243–74).

——— (1987b). 'Contemplation and Happiness: A Reconsideration.' *Synthese* 72: 187–216.

——— (1988a). 'Some Remarks on Aristotle's Moral Psychology.' *Southern Review of Philosophy* 27, Supplement: 25–42.

——— (1988b). Review of *The Fragility of Goodness: Luck and Ethics in Greek Tragedy and Philosophy* by Martha C. Nussbaum. *Philosophical Review* 97: 543–64.

210   *References*

—— (1988c). 'Metaphysics in Aristotle's Embryology.' *Proceedings of the Cambridge Philological Society* 214: 14–41.

DAHL, N. O. (1984). *Practical Reason, Aristotle, and Weakness of Will.* Minneapolis: University of Minnesota Press.

DANCY, R. M. (1975). *Sense and Contradiction.* Dordrecht: Reidel.

DEFOURNY, P. (1937). 'Contemplation in Aristotle's Ethics.' Repr. in Barnes, Schofield, and Sorabji (1975: 2, 25–32).

DESOUSA R. (1979). 'The Rationality of Emotions.' Repr. in A. Rorty (ed.), *Explaining Emotions,* 127–51. Berkeley, Calif.: University of California Press, 1980.

DEVEREUX, D. (1981). 'Aristotle on the Essence of Happiness.' O'Meara (1981, 247–60).

DÜRING, I. (1961) (ed.). *Aristotle's Protrepticus.* Göteborg.

ENGBERG-PEDERSEN, T. (1979). 'More on Aristotelian *Epagoge.*' *Phronesis* 24: 301–17.

—— (1983). *Aristotle's Theory of Moral Insight.* Oxford: Clarendon Press.

—— (1985). 'Practical Inquiry and Practical Philosophy in Aristotle.' *Danish Yearbook of Philosophy* 22: 57–63.

EVANS, J. D. G. (1977). *Aristotle's Concept of Dialectic.* Cambridge: Cambridge University Press.

FORSTER, E. S. (1955) (ed.). *Aristotle: On Coming-To-Be and Passing-Away.* Cambridge, Mass.: Loeb Classical Library.

FORTENBAUGH, W. W. (1975). *Aristotle on Emotion.* New York: Barnes and Noble.

FREDE, M. (1987). *Essays in Ancient Philosophy.* Minneapolis: University of Minnesota Press.

FURLEY, D. J. (1955) (ed.). *Aristotle: On the Cosmos.* Cambridge, Mass.: Loeb Classical Library.

FURTH, M. (1985). *Aristotle Metphysics: Books Zeta, Eta, Theta, Iota (VII–X).* Indianapolis: Hackett.

—— (1988). *Substance, Form and Psyche: An Aristotelian Metaphysics.* Cambridge: Cambridge University Press.

GAUTHIER, R. A. and JOLIF, J. Y. (1970). *L'Éthique à Nicomaque: Introduction, traduction et commentaire.* 2nd edn. Vols. i. 1–2, ii. 1–2. Louvain: Publications Universitaires.

GILL, M. L. (1989). *Aristotle on Substance: The Paradox of Unity.* Princeton, NJ: Princeton University Press.

GLASSEN, P. (1957). 'A Fallacy in Aristotle's Argument About the Good.' *Philosophical Quarterly* 7: 319–22.

GOMEZ-LOBO, A. (1981). 'Definitions in Aristotle's *Posterior Analytics.*' O'Meara (1981, 25–46).

GOSLING, J. C. B., and Taylor, C. C. W. (1982). *The Greeks on Pleasure.* Oxford: Clarendon Press.

GOTTHELF, A. (1985) (ed.). *Aristotle on Nature and Living Things*. Pittsburgh: Mathesis Publications.

—— and LENNOX, G. L. (1987) (eds.), *Philosophical Issues in Aristotle's Biology*. Cambridge: Cambridge University Press.

GRAHAM, D. W. (1987). *Aristotle's Two Systems*. Oxford: Clarendon Press.

GRANT, A. (1885) (ed.). *The Ethics of Aristotle*. 2 vols. 4th edn. London: Longmans, Green, and Co.

GREENWOOD, L. H. G. (1909) (ed.). *Aristotle: Nicomachean Ethics Book Six*. Repr. New York: Arno Press, 1973.

HAMLYN, D. W. (1968) (tr.) *Aristotle's De Anima*. Oxford: Clarendon Press.

HARDIE, W. F. R. (1968). *Aristotle's Ethical Theory*. Oxford: Clarendon Press.

HETT, W. S. (1936) (ed.). *Aristotle: Parva Naturalia*. Cambridge, Mass.: Loeb Classical Library.

HICKS, R. D. (1907) (ed.). *Aristotle: De Anima*. Cambridge: Cambridge University Press.

HUME, D. (1739). *A Treatise of Human Nature*. Oxford: Clarendon Press, 1967.

HURSTHOUSE, R. (1980). 'A False Doctrine of the Mean.' *Proceedings of the Aristotelian Society* 81 (1980–1): 57–72.

——(1988). 'Moral Habituation: A Review of Troels Engberg-Pedersen, *Aristotle's Theory of Moral Insight*.' *Oxford Studies in Ancient Philosophy* 6: 201–19.

IRWIN, T. H. (1977). 'Aristotle's Discovery of Metaphysics.' *Review of Metaphysics* 31: 210–29.

—— (1978). 'First Principles in Aristotle's Ethics.' *Midwest Studies in Philosophy* 3: 252–72.

—— (1982). 'Aristotle's Concept of Signification.' Schofield and Nussbaum (1982, 241–66).

—— (1985a). 'Permanent Happiness.' *Oxford Studies in Ancient Philosophy* 3: 89–124.

—— (1985b) (tr.). *Aristotle, Nicomachean Ethics*. Indianapolis: Hackett.

—— (1986). 'Aristotle's Conception of Morality.' *Proceedings of the Boston Area Colloquium in Ancient Philosophy* 1: 115–43.

—— (1987). 'Ways to First Principles: Aristotle's Methods of Discovery.' *Philosophical Topics* 15: 109–34.

—— (1988a). 'Disunity in the Aristotelian Virtues.' *Oxford Studies in Ancient Philosophy* (Supplementary Volume): 61–78.

—— (1988b). *Aristotle's First Principles*. Oxford: Clarendon Press.

JOACHIM, H. H. (1951). *The Nicomachean Ethics*. Oxford: Clarendon Press.

KAHN, C. H. (1981). 'The Role of *Nous* in the Cognition of First Principles in *Posterior Analytics* II. 19.' Berti (1981, 385–414).

—— (1985). 'The Place of the Prime Mover in Aristotle's Teleology.' Gotthelf (1985, 183–205).

KASSEL, R. (1966). *Aristotelis: De Arte Poetica.* Oxford: Clarendon Press.

KENNY, A. J. P. (1978). *The Aristotelian Ethics.* Oxford: Clarendon Press.

KEYT, D. (1978). 'Intellectualism in Aristotle.' In *Essays in Ancient Greek Philosophy*, ii, ed. J. P. Anton and A. Preus, 364–87. Albany, NY: State University of New York Press, 1983.

KOSMAN, L. A. (1973). 'Understanding, Explanation, and Insight in the *Posterior Analytics*.' In *Exegesis and Argument*, ed. E. N. Lee, A. D. Mourelatos, and R. M. Rorty, 374–92. Assen: Van Gorcum,

—— (1984). 'Substance, Being, and *Energeia*.' *Oxford Studies in Ancient Philosophy* 2: 121–49.

—— (1987). 'Animals and Other Beings in Aristotle.' Gotthelf and Lennox (1987, 360–91).

KRAUT, R. (1979). 'The Peculiar Function of Human Beings.' *Canadian Journal of Philosophy* 9: 467–78.

—— (1988). 'Comments on "Disunity in the Aristotelian Virtues".' *Oxford Studies in Ancient Philosophy* (Supplementary Volume): 79–86.

—— (1989). *Aristotle on the Human Good.* Princeton, NJ: Princeton University Press.

KRIPKE, S. A. (1980). *Naming and Necessity.* Cambridge, Mass.: Harvard University Press.

LEAR, J. (1988). *Aristotle: The Desire to Understand.* Cambridge: Cambridge University Press.

LEE, H. D. P. (1952) (ed.). *Aristotle's Meteorologica.* Cambridge, Mass.: Loeb Classical Library.

LEIGHTON, S. (1982). 'Aristotle on the Emotions.' *Phronesis* 27 : 144–74.

—— (1988). 'Aristotle's Courageous Passions.' *Phronesis* 33: 76–99.

LENNOX, J. G. (1987). 'Kinds, Forms of Kinds, and the More and the Less in Aristotle's Biology.' Gotthelf and Lennox (1987, 339–59).

LESHER, J. H. (1973). 'The Meaning of *Nous* in the *Posterior Analytics*.' *Phronesis* 18 (1973): 44–68.

LIDDELL, H. G., SCOTT, R., AND JONES, H. S. (1966). *A Greek–English Lexicon.* 9th edn. Clarendon Press: Oxford.

LOSIN, P. (1987). 'Aristotle's Doctrine of the Mean.' *History of Philosophy Quarterly* 4: 329–41.

LULOFS, H. J. D. (1965) (ed.). *Aristotelis: De Generatione Animalium.* Oxford: Clarendon Press.

MCDOWELL, J. (1979). 'Virtue and Reason.' *Monist* 62: 331–50.

—— 1980. 'The Role of Eudaimonia in Aristotle's Ethics.' Repr. in Rorty (1980, 359–76).

MATTHEN, M. (1987) (ed.). *Aristotle Today: Essays on Aristotle's Ideal of Science.* Edmonton: Academic Printing and Publishing.

MIGNUCCI, M. (1981). '*Hōs epi to polu* et nécessaire dans la conception aristotélicienne de la science.' Berti (1981, 173–203).

MILLGRAM, E. (1987). 'Aristotle on Making Other Selves.' *Canadian Journal of Philosophy* 17: 361–76.

MINIO-PALUELLO, L. (1949) (ed.). *Aristotelis: Categoriae et De Interpretatione*. Oxford: Clarendon Press.

MODRAK, D. K. W. (1987). *Aristotle: The Power of Perception*. Chicago: University of Chicago Press.

NORMAN, R. (1969). 'Aristotle's Philosopher-God.' Repr. in Barnes, Schofield, and Sorabji (1975, 4: 93–102).

NOZICK, R. (1989). *The Examined Life: Philosophical Meditations*. New York: Simon and Schuster.

NUSSBAUM, M. C. (1978). *Aristotle's De Motu Animalium: Text with Translation, Commentary, and Interpretative Essays*. Princeton, NJ: Princeton University Press.

—— (1986*a*). *The Fragility of Goodness*. Cambridge: Cambridge University Press.

—— (1986*b*). 'The Discernment of Perception: An Aristotelian Conception of Private and Public Rationality.' *Proceedings of the Boston Area Colloquium in Ancient Philosophy* 1: 151–201.

O'MEARA, D. J. (1981) (ed.). *Studies in Aristotle*. Washington, DC: Catholic University of America Press.

OWEN, G. E. L. (1961). '*Tithenai ta Phainomena*.' Repr. in Owen (1986, 239–51).

—— (1978). 'Particular and General.' Repr. in Owen (1986, 279–94).

—— (1986). *Logic, Science and Dialectic*. Ithaca, NJ: Cornell University Press.

PATZIG, G. (1960). 'Theology and Ontology in Aristotle's *Metaphysics*.' Repr. in Barnes, Schofield, and Sorabji (1975, 2: 33–49).

PECK, A. L. (1965) (ed.). *Aristotle: Historia Animalium*. Cambridge, Mass.: Loeb Classical Library.

—— (1968; (ed.). *Aristotle: The Parts of Animals*. Cambridge, Mass.: Loeb Classical Library.

PENNER, T. (1970). 'Verbs and the Identity of Actions – A Philosophical Exercise in the Interpretation of Aristotle.' In *Ryle: A Collection of Critical Essays*, ed. O. P. Wood and G. Pitcher, 393–453. Garden City, NY: Doubleday, 1970.

PRICE, A. W. (1989). *Love and Friendship in Plato and Aristotle*. Oxford: Clarendon Press.

PUTNAM, H. (1975). *Mind, Language and Reality: Philosophical Papers*. Vol. 2. Cambridge: Cambridge University Press.

QUINE, W. V. O. (1969). 'Epistemology Naturalized.' In id., *Ontological Relativity and Other Essays*, 69–90. New York: Columbia University Press.

RACKHAM, H. (1934). *Aristotle: The Nicomachean Ethics*. New and rev. edn. Cambridge, Mass.: Harvard University Press.

REEVE, C. D. C. (1988). *Philosopher-Kings: The Argument of Plato's Republic*. Princeton, NJ: Princeton University Press.

—— (1989). *Socrates in the Apology: An Essay on Plato's Apology of Socrates*. Indianapolis: Hackett.

RORTY, A. O. (1980) (ed.). *Essays on Aristotle's Ethics*. Berkeley, Calif.: University of California Press.

ROSS, W. D. (1923). *Aristotle*. London: Methuen.

—— (1924) (ed.). *Aristotle: Metaphysics*. 2 Vols. Oxford: Clarendon Press.

—— (1936) (ed.). *Aristotle: Physics*. Oxford: Clarendon Press.

—— (1949) (ed.). *Aristotle's Prior and Posterior Analytics*. Oxford: Clarendon Press.

—— (1956) (ed.). *Aristotelis: De Anima*. Oxford: Clarendon Press.

—— (1957) (ed.). *Aristotelis: Politica*. Oxford: Clarendon Press.

—— (1959) (ed.). *Aristotelis: Ars Rhetorica*. Oxford: Clarendon Press.

—— (1980) (tr.). *Aristotle: The Nicomachean Ethics*. Rev. edn. Oxford: Oxford University Press.

—— (1984) (ed.). *Aristotelis: Topica et Sophistici Elenchi*. Oxford: Clarendon Press.

SCHOFIELD, M. and NUSSBAUM, M. (1982) (eds.). *Language and Logos: Studies in Ancient Greek Philosophy*. Cambridge: Cambridge University Press.

SCHOLZ, H. (1930). 'The Ancient Axiomatic Theory.' Repr. in Barnes, Schofield, and Sorabji (1975, 1: 50–64).

SHERMAN, N. (1989). *The Fabric of Character*. Oxford: Clarendon Press.

SLOTE, M. (1989). *Beyond Optimizing*. Cambridge, Mass.: Harvard University Press.

SORABJI, R. (1980). *Necessity, Cause, and Blame: Perspectives on Aristotle's Theory*. Ithaca, NY: Cornell University Press.

—— (1981). 'Definitions: Why Necessary and In What Way?' Berti (1981, 205–44).

STEWART, J. A. (1892). *Notes on the Nicomachean Ethics*. 2 vols. Repr. New York: Arno Press, 1973.

STICH, S. (1990). *The Fragmentation of Reason*. Cambridge, Mass.: MIT Press.

SUSEMIHL, F. (1884) (ed.). *Aristotelis: Ethica Eudemia*. Repr. Amsterdam: Hakkert, 1967.

URMSON, J. O. (1973). 'Aristotle's Doctrine of the Mean.' Repr. in Rorty (1980, 157–70).

WEDIN, M. V. (1988). *Mind and Imagination in Aristotle*. New Haven, Conn.: Yale University Press.

WHITEHEAD, D. (1975). 'Aristotle the Metic.' *Proceedings of the Cambridge Philological Society* 21: 94–9.

WHITING, J. (1988). 'Aristotle's Function Argument: A Defense.' *Ancient Philosophy* 8: 33–48.

WIGGINS, D. (1975). 'Deliberation and Practical Reason.' Repr. in Rorty (1980, 221–40).

—— (1978). 'Weakness of Will, Commensurability, and the Objects of Deliberation and Desire.' Repr. in Rorty (1980, 241–65).

WILKES, K. V. (1978). 'The Good Man and the Good for Man in Aristotle's Ethics.' Repr. in Rorty (1980, 341–57).

WITT, C. (1989). *Substance and Essence in Aristotle: An Interpretation of Metaphysics VII–IX.* Ithaca, NY: Cornell University Press.

WOODS, M. (1982) (tr.). *Aristotle's Eudemian Ethics, Books I, II, and VIII.* Oxford: Clarendon Press.

YOUNG, C. M. (1988). 'Aristotle on Temperance.' *The Philosophical Review* 97: 521–42.

INDEX LOCORUM ARISTOTELIS

GENERAL INDEX